READ AND RESPOND

A Text/Anthology

Third Edition

Janet R. Swinton

Spokane Falls Community College

William J. Agopsowicz

San Joaquin Delta College

ROXBURY PUBLISHING COMPANY

NOTE TO INSTRUCTORS

A comprehensive **Instructor's Manual** is available

Library of Congress Card Cataloging-in-Publication Data

Swinton, Janet R., 1948-
    Read and respond: a text/anthology/Janet R.
    Swinton, William J. Agopsowicz. —3rd. ed.
      p. cm.
    Includes bibliographical references (p.) and index.
    ISBN 0-935732-63-2
    1. Reading (Higher education) 2. College readers
  I. Agopsowicz, William J., 1943- . II. Title
  LB2395.3.S95   1995
  428.4'071'1—dc20

                             94-42934
                                CIP

READ AND RESPOND (THIRD EDITION)

ISBN 0-935732-63-2

Publisher and Editor: Claude Teweles
Copy Editor: Ingrid Herman Reese
Associate Editors: Dawn VanDercreek and Sacha A. Howells
Typography and Design: Ingrid Herman Reese
Cover Design: Greg Cammack & Allan Miller

Printed on acid-free paper in the United States of America. This paper meets the standards for recycling of the Environmental Protection Agency.

ROXBURY PUBLISHING COMPANY
P.O. Box 491044
Los Angeles, California 90049-9044
(213) 653-1068

We dedicate the Third Edition of *Read and Respond* to our students. They provided the original impetus for the book, and they suggested most of the articles included in the three editions. They continue to inspire us.

PREFACE

To the Instructor

We are pleased at the enthusiastic reception of the first two editions of *Read and Respond*, a combination text/anthology designed to improve reading and writing skills. The Third Edition has been significantly expanded and revised.

The book's approach is unique because students' comprehension is assessed by summary writing rather than objective testing. After summarizing an article, students write a personal response to it, learning basic essay-writing techniques in the process.

The Third Edition offers a variety of useful new features, including

- a new chapter on how to read and study textbook chapters.

- revisions and new models in Part One to aid classroom instruction in finding the topic, main idea, and major details of an article.

- more instruction and models in Chapter Five, "Writing a Response," on brainstorming and writing paragraphs and essays in response to articles.

- an anthology section with many recent articles, including a new section on topics representing various cultural viewpoints. Over half of the articles in Part Two are new to the Third Edition.

- an appendix featuring expanded instruction on summarizing narrative essays and *new* instruction on improving vocabulary.

While its design has been updated, the organization and philosophy of the Third Edition are in keeping with the First and Second Editions. The use of written summaries tests the student's ability to state main points rather than simply recognize them. Furthermore, since the summary and personal response are written in the student's own words, the instructor gains insight into the student's vocabulary and writing ability. Topics of student interest become evident, and the instructor can make recommendations for further reading. In this way, the crucial student-teacher relationship is enhanced, which helps build students' self- esteem as they develop proficiency in reading, writing, and critical thinking.

Chapter Six includes a sample chapter from *Biology: A Journey into Life*, an introductory biology textbook. The study techniques discussed in Chapter Six are demonstrated on the first section of the chapter, and students have an opportunity to practice these techniques on two following sections.

Part Two—the anthology—is comprised of 33 articles for practice in reading, summarizing, and writing responses. These articles, most of which were selected *by students* from the popular press, are grouped by subject, allowing students to choose topics of interest and to read several viewpoints on the same subject. The selections are arranged from easiest to most difficult. Each article is preceded by a preview section to help focus the reader's attention and pique curiosity. Also, difficult or unusual words are listed and are underlined within the article.

To the Student

The ability to read well can make your school work and job easier as well as provide hours of relaxing pleasure. As with other skills, it takes lots of practice to improve your reading ability. A good tennis player stays in practice by hitting tennis balls on a regular basis; a pianist practices piano at least an hour a day; a dancer rehearses for hours each week.

In addition to practice, you need a method to help guide you as you improve. ***Read and Respond*** provides you with a step-by-step reading method. You will learn how to state the main idea and details of an article in your own words and how to develop a summary. Your summary then becomes a measure of how much you understand of what you read. You are also given the opportunity to "respond" to the author, that is, to write your personal reaction to the author's ideas. By summarizing what you have read and responding to it, you become a better reader. The Third Edition of this book includes an entire chapter on textbook reading to help you learn and practice strategies for understanding textbooks. At the end of this chapter we have included an actual chapter from an introductory biology textbook, *Biology: A Journey into Life*. By practicing with this "real" chapter you will gain the confidence and skills to read your own textbooks. The book also includes an appendix on learning vocabulary.

The articles in ***Read and Respond*** were chosen—primarily by students—from popular magazines and newspapers and were tested in classes for interest, readability, and potential for evoking thoughtful responses. You will see that these nonfiction articles represent a wide variety of styles and topics. It is our hope that you will enjoy working with them.

Janet R. Swinton
William J. Agopsowicz

TABLE OF CONTENTS

PART ONE

CHAPTER ONE: DISCOVERING THE TOPIC

CHAPTER TWO: LOCATING THE MAIN IDEA

CHAPTER THREE: LOCATING MAJOR DETAILS

CHAPTER FOUR: WRITING A SUMMARY

CHAPTER FIVE: WRITING A RESPONSE

CHAPTER SIX: READING TEXTBOOKS

PART TWO

LEARNING STRATEGIES

HEALTH AND FITNESS

PARENTING/FAMILY

THE SEXES

CULTURAL VIEWPOINTS

APPENDICES

PART ONE

Part One consists of six chapters, each containing instruction, models, and exercises. For each chapter, first carefully read the instruction and study the models. Then complete the exercises. These exercises will help you evaluate your understanding of each chapter.

Chapter One

DISCOVERING THE TOPIC

The models and exercises in this chapter will help you to

- Locate the topic of an article.
- State the topic of an article using specific language.

To understand what you read, you must first identify the topic. **Topic** is another word for subject matter; it means "what the article is about." In most cases, you have to know what topic is being discussed before you can determine what the author thinks about it.

GENERAL AND SPECIFIC TOPICS

A topic can be stated in a single word such as ***tests, dating, or boating.*** These words are very general. ***Tests,*** for example, does not reveal whether the article is about taking tests, creating them, or cheating on them. It does not indicate whether the author is concerned with essay tests or multiple-choice tests. ***Dating*** does not, by itself, reveal if the author will discuss dating practices in different cultures or offer hints on how to find the ideal mate. ***Boating*** provides no clues about the type of boats being discussed or whether the article is for a skilled sailor or a beginner. There is still much to discover about these topics if you want to know what the article is actually about.

After you read an article it is a good idea to state the topic, and you will find it helpful to make your statement as precise, or specific, as possible. Reading is more useful and pleasurable when you quickly comprehend, or understand, what you are reading. Identifying the specific topic of your reading is the first step to understanding and the enjoyment it brings.

Compare the general and specific topics listed below:

General:	**Specific:**
Tests	Using essay tests in college math
Dating	Dating practices in Mexico
Boating	Sailboats for beginners

Adding specific information about a topic shows that you understand more about it than is indicated when you state only the general topic. To state a topic specifically, simply add information; instead of a single word, write a short phrase.

HOW TO LOCATE THE TOPIC

To locate the topic of an article, ask yourself, "What is the article about?" The answer can often be found in the title, so you should look there first. Reading the title is the first step in a **preview,** a quick look at an article before reading it. Sometimes the title states the topic specifically: "Saving the Humpback Whale." If the topic is not specifically stated in the title ("Whales"), you will want more information before reading the entire article. In this case, continue to preview by reading the first and last paragraphs of the article. For more information, read the first sentence of each paragraph. If the article is only one paragraph long, read the first and last sentences. The point is to *quickly* gain as much understanding as possible. You will read with more comprehension and pleasure if you have the specific topic in mind while reading the rest of the article.

MODEL ONE: Locating the topic of an article

RE-ENTRY STUDENTS

Re-entry students have a positive effect on college students, instructors, and the community. They are called "re-entry" students because they have been out of school for a period of time and now have come back. No longer are college classes primarily made up of 18- to 20-year-old recent high school graduates. The average age of students in many colleges is closer to 30. Occasionally a student graduates from college for the first time at the age of 70 or even older. For younger students, re-entry students are often models of dedication and hard work. Instructors enjoy the variety of life experiences that these students bring to the classroom. Finally, it might be the community at large that benefits most, for the re-entry students truly exemplify the saying that we are learners all our lives.

What is the article about? (Topic)

The positive effects of re-entry students

Or you might write

Re-entry college students' positive effects on others

COMMENTS: The title provides the general topic, re-entry students. You can discover the specific topic by reading the first sentence, which states that these students have positive effects on many people. As indicated, the specific topic can be stated in more than one way.

Reading comprehension is greatly improved when you know the specific topic. From now on, when we use the term **topic** we are referring to the specific topic.

EXERCISE ONE

Preview the following article and write the topic.

THE KEY TO GOOD MEMORY

Good memory depends on how interested you are in what you are trying to remember. If you are interested in baseball, you are likely to remember batting averages, earned run averages, and World Series results. On the other hand, if you are not interested in baseball, you might think you have a poor memory because you cannot remember vital baseball statistics. It is likely that you will remember names of popular recording stars if you are interested enough in them—items that the baseball fan might easily forget. In short, interest is the key to a good memory.

MODEL TWO: Locating the topic of an article

> ### HOPI KACHINA DOLL
> by Delphine Hirasuna
> *from Hemispheres*
>
> A popular item sold at every trading post and curio shop in the South-west is the colorful, elaborately costumed kachina doll, carved by Hopi Indians who inhabit the mesas of northeast Arizona.
>
> These intriguing wooden figurines are far more than souvenirs. They depict the masked dancers of the kachina ceremonial rites that are held in Hopi villages from late December through July. Meaning "life father," a kachina is considered a spiritual messenger for mortals. The original kachinas, according to folklore, were killed by ancient Hopi enemies and returned to the Underworld, leaving their sacred paraphernalia behind. In kachina ceremonies, impersonators take on supernatural qualities by wear-ing the masks of these spirits, which gives them the power to petition the gods for such things as rain and a plentiful harvest. According to Hopi custom, only males can be initiated into the kachina cult. To share the benefits of their spiritual association, the men often make kachina like-nesses to give to women and children at dance time.
>
> Carved from cottonwood roots and coated with a primer of clay, true kachina dolls are painted with colors symbolic of the six cardinal direc-tions. More than 250 kachinas are said to exist, but doll designs may vary depending on the skill and artistic ability of the craftsman. Avidly sought by visitors to the Southwest, kachina dolls are now treasured as art ob-jects, made all the more meaningful when one takes the time to learn the function and legends attached to each type of kachina.

What is the article about? (Topic)

Facts about the Hopi kachina doll

Or you might write

The lore of the Hopi kachina doll

Or perhaps

The kachina doll: more than just a souvenir

EXERCISE TWO

Preview the following article and write the topic.

DO THE FACTS EVER LIE?

In many controversial articles, there is one set of facts, but two different interpretations. The readers of such articles must question both the facts and the interpretations and make up their own minds. Good readers think and read critically; they do not blindly accept someone else's conclusions.

A recent study by the National Center for Health Statistics is a good example of why critical thinking is so important. The study concludes that children in non-smoking households are likely to be healthier than children who live with smokers. The study shows that 4.1 percent of young children in households with smokers were in fair to poor health. Only 2.4 percent of the children never exposed to tobacco smoke were in fair to poor health. However, this conclusion is disputed by the tobacco industry.

The claim by the tobacco industry is that the difference is really one of income levels. In other words, they believe that the study does not take all factors into consideration. It is unfair, they say, to single out smoking as the big cause of the health problems.

The two sides in this dispute are using the same facts, but are interpreting them differently. Therefore, it is up to the readers to question all aspects of the controversy. They need to ask a number of questions: "What is the bias or motive of the tobacco industry in this case?" "Why would a government agency interpret statistics this way?" "How was the study conducted?" "Are there other reasons why these children have poorer health?" These and other questions must be asked in order to make a judgment about such a dispute. Good readers evaluate information; they do not just accept it.

EXERCISE THREE

Preview the following articles and write the topic of each.

A MIDTERM NIGHT'S DREAM

from *New Choices*

William Miller of Parma, Ohio, has some fretful nights. The 57-year-old accountant stumbles through a classroom building, looking for the room where his final exam is to be given. He can't find it; no one will help him. Then he wakes up in a cold sweat.

Although 35 years have passed since Miller graduated from Denison University in Ohio, he still has this dream about twice a year. Sometimes he talks about it with his fellow members of MENSA, the national organization for men and women with IQs of 140 and higher. "About 10 percent of the folks in my chapter have exam dreams too," he reports.

A few months ago Miller read a newspaper article about Anne Shurling, a psychologist at Transylvania University in Lexington, Ky., who has been surveying hundreds of Transylvania alumni about what she calls "exam-anxiety dreams." Shurling, 41, has never had such a nightmare, but 27 percent of her respondents have.

The researcher has a mailbag full of letters from men and women like Miller, grateful to have found someone who understands their dreams. In one letter, for example, an industrial consultant in his mid-40s was livid: Why should a grown man making $200,000 a year, he demanded, still be dreaming about a stupid science exam after all this time?

Shurling thinks the dreams are stress-related. When we are nervous about something in our present-day lives, she says, our brains search for other, perhaps earlier, stressful situations—like final examinations.

This explanation makes perfect sense to Larry Shepherd, a 52-year-old technical manager for AT&T in Reading, Pa., who also wrote to Shurling. Lately he's been having a dream in which he shows up for a math test unprepared. Shepherd struggled through math courses right through the last requirement for his master's degree in engineering from Clarkson College in New York. Now he is considering taking early retirement—and spawning the nightmares of the next generation by becoming a math teacher.

The dreams seem to occur even into later years, Shurling says. And men are more likely to have them than women are—probably because men tend to remember more of their dreams than women do. "Also, men are poorer students," Shurling adds, "so they have more to be anxious about."

Scary as the exam dreams can be, they could be worse. Consider poor William Miller. In his other recurring dream, he has been called to boot camp and can't convince anyone he's already done his duty.

Now, that's a nightmare.

READING MORE, UNDERSTANDING LESS

by Jeff Meer

from *Psychology Today*

Increase your reading speed two to three times with no loss of comprehension! Is such a claim valid? Psychologists Marcel Just, Patricia A. Carpenter and Michael Masson think not, especially if complex or unfamiliar material is involved. They compared the reading abilities of three groups who read passages presented on a television monitor: eleven people who had completed a seven-week Evelyn Wood Reading Dynamics course, 12 who were told to "skim" and 13 others who read at average rates.

Each group read both relatively easy and difficult passages. The readers then briefly summarized the passages and answered 10 general and 10 detailed questions about each one.

Just, Carpenter, and Masson report that the speed-readers covered the material quickly, averaging almost 700 words per minute. The skimmers were timed at about 600 wpm and the average readers at 240 wpm. But speed hurt comprehension.

On the relatively easy material, the speed-readers answered only 65 percent of the general and 29 percent of the specific questions correctly. Average readers answered 80 percent of the general and 48 percent of the specific questions correctly. On the more difficult reading, average readers got half of the general questions correct, while speed-readers could manage just one in three. Both groups had trouble with the specific questions in the difficult passages, but the average readers still out-scored the speed-readers 23 percent to 17 percent. On all of the tests, skimmers answered questions about as well as did speed-readers.

The researchers also tracked eye movements to learn how speed-reading works. They found that for both passages, the speed-readers focused on approximately on one-third of the words and spent about 230 milliseconds on each, while average readers paused on twice as many words for an average of 330 milliseconds apiece. Skimmers, again, were similar to speed-readers.

Speed-reading may work well with easy or familiar material, the researchers say, but can lead to problems with dense or unfamiliar passages. Also, since speed-readers spend less time on words, they probably stop mulling over some of the more complicated words too soon to comprehend them.

"If you need to fully understand a passage you're better off reading normally than skimming," Just says, "and even if you are a trained speed-reader, you might want to read normally, especially on difficult material."

Marcel Just, Ph.D., and Patricia A. Carpenter, Ph.D., are at Carnegie-Mellon University. They have published some of these results in The Psychology of Reading and Language Comprehension *(Allyn & Bacon, 1987). Michael Masson, Ph.D., is at the University of Victoria in British Columbia, Canada.*

REMEMBER:

- To find the topic, ask "What is the article about?"

- To answer this question, preview by reading the title, subtitle, and bold-face headings. Also look at aids such as pictures or graphs.

- If more information is needed, read the first and last paragraphs of the article.

- If necessary, read the first sentence of all other paragraphs.

Chapter Two

LOCATING THE MAIN IDEA

The models and exercises in this chapter will help you to

- Determine the main idea of an article.
- State the main idea of an article in your own words.

The **main idea** of an article is the major point the author makes about a topic. In an article, the main idea is often called the **thesis statement.** In a paragraph, the main idea is often called the **topic sentence.**

The difference between the main idea and the topic is that in the main idea, the author states an opinion about the topic. In examples shown below, the topic is written in italics and the author's opinion is shown in boldface type. Notice that the opinion can be stated before or after the topic.

Americans are more concerned with *saving the whales* **than with saving jobs.**

Dating practices in Mexico **are considerably different than those in the United States.**

A person has to be careful when choosing *sailboats for beginners.*

HOW TO FIND THE MAIN IDEA

To find the main idea, ask, "What is the author's main point about the topic?" To answer this question, begin by looking at the clues that helped you identify the topic (the title, headings, pictures). For further clues, read the first and last paragraphs of the article (or the first and last sentences of a short article) because authors often state the main idea near the beginning or end of an article. If you find a sentence that states the main idea, underline it.

CAUTION: Often the main idea is not stated in one sentence. You may have to write it yourself. Even if it is stated, you should rewrite it in your own words to be sure you understand it.Whether you rewrite a sentence by the author or write your own main idea sentence, you need to read the article to discover if you have identified the main idea correctly. If you are correct, most of the information in the article will in some way describe, explain, or offer examples of the main idea.

The **main idea** is sometimes called the **controlling idea,** which makes sense because the main idea *controls* the information that the author selects for the article.

If most of the information does not relate to the main idea statement you have written, you should write a new sentence based on your careful reading of the article.

MODEL ONE: Finding the topic and main idea of an article

TAKING TESTS

What is the first thing you do when you take a test? If you are like most students, you probably start by answering the first question, then proceed through the test, answering the rest of the questions in order. However, there is a better way. If you follow a few simple steps, you can make test-taking easier and improve your grades.

The first step is to preview. Spend a few minutes scanning the test to find out how many questions there are and what types of questions are asked (multiple choice, true-false, essay, etc.). Pay attention to all directions. Notice how many points are assigned to different questions or sections. With this information in mind, next make a plan of how much time to spend on each question of the test and of which questions to answer first. Allow more time for sections worth the most points.

The third step is to begin with the section that is easiest for you. This will insure a few quick, easy points for you and will probably give you a positive feeling that will help get you through the test. Confidence is important to good performance on a test, and tackling questions you know the answers to will help your confidence.

Finally, when you come to questions that you cannot answer or are unsure about, skip them for the time being. After you have finished the rest of the test, you can come back to these questions, try to answer them, or guess if there is no penalty for guessing.

What is the article about? (Topic)

The value of a test-taking system

Or you might write

A good procedure for taking tests

What is the author's main point about the topic? (Main Idea)

A test-taking system can help you get better grades.

Or you might write

Four easy steps can help you get better grades on tests.

MODEL TWO: Finding the topic and main idea of an article

THE VALUE OF A SPEED READING COURSE

Leon was a typical college student, or at least he thought he was. He got fairly good grades, mostly C's and B's, but his grades began falling when he was swamped with reading assignments. He thought about quitting school, and he walked to the student union building to play pool. Instead, he decided to talk with a counselor. The counselor suggested that Leon take a speed reading course offered through the school's reading lab. Leon followed the advice and learned several skills which helped him improve his reading ability and self-confidence.

First, Leon learned to preview reading material by reading the title and by looking at pictures, charts, headings, or anything else that gave him some sense of the subject and main idea. Then, before he read the article, he would think about the subject to discover what he knew about it. He usually found that he already knew something about the subject matter and sometimes quite a lot. In either case, he found it helpful to briefly think about his own feelings and knowledge of the subject. It not only made the reading material interesting, but he found he understood it better.

Next, Leon developed the ability to vary his reading rate according to the material and his purpose for reading it. For example, Leon realized it does not make sense to speed read poetry or textbooks. Nor does it make sense to speed read material that is to be learned for a test the next day. However, when Leon was reading a novel or an article for pleasure or general information, speed reading techniques saved him a great deal of time.

Leon also learned how to read entire phrases instead of word-by-word. His instructor called this "clustering," and Leon soon found it easy to look at two or three words at a time instead of just one. Since the eyes stop when they focus, the fewer times Leon focused, the faster he read.

Finally, Leon learned not to waste eye movement. Instead of moving his eyes all the way to the end of each line, he practiced making his last eye-stop two or three words from the end of the line. He also learned to focus his eyes two or three words away from the left-hand margin of each new line rather than on the first word of the line.

Leon soon overcame his feeling of being overwhelmed by reading assignments. He realized that he had to determine what type of material he was being asked to read and analyze his purpose for reading it. He then felt free to use speed reading techniques when they were appropriate.

What is the article about? (Topic)

The benefits of a speed reading course

Or you might write

Ways to improve reading speed

What is the author's main point about the subject? (Main Idea)

Leon learned four skills that helped him read faster.

Or you might write

A reading course can provide help in increasing reading rate.

EXERCISE ONE

Preview the following article to discover the topic and main idea. Then read to determine if you are correct. Underline the main idea sentence and write it in your own words.

DYSLEXIA: RECOGNIZING SHAPES, NOT SOUNDS
by Sarah Vandershaf
from *Psychology Today*

Read these words. You probably can almost hear them as you read. Dyslexics, however, may lack this inner ear for language, making reading more difficult for them than it is for most people.

A preliminary study by psychologist Karen Gross-Glenn and others has shown differences in the patterns of brain activity in dyslexic and nondyslexic readers. The researchers pinpointed 60 structures throughout the brain thought to be involved in aspects of reading—eye movements, language and memory, among others—and measured their activity in six dyslexic and eight nondyslexic readers.

Gross-Glenn and her colleagues found that reading stimulates different regions in dyslexics' brains than it does in the nondyslexics. In both groups, visual regions in the brain were activated. But dyslexics' brains showed less activity than the others' in the posterior peri-insular cortex, a region important for interpreting the sound of words.

The pattern of activity in the dyslexics' brains did resemble that of one group of nondyslexics that the researchers also studied: five people who viewed pictures but did not read. This leads Gross-Glenn to believe that these dyslexics recognize words by how they look, not by how they sound.

"Many dyslexics read holistically," says Gross-Glenn. "They look at the 'envelope' of the word, the overall configuration." In this way, a dyslexic person could easily confuse a word like "publish" with "polish," since the two are very similar in their outward "shape."

Gross-Glenn also found differences in brain activity among the dyslexics themselves, perhaps reflecting different subgroups of dyslexia. Nonetheless, she is already applying her findings in remedial-reading programs that she hopes will help many types of dyslexics overcome their difficulties with the written word.

Karen Gross-Glenn, Ph.D., is at the University of Miami School of Medicine. She and her colleagues presented this research at the most recent meeting of the Society for Neuroscience.

EXERCISE TWO

Preview the following article to determine the topic and main idea. In this article the main idea is clearly stated by the author, Bill Cosby. **First,** underline the main idea sentence(s). **Second,** write the main idea in your own words.

HINT: Sometimes an author writes the main idea in two sentences. When this is the case, try to combine the two sentences into one of your own.

HOW TO READ FASTER
by Bill Cosby
'Power of the Printed Word' Program
International Paper Company

When I was a kid in Philadelphia, I must have read every comic book ever published. (There were fewer of them than there are now.)

I zipped through all of them in a couple of days, then reread the good ones until the next issues arrived.

Yes indeed, when I was a kid, the reading game was a snap. But as I got older, my eyeballs must have slowed down or something! I mean, comic books started to pile up faster than my brother Russell and I could read them!

It wasn't until much later, when I was getting my doctorate, I realized it wasn't my eyeballs that were to blame. Thank goodness. They're still moving as well as ever.

The problem is, there's too much to read these days, and too little time to read every word of it.

Now, mind you, I still read comic books. In addition to contracts, novels, and newspapers. Screenplays, tax returns, and correspondence. Even textbooks about how people read. And which techniques help people to read more in less time.

I'll let you in on a little secret. There are hundreds of techniques you could learn to help you read faster. But I know of three that are especially good. And if I can learn them, so can you—and you can put them to use immediately.

They are commonsense, practical ways to get the meaning from printed words quickly and efficiently. So you'll have time to enjoy your comic books, have a good laugh with Mark Twain or a good cry with *War and Peace*. Ready?

Okay. The first two ways can help you get through tons of reading material fast—without reading every word.

They'll give you the overall meaning of what you're reading. And let you cut out an awful lot of unnecessary reading.

1. PREVIEW—IF IT'S LONG AND HARD

Previewing is especially useful for getting a general idea of heavy reading like long magazine articles, business reports, and nonfiction books.

It can give you as much as half the comprehension in as little as one-tenth the time. For example, you should be able to preview eight or ten 100-page reports in an hour. After previewing, you'll be able to decide which reports (or which parts of reports) are worth a closer look.

Here's how to preview: Read the entire first two paragraphs of whatever you've chosen. Next read only the first sentence of each successive paragraph. Then read the entire last two paragraphs.

Previewing doesn't give you all the details. But it does keep you from spending time on things you don't really want—or need—to read.

Notice that previewing gives you a quick, overall view of long unfamiliar material. For short, light reading, there's a better technique.

2. SKIM—IF IT'S SHORT AND SIMPLE

Skimming is a good way to get a general idea of light reading—like the popular magazines or the sports and entertainment sections of the paper.

You should be able to skim a weekly popular magazine or the second section of your daily paper in less than half the time it takes you to read it now.

Skimming is also a great way to review material you've read before.

Here's how to skim: Think of your eyes as magnets. Force them to move fast. Sweep them across each and every line of type. Pick up only a few key words in each line.

Everybody skims differently.

You and I may not pick up exactly the same words when we skim the same piece, but we'll both get a pretty similar idea of what it's all about.

To show you how it works, I put brackets around the words I picked out when I skimmed the following story. Try it. It shouldn't take you more than ten seconds.

My brother [Russell] [thinks monsters] [live] in our [bedroom closet]

[at night.]

But I told him [he is crazy.]

"Go and [check then,"] he said.

[I didn't want] to.

Russell said [I was chicken.]

["Am not,"] I said.

["Are so,"] he said.

So [I told him] the monsters were going to [eat him] at [midnight.]
He started to cry. My [dad came in] and [told] the monsters [to beat it.]
Then he told us to [go to sleep.]

["If I hear] any more about monsters," he said, ["I'll spank you."]

We went to [sleep fast.] And you [know something?] They [never
did] [come back.]

Skimming can give you a very good idea of this story in about half the
words—and in less than half the time it'd take you to read every word.

So far, you've seen that previewing and skimming can give you a general idea about content—fast. But neither technique can promise more
than 50 percent comprehension, because you aren't reading all the words.
(Nobody gets something for nothing in the reading game.)

To read faster and understand most—if not all—of what you read, you
need to know a third technique.

3. CLUSTER—TO INCREASE SPEED
AND COMPREHENSION

Most of us learn how to read by looking at each word in a sentence—
one at a time. Like this:

My—brother—Russell—thinks—monsters...

You probably still read this way sometimes, especially when the words
are difficult. Or when the words have an extra-special meaning—as in a
poem, a Shakespearean play, or a contract. And that's okay.

But word-by-word reading is a rotten way to read faster. It actually
cuts down on your speed.

Clustering trains you to look at groups of words instead of one word at
a time—to increase your speed enormously. For most of us, clustering is a
totally different way of seeing what we read.

Here's how to cluster: Train your eyes to see all the words in clusters of up to three or four words at a glance. Here's how I'd cluster the story we just skimmed:

[My brother Russell] [thinks monsters] [live in] [our bedroom closet]

[at night.]

[But I told him] [he is crazy.]

["Go and] [check then,"] [he said.]

[I didn't want to.] [Russell said I was chicken.]

["Am not,"] [I said.]

["Are so,"] [he said.]

[So I told him] [the monsters] [were going to] [eat him] [at

midnight.] [He started to cry.] [My dad came in] [and told the

monsters] [to beat it.] [Then he told us] [to go to sleep.]

["If I hear] [any more about monsters,"] [he said,] ["I'll spank you."]

[We went] [to sleep fast.] [And you] [know something?] [They]

[never did] [come back.]

Learning to read clusters is not something your eyes do naturally. It takes constant practice.

Here's how to go about it: Pick something light to read. Read it as fast as you can. Concentrate on seeing three to four words at once rather than one word at a time. Then reread the piece at your normal speed to see what you missed the first time.

Try a second piece. First cluster, then reread to see what you missed in this one.

When you can read in clusters without missing much the first time, you'll know that your speed has increased. Practice 15 minutes every day and you might pick up the technique in a week or so. (Don't be disappointed if it takes longer. Clustering everything takes time and practice.)

So now you have three ways to help you read faster. <u>Preview</u> to cut down on unnecessary heavy reading. <u>Skim</u> to get a quick, general idea of light reading. And <u>cluster</u> to increase your speed and comprehension.

With enough practice, you'll be able to handle more reading at school or work—and at home—in less time. You should even have enough time to read your favorite comic books—and *War and Peace*!

EXERCISE THREE

Preview the following articles and write the topic of each. If you can determine a main idea sentence from the preview, underline it. Otherwise, read enough of the article to locate and underline the main idea sentence if one is stated clearly. Finally, write the main idea in your own words.

A CHEATER'S GUIDE TO HIGH MARKS

by Marc Peyser
from *Newsweek*

Whoever said cheaters never prosper never met Michael Moore. A junior at New Jersey's Rutgers University, Moore is the author of "Cheating 101: The Benefits and Fundamentals of Earning the Easy 'A'," one of the most talked-about books to hit college campuses this year. An 87-page guide to academic guile, "Cheating" offers the finer points of plagiarizing, swiping exams and passing answers right under the professor's nose. Among its lowlights: "Splitting," where a number of conspirators signal each other during an exam with carefully choreographed foot steps; and "Doctoring," where intricately coded crib notes are inscribed on desks, floors, umbrellas, candy-bar wrappers, eyeglass cases and the bottoms of soda cans.

Obviously, many of the book's 65 recipes work best when the professor doesn't pay attention or know the students very well. In fact, Moore spends considerable time lambasting colleges for such sins. "Cheating is a natural defense mechanism triggered by irrelevant courses and professors who look forward to their paychecks more than they do teaching," he claims.

Not surprisingly, that sort of talk—not to mention this kind of book—has rankled a few academics. Rutgers dean James Reed concedes that classes are often too large and that a few professors are too lazy to proctor their exams. He also acknowledges that 29 Rutgers College students were convicted of "academic dishonesty" last year. But, adds Reed, a how-to book on deceit hardly qualifies as a cure-all: "I understand the animus, but I don't respect his methods. There are more constructive ways to effect change."

Moore agrees he could have raked the muck more constructively. But that wouldn't have made as salutary an impact where he wanted it most: his wallet. At $6 a pop, "Cheating" sold 1,000 copies in five days, and a second printing of 2,000 is going fast. Besides, Moore really doesn't see himself as a Fagin or a fink. "I don't think I'm making a cheater out of anybody," he says. "It's their choice, like drunk driving. It's only wrong if you get caught." Maybe the '80s aren't over after all.

THE SECRET OF GETTING KIDS TO LISTEN
by Mary Beth Spann (with Adele Faber)
from *Instructor*

"Kids tune out commands, threats, warnings, and lectures," Adele Faber, co-author of the parenting classic *How to Talk So Kids Will Listen & Listen So Kids Will Talk* (Avon, 1980), tells INSTRUCTOR. "If we want children to listen respectfully to us, we have to use language that makes it possible for them to listen." Faber should know—she's spent two decades helping teachers and parents learn how to communicate effectively with children. We asked her to share her strategies for developing and delivering the kinds of messages that are especially effective with young children. Her advice follows:

1. Encourage listening through play and humor.

Use fanciful techniques to turn learning to listen into a chance to play, a chance to use imagination, and a chance to have fun. If, for example, you want children to walk quietly through the halls, suggest that all of you walk on "marshmallow shoes" or ask kids to reach into their pockets for their "magic mouth-locking keys."

2. Ask students to help figure out solutions to problems.

When it's circle time, do your students do more fidgeting and squirming than listening? Instead of reminding them to be polite and listen to one another *again,* it's helpful to put the problem out on the table for the whole class to tackle. Start by saying something like, "At circle time, I can tell it's hard for some of you to stop yourselves from wriggling." Then ask students for input on how to resolve this problem and write down each of their suggestions. Students may suggest taking a jumping jack or wriggling break, skipping circle time altogether, or having two circle times instead of one long one. At this stage, anything goes—even suggestions that seem silly or impossible—because an inappropriate idea may lead to an appropriate one.

Next, ask for students' help in sorting through the list, eliminating suggestions that won't work and settling on a solution that all or most of you are comfortable with. If what you try solves the problem, point this out to the class by saying something like, "I notice that your solution works!" If what you try doesn't work, give another idea from your list a whirl.

3. Remember to use descriptive—not judgmental—praise.

All praise is not created equal. Praise that judges children or their efforts—such as "that's good" or "you're a good writer"—encourages students to be dependent on us for feedback. Or kids will tune out that kind of global praise, not holding much stock in it.

On the other hand, descriptive praise—simple statements that describe what a child is doing or making—offers students realistic snapshots of their strengths and abilities. If you tell a child, "The end of your story surprised me. Because I didn't think it would turn out that way, it really made me laugh"—the child will also hear, "You have good storytelling skills." This kind of descriptive praise empowers children because it helps them learn more about themselves and their own work.

4. To help tune kids in, offer choices.

Picture this: All the children in your class are happily engaged in creating a colorful dinosaur mural—except David. While the others are planning and painting, he's busy teasing classmates and pretending the paintbrushes are drumsticks. Reminders to start working fall on deaf ears.

While it's easy to reproach David in front of the other students, a quiet, more personal approach that offers choices will more likely engage his attention and help him save face—or avoid giving him the negative attention he may crave. For example, you might take David aside and whisper,

"David, we need everybody's help with this mural. Would you rather paint the grass or the clouds?" If David doesn't care to paint—and keep in mind that some children don't—try offering him another option by saying something like, "So painting doesn't interest you, David. Maybe you'd rather be a researcher. We need someone to find fun facts about dinosaurs to add to the mural." By offering David a choice and avoiding placing the blame on him, he will probably be more likely to hear and to act on what you have to say.

REMEMBER:

- To understand what you read, you must determine the main idea of an article.

- To discover the main idea, ask the question, "What is the author's main point about the topic?"

- To answer this question, preview by reading the title, subtitles, and boldface headings. Look at any charts or graphs. Then read the first sentence of each paragraph and the entire first and last paragraph.

- When you locate a sentence you believe states the main idea, underline it.

- Write the main idea in a complete sentence, using your own words.

Chapter Three

LOCATING MAJOR DETAILS

The models and exercises in this chapter will help you to

- Locate the major details of an article.
- Restate the major details of an article in outline form.

You have a natural curiosity that makes you want to understand both an author's point and the reasoning or support for that point. This sense of curiosity should be developed, for it is the key to critical thinking. Only by examining an author's logic can you intelligently agree or disagree with the main point.

Major details answer the question, "How does the author support the main idea?" Authors use facts, examples, explanations, scientific proof, or combinations of these to support and clarify the main idea of an article. Often explanations of the major details are also added; these are called **minor details**. While minor details can be interesting and informative, they are usually not essential to an understanding or evaluation of the main idea. Therefore, this chapter will concentrate on major details only.

A simplified outline of an article might look something like this:

Topic
   Main Idea
      Major Detail
         Minor Detail
      Major Detail
         Minor Detail
         Minor Detail
      Major Detail
         Minor Detail

If you know the topic, the main idea, and the major details of an article, you understand it well. One way readers recognize major details is by looking for signal words.

SIGNAL WORDS

Major details are often indicated by **signal words and phrases** (sometimes called **transitions**). For example, the word "finally" usually indicates that the author is about to state the final point. In the sentence you just read, the signal phrase "for example" is used to indicate that an example follows.

The following signal words and phrases are grouped according to their function.

Words that signal time or order of importance:

first	finally	before
in the first place	when	after that
second	then	later on

Words that signal contrast or an opposite point:

however	in contrast	despite
but	by contrast	although
on the contrary	in spite of	nevertheless

Words that signal the conclusion of an idea:

in conclusion	to sum up	finally
therefore	in short	as a result
consequently	in summary	

Words that signal the same or a similar idea:

and	more than that	likewise
furthermore	also	similarly
moreover	in the same manner	

Words that signal causes and effects:

because	due to	consequently
since	therefore	as a result

Words that signal examples:

for example	for instance	to illustrate

CAUTION: Even though major details are often introduced by signal words and phrases, authors also use them for other purposes. Therefore, you need to read carefully; don't assume that behind every signal word is a major detail.

Once you have identified the main idea of an article, you will want to identify the major details. Since signal words often help identify major details, it is a good idea to underline them. In the following model, the first sentence is underlined to indicate the main idea, and the signal words (or phrases) which help identify major details are in bold print.

MODEL ONE: Identifying major details with the help of signal words

Read the following article and notice the signal words and phrases which indicate major details.

DRIVING IN EUROPE

<u>Driving experiences vary from one European country to the next</u>. **For example**, in England people drive on the left-hand side of the road. This gets confusing for Americans, especially when they are turning at intersections. **On the other hand**, the French drive on the right-hand side of the road, but their roads are narrow and many of them wind through small villages. **In contrast**, Germany has autobahns (freeways) without speed limits. For instance, it is not uncommon for Germans to drive 100 miles an hour or more on autobahns. **Finally**, in Switzerland the roads are wide and in good condition, but travel on them is often slow because of the many mountain passes.

COMMENTS: The signal words and phrases in bold print indicate the four major details in this article. "For instance" is also a signal phrase, but in this article it does not introduce a major detail. It precedes an example (minor detail) of how fast some Germans drive.

MODEL TWO: Identifying major details with the help of signal words

You read "Taking Tests" in Chapter Two. Read it again here, noticing the underlined signal words which indicate major details.

TAKING TESTS

What is the first thing you do when you take a test? If you are like most students, you probably start by answering the first question, then proceed through the test, answering the rest of the questions in order. However, there is a better way. If you follow a few simple steps, you can make test-taking easier and improve your grades.

The <u>first</u> step is to preview. Spend a few minutes scanning the test to find out how many questions there are and what types of questions are asked (multiple choice, true-false, essay, etc.). Pay attention to all directions. Notice how many points are assigned to different questions or sections. With this information in mind, <u>next</u> make a plan of how much time to spend on each question of the test and of which questions to answer first. Allow more time for sections worth the most points.

The <u>third</u> step is to begin with the section that is easiest for you. This will insure a few quick, easy points for you and will probably give you a positive feeling that will help get you through the test. Confidence is important to good performance on a test, and tackling questions you know the answers to will help your confidence.

<u>Finally,</u> when you come to questions that you cannot answer or are unsure about, skip them for the time being. After you have finished the rest of the test, you come back to these questions, try to answer them, or guess if there is no penalty for guessing.

A complete outline of this article would look like this:

Topic: Test-taking made easier

Main Idea: Four easy steps can help you earn better grades

    Major Detail: First preview before answering

        Minor Detail: How to preview

    Major Detail: Plan so you can work efficiently

        Minor Detail: How to use time wisely

    Major Detail: Begin with easiest section

        Minor Detail: Get quick points

        Minor Detail: Get positive feeling

    Major Detail: Skip questions you don't know

        Minor Detail: Return to these items later

Notice that a good understanding of the article can be shown with just the main idea and major details. While you will often enjoy reading minor details, stating the main idea and major details will show your basic comprehension of the article. From now on, model outlines will include only **major details.**

EXERCISE ONE

The main idea of the following article is underlined. First, underline the signal words which indicate major details. Second, make an outline of the topic, main idea, and major details. Remember to write the outline in your own words to be sure you understand the material.

HOW TO PREVIEW A TEXTBOOK

One of the most helpful things you can do when you begin a new class in college is to preview your textbook. To do this, follow these simple steps. First, examine the table of contents. This will quickly tell you how many chapters are in the book and the nature of the material covered. Second, read the "To the Student" section or the preface, if there is one, to see how the book is organized and how the author approaches the material. Among other things, this will tell you if the book is practical or theoretical in approach. Then examine the copyright date to see how recent the text is. Finally, check to see what special features the book contains. For example, is there an index at the back listing important terms and concepts? Is there a glossary where terms are defined? Is the book arranged chapter-by-chapter or alphabetically? Is there an appendix of additional information? Are there summaries at the end of each chapter? By taking just a few minutes to preview your next textbook, you can get more out of your book in a shorter amount of time.

KEY SENTENCES

An author does not always write signal words before major details. When there are few or no signal words, you must look for key sentences which contain reasons, causes, effects, examples, or steps of a process. Ask yourself, "Which sentences in the article make the main idea understandable or believable?"

MODEL THREE: Locating major details without the aid of signal words

Read the following article and notice the major details which are in italics. The first sentence is underlined because it is the main idea.

TEST ANXIETY

<u>Whenever I take a test I get nervous, and it shows.</u> I can't help it. *My hands shake so much I can hardly hold my pen.* I'm sure everyone notices, but I can't control it. They must think I have some disease of the muscles, but it only happens at test time. *The palms of my hands get sweaty, and I have to keep wiping them on my pants to keep them dry.* Shaky, sweaty hands do not write good tests.

My stomach tightens up and my head aches. I feel as if I have eaten too much, even when I have an empty stomach. It's very distracting, even painful. If I take a pain reliever for my headache, it often further irritates my stomach. I am just not able to think about the test.

I am working to control my nervousness but have not had much luck. I will keep trying, but I may need to get some help. It is a problem too big for me to tackle alone right now.

COMMENTS: Even though no signal words are used to indicate major details, it is clear that the major details describe physical reactions to nervousness about taking tests. The last paragraph is a re-statement of the main idea expressing the author's intention to keep working on the problem.

EXERCISE TWO

Read the following article. Underline the main idea and any signal words which indicate major details. Then write an outline listing the Topic, Main Idea, and Major Details.

WHY TAKE GOOD NOTES?

Perhaps you have been told to take good notes in order to get better grades. "Oh sure," you think, "it might help, but it's a lot of work. It may not be worth the effort." Actually, taking good class notes is important for several reasons and is almost always worth its weight in gold.

For one thing, note-taking helps you keep your mind on what the instructor is saying. If you are trying to write the important ideas of the lecture, you have to keep your mind focused. We all know how easy it is to let our minds wander during some classes.

Second, notes are a good memory aid. They remind you of future assignments and due dates, and they provide you with review sheets before tests. Most of us do not have photographic memories, but good notes can remind us of the classroom experience.

Sometimes an instructor lectures on the same ideas as those in your textbook. Often the textbooks are long and difficult to read. Good notes can help clarify material in the textbook when your instructor covers ideas from the book. It is important to get the necessary information, but it usually does not matter where you get it.

Last, good notes are a record of information that might not be included in your textbook but which your instructor expects you to know. Often, instructors test primarily on class lectures, even when a textbook is assigned. You will find that, with very few exceptions, good class notes are more than worth all the effort it takes to produce them. The rewards are called good grades and pride in your accomplishment.

EXERCISE THREE

Read the following article. Underline the main idea and any signal words which indicate major details. Then write an outline listing the Topic, Main Idea, and Major Details.

HOW TO TAKE GOOD NOTES

So you are convinced that good note-taking is important to your success in academics. However, no one has taught you how to take good notes. Teachers have just expected you to do this since you have been in school. It's important to find the style that works for you, but several steps are involved in almost all good note-taking systems.

The first step is to date and label your notes. This is simple and quick, but it is important. It keeps your notes organized. If an instructor says you will be tested on the material from the two previous weeks which cover the human skeleton, you will be able to quickly identify what to study.

Next, consider how your notes look. Two things are important here. Leave plenty of space as you take notes. This allows you to fill in words or ideas you may have missed and still keep your notes neat and readable. Furthermore, you should devise a method for indicating key points. Some people underline these points; others put a star or check beside them; still others indicate them by indenting either the major points or the subpoints. The important thing is not *how* you identify them but that you *do* identify them.

Be sure you always take notes in your own words. To do this, develop your own shorthand or system of abbreviations so that you can concentrate on listening rather than on writing. Putting ideas in your own words, even in abbreviations, is the only way to be sure you understand the material.

Perhaps the most important step is to get in the habit of editing your notes soon after class. By doing this you will automatically review the important ideas from class, fill in any information you wrote down in sketchy form, and realize what you missed so that you can ask questions later. Try to review notes within twenty-four hours after class.

STRATEGIES FOR LONGER ARTICLES

So far the articles in the models and exercises in this chapter have been rather short. Most articles you will read are much longer, and identifying the main idea and major details usually becomes a greater challenge due to the increased length. Like any other skill, the ability to find major details improves with practice. Here are some suggestions to help you develop this skill.

1. Follow *all* of the preview steps discussed in Chapters One and Two:
   - read the title
   - look at pictures, subtitles, and headings
   - read the first and last paragraphs
   - read the first sentence of each of the other paragraphs

2. Divide the article into sections which indicate the introduction, main idea, major details, and conclusion. The sections may consist of one or more paragraphs. Check the main idea of each paragraph to see if it is a major detail of the article. Do not assume that each paragraph contains a major detail.

3. Label each section on the article itself.

MODEL FOUR: Identifying major details in an article

IMPROVING YOUR MEMORY

Section One:
Introduction

At a party, Nora was introduced to five friends of the host. The host said, "Nora, I'd like you to meet Teresa and her husband Juan. Teresa works at the reading lab with me; I'm sure I've told you about her. And this is Sherry, Alexis, and Maria." Nora said hello to each one and went into the kitchen to find her roommate. A few minutes later, Nora could not remember the names of any of the people she had just met. She complained to her roommate, "I just don't have a good memory."

Main Idea

How is your memory? It is probably only when your memory fails you that you think about it. An occasional lapse is normal. The key to "managing" your memory and improving it is to understand how memory works.

Section Two:
Major Detail

In order to remember something, you need to have sensory input; that is, a sensation needs to be recorded by one of your senses. For example, a plane flies over your house and you hear it, or a cake is burning in the oven and you smell it.

Section Three:
Major Detail

But sensory input is not enough. Your eyes and ears might be seeing and hearing numerous sights and sounds, but you can only focus on a few at any one time. The ones you focus on are the ones you are most likely to remember.

Section Four:
Major Detail

To improve your memory retention, you must consciously *intend* to remember certain sights, sounds, smells, or other stimuli and then focus on them. For example, at a party like the one Nora attended, you might be introduced to several people. If you feel it is important to remember their names, focus on their names and faces and make an effort to remember them. If necessary, use word associations to help you remember. (For example, to remember Alexis' name, you might associate her with the television character on "Dynasty.") Without the intention to remember, you probably won't retain the name in the first place. Or you may forget it as soon as you hear it because you did not make any special effort to remember.

Section Five:
Major Detail

This conscious effort is not enough for lasting memory, however. You will not remember the sensory input for very long if you do not do something to place it in your long-term memory. You need to review the new information within 24 to 48 hours to remember it over time. Periodic review will ensure that you never forget the information.

Section Six:
Conclusion

Improving your memory using this technique is not difficult. Practice it often to improve your retention skills. Pay attention to the input, your intent to remember, and, of course, review. You have the power to remember anything you want—if you choose to.

What is the article about? (Topic)

How memory works

What is the author's main point about the topic? (Main Idea)

Everyone has a "good" memory but can improve it by understanding how memory works.

How does the author support the main idea? (Major Details)

—We receive input via one of the senses.
—We focus on certain input.
—In order to remember, we must intend to remember.
—Reviewing within 24 hours is important.

COMMENTS: Section One (the first two paragraphs) of this article introduces the topic and states the main idea of the entire article. Sections Two, Three, Four and Five each contain one major detail. Section Six (the conclusion) restates the main idea and major details.

MODEL FIVE: Identifying major details in an article

THE IMPORTANCE OF CHILDHOOD MEMORIES
by Norman M. Lobsenz
from *Reader's Digest*

Section One:
Introduction

Some years ago, when my young wife became desperately ill, I wondered how I would be able to cope with the physical and emotional burden of caring for her. One night, when I was drained of strength and endurance, a long forgotten incident came to mind.

I was about ten years old at the time and my mother was seriously ill. I had gotten up in the middle of the night to get a drink of water. As I passed my parents' bedroom, I saw the light on. I looked inside. My father was sitting in a chair in his bathrobe next to Mother's bed, doing nothing. She was asleep. I rushed into the room.

"What's wrong?" I cried. "Why aren't you asleep?"

Dad soothed me. "Nothing's wrong. I'm just watching over her."

I can't say exactly how, but the memory of that long-ago incident gave me the strength to take up my own burden again. The remembered light and warmth from my parents' room were curiously powerful and my father's words haunted me: "I'm just watching over her." The role I now assumed seemed somehow more bearable, as if a resource has been called from the past or from within.

Section Two:
Main Idea

In moments of psychological jeopardy, such memories often turn out to be the ultimate resources of personality, dark prisms which focus our basic feeling about life. As Sir James Barrie once wrote, "God gives us memory so that we may have roses in December."

Section Three:
Major Detail
*Can't predict
what makes
lasting
memories*

No parent can ever really know which memory, planted in childhood, will grow to be a rose. Often our most vivid and enduring remembrances are of apparently simple, even trivial things. I did not discover this myself until one bright, leaf-budding spring daywhen my son Jim and I were putting a fresh coat of paint on the porch railing. We were talking about plans to celebrate his approaching 15th birthday, and I found myself thinking how quickly his childhood had passed.

"What do you remember best?" I asked him.

He answered without a moment's hesitation. "The night we were driving somewhere, just you and me, on a dark road, and you stopped the car and helped me catch fireflies."

Fireflies? I could have thought of a dozen incidents, both pleasant and unpleasant, that might have remained vivid in his mind. But fireflies? I searched my memory—and eventually it came back to me.

I'd been driving cross-country, traveling late to meet a rather tight schedule. I had stopped to clean the windshield, when all at once a cloud of fireflies surrounded us. Jim, who was five years old then, was tremendously excited. He wanted to catch one. I was tired and tense, and anxious to get on to our destination. I was about to tell him that we didn't have time to waste when something changed my mind. In the trunk of the car I found an empty glass jar. Into it we scooped dozens of the insects. And while Jim watched them glow, I told him of the mysterious cold light they carried in their bodies. Finally, we uncapped the jar and let the fireflies blink away into the night.

"Why do you remember that?" I asked. "It doesn't seem terribly important."

"I don't know," he said. "I didn't even know I did remember it until just now." Then a few moments later: "Maybe I do know why. Maybe it was because I didn't think you were going to stop and catch any with me—and you did."

Since that day I have asked many friends to reach back into their childhoods and tell me what they recall with greatest clarity. Almost always they mention similar moments—experiences or incidents not of any great importance. Not crises or trauma or triumphs, but things which, although small in themselves, carry sharp sensations of warmth and joy, or sometimes pain.

One friend I spoke with was the son of an executive who was often away from home. "Do you know what I remember best?" he said to me. "It was the day of the annual school picnic when my usually very dignified father appeared in his shirt-sleeves, sat on the grass with me, ate a box lunch, and then made the longest hit in our softball game. I found out later that he postponed a business trip to Europe to be there." My friend is a man who experiences the world as a busy, serious place but who basically feels all right about it and about himself. His favorite childhood memory is both clue to and cause of his fundamental soundness.

Section Four:
Major Detail
*Parents
can help
shape
memories*

Clearly, the power parents have to shape the memories of their children involves an awesome responsibility. In this respect nothing is trivial. What to a grownup might seem a casual word or action often is, to a child, the kernel of a significant memory on which he will build. As grownups, we draw on these memories as sources of strength or weakness. Author Willa Cather saw this clearly. "There are those early memories," she wrote. "One cannot get another set; one has only those."

Not long ago, I talked with a woman who has married a young and struggling sculptor. She cheerfully accepted their temporary poverty. "I grew up during the depression," she said. "My dad scrambled from one job to another. But I remembered that each time a job ended, my mother would scrape together enough money to make us an especially good dinner. She used to call them our 'trouble meals.' I know now that they were her way of showing Dad she believed in him, in his ability to fight back. I learned that loving someone is more important than having something."

If childhood memories are so important, what can parents do to help supply their children with a healthy set?

Section Five
Major Detail
Steps to provide good memories

■ For one thing, parents should be aware of the importance of the memory-building process. In our adult preoccupation, we tend to think that the "important" experiences our children will have are still in their future. We forget that, to them, childhood is reality rather than merely a preparation for reality. We forget that childhood memories form the adult personality. "What we describe as 'character,' " wrote Sigmund Freud, "is based on the memory traces of our earliest youth."

■ Parents can try to find the extra energy, time, or enthusiasm to carry out the small and "insignificant" plan that is so important to a child. The simple act of baking that special batch of cookies or helping to build that model car, even though you are tired or harried, may make an important memory for your youngster.

Conversely, parents can try to guard against the casual disillusionments and needless disappointments which they often unthinkingly inflict on children. I would venture that almost everyone has a memory of an outing canceled or a promise broken without a reason or an explanation. "My father always used to say, 'We'll see.' " one man told me. "I soon learned that what that meant was 'no,' but without any definite reason."

■ Parents can think back to their own childhoods and call up their own memories. By remembering the incidents that made important impressions on them, parents can find guideposts to ways in which they can shape the future memories of their own youngsters.

■ Finally, parents can, by their own actions and words, communicate emotions as well as exper-iences to their children. We can give them a

> memory of courage rather than fear; of strength rather than weakness; of an appetite for adventure rather than a shrinking from new people and places; of warmth and affection rather than rigidity and coldness. In just such memories are rooted the attitudes and feeling that characterize a person's entire approach to life.

What is the article about? (Topic)

Childhood memories

Or you might write

Why childhood memories are important

What is the author's main point about the topic? (Main Idea)

Childhood memories can help us get through tough times.

Or you might write

In tough times, childhood memories can give us strength.

How does the author support the main idea? (Major Details)

—*Parents can't predict what makes lasting memories.*
—*Parents can help shape their children's memories in four ways:*
   1. be aware of the importance of memory process
   2. try to find extra time & energy for children's activities
   3. recall own childhood memories
   4. share both your emotions & experiences w/children

COMMENTS: Notice that not every paragraph contains a major detail. For example, Section One (the introduction) is five paragraphs long and Section Three (one long example) is nine paragraphs long.

EXERCISE FOUR

In Chapter Two you read "How to Read Faster" and wrote the topic and main idea. This time, divide the article into sections and label them. Then write an outline, providing the topic, main idea, and major details.

HOW TO READ FASTER
by Bill Cosby
'Power of the Printed Word' Program
International Paper Company

When I was a kid in Philadelphia, I must have read every comic book ever published. (There were fewer of them than there are now.)

I zipped through all of them in a couple of days, then reread the good ones until the next issues arrived.

Yes indeed, when I was a kid, the reading game was a snap. But as I got older, my eyeballs must have slowed down or something! I mean, comic books started to pile up faster than my brother Russell and I could read them!

It wasn't until much later, when I was getting my doctorate, I realized it wasn't my eyeballs that were to blame. Thank goodness. They're still moving as well as ever.

The problem is, there's too much to read these days, and too little time to read every word of it.

Now, mind you, I still read comic books. In addition to contracts, novels, and newspapers. Screenplays, tax returns, and correspondence. Even textbooks about how people read. And which techniques help people to read more in less time.

I'll let you in on a little secret. There are hundreds of techniques you could learn to help you read faster. But I know of three that are especially good. And if I can learn them, so can you—and you can put them to use immediately.

They are commonsense, practical ways to get the meaning from printed words quickly and efficiently. So you'll have time to enjoy your comic books, have a good laugh with Mark Twain or a good cry with *War and Peace*. Ready?

Okay. The first two ways can help you get through tons of reading material fast—without reading every word.

They'll give you the overall meaning of what you're reading. And let you cut out an awful lot of unnecessary reading.

1. PREVIEW—IF IT'S LONG AND HARD

Previewing is especially useful for getting a general idea of heavy reading like long magazine articles, business reports, and nonfiction books.

It can give you as much as half the comprehension in as little as one-tenth the time. For example, you should be able to preview eight or ten 100-page reports in an hour. After previewing, you'll be able to decide which reports (or which parts of reports) are worth a closer look.

Here's how to preview: Read the entire first two paragraphs of whatever you've chosen. Next read only the first sentence of each successive paragraph. Then read the entire last two paragraphs.

Previewing doesn't give you all the details. But it does keep you from spending time on things you don't really want—or need—to read.

Notice that previewing gives you a quick, overall view of long unfamiliar material. For short, light reading, there's a better technique.

2. SKIM—IF IT'S SHORT AND SIMPLE

Skimming is a good way to get a general idea of light reading—like the popular magazines or the sports and entertainment sections of the paper.

You should be able to skim a weekly popular magazine or the second section of your daily paper in less than half the time it takes you to read it now.

Skimming is also a great way to review material you've read before.

Here's how to skim: Think of your eyes as magnets. Force them to move fast. Sweep them across each and every line of type. Pick up only a few key words in each line.

Everybody skims differently.

You and I may not pick up exactly the same words when we skim the same piece, but we'll both get a pretty similar idea of what it's all about.

To show you how it works, I circled the words I picked out when I skimmed the following story. Try it. It shouldn't take you more than ten seconds.

My brother [Russell] [thinks monsters] [live] in our [bedroom closet]

[at night.]

But I told him [he is crazy.]

"Go and [check then,"] he said.

[I didn't want] to.

Russell said [I was chicken.]

["Am not,"] I said.

["Are so,"] he said.

So [I told him] the monsters were going to [eat him] at [midnight.] He started to cry. My [dad came in] and [told] the monsters [to beat it.] Then he told us to [go to sleep.]

["If I hear] any more about monsters," he said, ["I'll spank you."]

We went to [sleep fast.] And you [know something?] They [never did] [come back.]

Skimming can give you a very good idea of this story in about half the words—and in less than half the time it'd take you to read every word.

So far, you've seen that previewing and skimming can give you a general idea about content—fast. But neither technique can promise more than 50 percent comprehension, because you aren't reading all the words. (Nobody gets something for nothing in the reading game.)

To read faster and understand most—if not all—of what you read, you need to know a third technique.

3. CLUSTER—TO INCREASE SPEED AND COMPREHENSION

Most of us learn how to read by looking at each word in a sentence—one at a time. Like this:

My—brother—Russell—thinks—monsters...

You probably still read this way sometimes, especially when the words are difficult. Or when the words have an extra-special meaning—as in a poem, a Shakespearean play, or a contract. And that's okay.

But word-by-word reading is a rotten way to read faster. It actually cuts down on your speed.

Clustering trains you to look at groups of words instead of one word at a time—to increase your speed enormously. For most of us, clustering is a totally different way of seeing what we read.

Here's how to cluster: Train your eyes to see all the words in clusters of up to three or four words at a glance. Here's how I'd cluster the story we just skimmed:

[My brother Russell] [thinks monsters] [live in] [our bedroom closet]

[at night.]

[But I told him] [he is crazy.]

["Go and] [check then,"] [he said.]

 [I didn't want to.] [Russell said I was chicken.]

["Am not,"] [I said.]

["Are so,"] [he said.]

[So I told him] [the monsters] [were going to] [eat him] [at

midnight.] [He started to cry.] [My dad came in] [and told the

monsters] [to beat it.] [Then he told us] [to go to sleep.]

["If I hear] [any more about monsters,"] [he said,] ["I'll spank you."]

[We went] [to sleep fast.] [And you] [know something?] [They]

[never did] [come back.]

Learning to read clusters is not something your eyes do naturally. It takes constant practice.

Here's how to go about it: Pick something light to read. Read it as fast as you can. Concentrate on seeing three to four words at once rather than one word at a time. Then reread the piece at your normal speed to see what you missed the first time.

Try a second piece. First cluster, then reread to see what you missed in this one.

When you can read in clusters without missing much the first time, you'll know that your speed has increased. Practice 15 minutes every day and you might pick up the technique in a week or so. (Don't be disappointed if it takes longer. Clustering everything takes time and practice.)

So now you have three ways to help you read faster. <u>Preview</u> to cut down on unnecessary heavy reading. <u>Skim</u> to get a quick, general idea of light reading. And <u>cluster</u> to increase your speed and comprehension.

With enough practice, you'll be able to handle more reading at school or work—and at home—in less time. You should even have enough time to read your favorite comic books—and *War and Peace*!

EXERCISE FIVE

Now is a good time to explore the essays in Part Two. Choose two essays (perhaps with advice from your instructor) and complete all of the steps you have learned so far. Preview the article, divide it into sections and label them. Then write an outline stating the topic, main idea, and major details.

REMEMBER:

- Major details support the author's main point; they are essential to your understanding of the main idea and your ability to evaluate it.

- Major details answer the question, "How does the author support the main idea?"

- To find major details:

  - Preview the article to determine the topic and main idea.

  - Use signal words and phrases to help you identify major details.

  - Divide longer articles into sections; read the first line of every paragraph to help you determine where to divide the sections.

  - Determine the main idea of each section; these are usually the major details of a longer article.

Chapter Four

WRITING A SUMMARY

The models and exercises in this chapter will help you to

- Write the topic, main idea, and major details in outline form.
- Write a summary of an article from an outline.

Knowing how to write a good summary can benefit you in several ways:

1. A written summary allows you to measure your understanding of an article because you have to write it in your own words.
2. You can improve your grades because many college courses require written summaries.
3. You can write better term papers because such assignments require you to summarize long articles and books before you write your paper.
4. A written summary is often part of an essay exam. Therefore, if you can write a good summary, you have a clear advantage over students who cannot.

When you write a summary of an article, you re-write what someone else has written. You write a shorter version, using your own words and sentence style. To write a shorter version of an article, you focus on the author's main idea and major details.

START WITH AN OUTLINE

The topic, main idea, and major details of an article are the elements of a good outline. You have practiced writing these elements in Chapters One, Two, and Three. Putting these elements together will form an outline from which you can write a good summary.

Your outline should include the following:

- the topic (stated in a word or phrase)
- the main idea (stated in a complete sentence)
- a list of major details (stated in phrases or sentences)

MODEL ONE: The outline of an article

Below is an article you read in Chapter Three. An outline of the article is modeled for you.

HOW TO PREVIEW A TEXTBOOK

<u>One of the most helpful things you can do when you begin a new class in college is to preview your textbook. To do this, follow these simple steps.</u> First, examine the table of contents. This will quickly tell you how many chapters are in the book and the nature of the material covered. Second, read the "To the Student" section or the preface, if there is one, to see how the book is organized and how the author approaches the material. Among other things, this will tell you if the book is practical or theoretical in approach. Then examine the copyright date to see how recent the text is. Finally, check to see what special features the book contains. For example, is there an index at the back listing important terms and concepts? Is there a glossary where terms are defined? Is the book arranged chapter-by-chapter or alphabetically? Is there an appendix of additional information? Are there summaries at the end of each chapter? By taking just a few minutes to preview your next textbook, you can get more out of your book in a shorter amount of time.

What is the paragraph about? (Topic)

How to preview a textbook

Or you might write

Previewing a textbook

What is the author's main point about the topic? (Main Idea)

Previewing a textbook involves four steps.

Major Details:

—*look at table of contents*

—*read any introductory material*

—*check copyright date*

—*look for special features*

HOW TO TURN YOUR OUTLINE INTO A SUMMARY

Your outline can be turned into a summary in three steps:

1. Write an opening sentence.
2. Change phrases of the outline into complete sentences.
3. Add necessary information.

Writing the Opening Sentence

The opening sentence of a summary should contain the article's title and author (if given) as well as the author's main idea.

Here are sample opening sentences for articles you read in previous chapters of this book:

A. Bill Cosby offers three ways to cut down on reading time in "How To Read Faster."

B. In "The Importance of Childhood Memories," Norman M. Lobsenz describes how childhood memories can help us get through difficult times.

C. In "Test Anxiety" the author describes the physical symptoms experienced before taking a test.

Notice that the verbs in each of these examples are written in present tense. Here are some other verbs you might use for these opening sentences:

Bill Cosby *explains*...
Norman Lobsenz *states*...
The author *relates*...

Later in the summary, you may wish to use the author's name again. Once you have given the full name, use only the author's last name throughout your summary.

Cosby also lists...
Lobsenz further examines...

After the Opening Sentence

A good summary contains major details of the article.

A good summary contains any minor details needed to explain or clarify the major details.

A good summary is written primarily in your own words. If you use more than three consecutive words from the article, use quotation marks. You might wish to quote an important phrase or sentence, but your summary should never be simply a string of quotations.

The length of a summary varies. It is usually no longer than **one-fourth** as long as the article you are summarizing.

MODEL TWO: Outline and summary of an article

Following this article is a model of an outline and a summary.

REVITALIZE YOUR MEMORY
by Mark Golin
from *Prevention*

Memory. People tend to think of it as the ability to dredge up the name of that mustached man they met in a Parisian pet shop 25 years ago. But in reality, we use our memory every minute of the day for everything we do. We use it every time we speak a word, drive a car, brush our teeth or shop for groceries.

Given the importance of memory, it's hard to understand why we do so little to keep this important commodity from declining as we get older. Maybe it's because we don't think there's anything we *can* do about it. But in fact, the regeneration of a fading memory is well within most people's power.

"Many of the everyday lapses we experience are more the fault of our poor memory techniques than of any physical problem with the brain," says Robin West, Ph.D., University of Florida psychologist and author of *Memory Fitness Over Forty* (Triad Publishing, 1985). "Given the use of good techniques, practice and daily mental stimulation, there's no reason why you can't improve your memory substantially.

Keeping your memory in top form is similar to keeping your body in shape. But instead of brisk morning strolls, you need to turn the task of memorizing into a creative adventure that makes your mind work up a healthy sweat. Here's how to set up your own memory training program.

Attenn-shun!

Start by memorizing a little one-liner penned by English writer Samuel Johnson: "The art of memory is the art of attention." When we can't remember a piece of information, frequently it's because we never really paid enough attention to it in the first place. Since we didn't encode it firmly in our memory, it's no surprise that it's not there when we look for it.

Taking the attention theme one step further, in 1890, psychologist William James wrote, "Habit diminishes the conscious attention with which our acts are performed." To put this ponderous statement into everyday clothes, try to remember in detail the sign above the first gas station that you pass on the way to the grocery store or work. Don't feel bad if you can't. Even though you pass it every day, chances are you never really see it. "People commonly turn off their minds when they are performing habitual actions," says Dr. West. "When you are in an 'automatic pilot mode,' new information has no way of encoding itself in your mind."

The way to combat automatic-pilot syndrome is to practice the fine art of observation—consciously pay attention to details that make an object or circumstance unique. Dr. West suggests starting with a magazine photo of a person. Look at the photo, then close the magazine. List the features in the photo. What color were the eyes? What shape was the nose? What about hairstyle and clothing? Was there anything in the background? Having made a list, go back to the photo and study it for two details you missed. Then start again. Do this until you've managed to list every aspect down to the most minute.

Another way to practice observation during the day is to think of a common item that you see regularly. It could be a fountain pen, a building you walk by, or a tile floor. Before you actually come across the item again, ask yourself some questions about it. What is it made of? How many windows? What color? If you can't answer the questions immediately, take a moment when confronted by the object to look for the answers.

With practice, observation can become second nature. The way you look at things changes as you focus in on details. And the attention you pay to detail makes each object unique enough that it will stand out in your mind and be easily encoded into your memory.

Off Automatic Pilot

Now you can apply your new-found powers of observation to your behavior. How many times have you left the house only to wonder 10 minutes later if you locked the front door? "To overcome an automatic-pilot behavior like this, you need to either change the pattern of your action or find something concerning this routine action that is new and unusual," says Dr. West.

If you're right-handed, for example, you could lock the front door with your left hand. Or, as you lock the door, note the sound of the lawn mower coming from your neighbor's yard. Twenty minutes later, as you're driving along wondering whether you locked the front door, you'll remember the lawn mower and then remember that you locked the door while listening to that sound.

Making Things Meaningful

Memory and learning are not far apart, notes Dr. West. When we learn, we take random information and arrange it in a manner that has meaning to us.

As we concentrate and note specific details, they become encoded in our memory. But many things we wish to remember, such as lists of items, phone numbers, dates and random facts, are difficult to organize into a cohesive whole because they have no order or inherent meaning. Rather than remembering one thing that naturally flows into another, we try to remember many different pieces of information that have no connection.

A better way—and the secret of most memory techniques—involves organizing those small pieces of material into larger groups, giving the items a context we can understand and making the information unique in our own minds.

"Many times, it's hard to draw a line of understanding between a word and its meaning," says Dr. West. "You might be hard put to remember that the medical prefix *blepharo-* refers to the eyelids, for example, because it provides no clues. But you can take the sound of the word and incorporate it into this sentence: I'd *bl*ink if I saw a *pharaoh*. The sentence reminds you of the word and blink suggests eyelid."

To remember an address, such as 1225 Turner Street, you might say to yourself, "I *turned* my life around on *Christmas*," (12/25). Can't seem to remember that there are 5,280 feet in a mile? Think of "5 tomatoes": 5, 2 *(to)*, 8 *(mat)*, 0 *(oes)*.

Interactive Imagery

Here's a good memory technique to practice at the supermarket. Suppose you have six items you need to pick up. To use mental imagery, picture the six items in your mind. Maybe they'd be on a shelf or lined up at the checkout counter, but the six items would be inactive.

Interactive imagery goes one step further, in that you picture a sequence of action events that include the items you want to remember. That way, when you're at the store, you can just replay the image in your mind like a video. It may sound confusing, but let's give it a whirl using a typical grocery list: milk, bread, celery, pepper, apples, and cucumbers. Keep in mind, the more flamboyant the image, the better you'll remember it.

Walking through the woods you come to the bank of a white river of milk. To make your journey easier you decide to sail down the river and do so on a raft made of a large slice of bread. The long green steering oar you're using is actually an enormous celery stalk. The weather starts to turn bad and soon dense flakes of black snow (pepper) and huge red hailstones (apples) begin to fall. Things go from bad to worse as your bread raft sails out to a milk sea where an enemy submarine is waiting. The sub fires and you see a cucumber torpedo heading straight for you.

Now close your eyes and try very hard to actually see yourself in the story. Once you have seen the image, try testing yourself and see if you remember all six items by replaying your mental video. Try again five days from now.

This technique can also be applied to other tasks, such as remembering names. "When I want people to remember my name," says Dr. West, "I have them picture a robin flying west. To connect the name to my person, I ask them to include my most memorable feature, long hair, in the image. The end result is a mental image of a robin flying west with long hair streaming behind it in the wind. When they see my long hair, it triggers the image that contains my name, Robin West."

If you are thinking that this is an awful lot of trouble just to remember a few things, note the other benefits that will accrue. "Storing information in a rich, elaborate form is the secret of sharp recall," says psychologist Endel Tulving, Ph.D., of the University of Toronto.

The process of making information rich and elaborate is also one of the finest ways to stimulate yourself intellectually. Your mind needs this stimulation to stay sharp just as your heart needs aerobic exercise to stay strong. And you may just find that tailoring information into sayings and images can be quite an entertaining way to stay in mental shape.

Finally, if you don't exercise your memory, you will begin to lose it. There's little doubt about that, experts agree. Most of the time, the process can be reversed, but why not start to recharge your memory now and enjoy it to the fullest?

OUTLINE

What is the article about? (Topic)

Techniques for making or keeping your memory sharp

What is the author's main point about the topic? (Main Idea)

Through regular practice of proven techniques, you can improve your memory and keep it in top shape.

Major Details

—*Good memory starts with attention. Memory blamed, but maybe never paid attention. Must practice.*

—*Apply attention by changing behavior. Get off automatic pilot by doing something different.*

—*Need to make abstract things or numbers meaningful. Things which seem random or meaningless are too hard to remember.*

—*Mental imagery is helpful, but interactive imagery is better. Put things in sequence and imagine them (making up a story with items that need to be remembered).*

—*With memory, it's use it or lose it.*

SUMMARY

In "Revitalize Your Memory," Mark Golin says that people can improve their memory or keep it sharp if they just use a few proven techniques. He begins with the importance of attention. Sometimes, he says, people blame forgetting on poor memory, but they really never techniques. He begins with the importance of attention. Sometimes, he says, people blame forgetting on poor memory, but they really never paid attention in the first place. It's sort of like they are on "automatic pilot," and they need to fight this by practicing paying attention to details such as color and shapes. Once they are off automatic pilot, they can practice doing something unusual. He gives examples such as doing things with their left hands if they are right-handed.

· Next, Golin explains the importance of making things meaningful. So many things seem meaningless or abstract, such as a list of numbers or a technical term. However, by looking at the sound a word makes or making seemingly silly connections to things, a person will remember things better.

Interactive imagery is similar to making things meaningful. One can put things in sequence or make up a story about items to be remembered. This also works for people's names. Golin reminds us that a memory must be exercised or it will become weaker.

COMMENTS: The first sentence of the summary identifies the title, author, and main idea of the article. The main idea is stated in the summary writer's own words. The major details in the outline and summary make use of some of the words used in the article. This is necessary because the terms themselves need to be identified. However, they are explained and described in the summary writer's own words.

Also, summaries of shorter articles are often only one paragraph. This article is over 1,500 words, so the summary is also a bit longer (approximately 230 words). Because of its length, it is written in more than one paragraph.

EXERCISE ONE

Read the article below. An outline is provided. Write a summary from the outline.

REPAIRING YOUR CAR

Good mechanics can save you a lot of money during the lifetime of your car. More important, they can save your life. Since good mechanics are so important to car owners, it is helpful to know where to find them. Good mechanics may be found working in a variety of places.

Dealers' service departments specialize in repairs of particular makes of cars, and their mechanics are given special training by the manufacturer. They are the highest paid in the industry. You would be wise to use your dealer while your warranty is in effect.

Independent garages can and often do charge less than a dealer due to lower overhead. Their reliability is largely dependent on the individual in charge. It is a good idea to check out a garage's reputation by questioning local residents and customers if possible.

Specialty shops service one part of the car only: radiators, tires, mufflers, automatic transmissions, ignitions, or brakes. Usually these mechanics are very skilled within their areas of expertise.

Service departments of chain department and discount stores are usually located near large shopping areas. Their mechanics are experienced in making fast, relatively simple repairs and replacements, particularly on popular U.S. cars—but lack training and experience to diagnose complex mechanical problems.

Gasoline stations offer the advantages of a close-in location and conveniently long hours. In addition, their owners are not likely to take advantage of good, regular customers. For routine maintenance and minor repair jobs, you would probably find a neighborhood service station satisfactory.

Automotive diagnostic centers possess highly sophisticated electronic equipment to evaluate the various mechanical systems of a car, diagnose existing problems, and predict future ones. Authentic diagnostic centers are usually not in the repair business themselves. Charges are quite low.

OUTLINE

What is the article about? (Topic)

Places to take your car for repair

What is the author's main point about the topic (Main Idea)

You can find a good mechanic at a number of places.

Or you might write

There are a number of good places to take your car for repair.

How does the author support the topic? (Major Details)

—Dealer service depts. good for warranty work

—Independent garages charge less but should be checked

—Specialty shops for just one type of repair

—Discount or dept. stores convenient for minor repairs

—Gas stations open long hours—best for routine work

—Automotive diagnostic centers only for diagnosing

COMMENTS: Notice that details about each of these locations are provided. You might consider these details minor; however, a list of repair places without this information would neither help you understand the article nor summarize it.

EXERCISE TWO

Read the following article. Outline it by writing the topic, main idea, and major details. Then write a summary of the article from your outline.

MUSIC SOOTHES THE SAVAGE BRAIN
by Joshua Cooper Ramo
from *Newsweek*

Hmm. Hmmmm-humm. Humm. That's the start of Mozart's Sonata for Two Pianos in D Major and, according to a neurobiology study, if you hum along, you could be a couple of IQ points smarter by the time you finish this magazine. The study, published in the British science journal *Nature,* found that listening to Mozart could actually increase your intelligence, at least temporarily. Thirty-six college students listened to the sonata, a relaxation tape, and nothing, and then took three different IQ tests. The post-Mozart scores showed a substantial boost: an average score of 119, as opposed to 111 for the relaxation tape and 100 for silence. Though the brain buzz seems to last only about 15 minutes, researchers say that exposing children to the music at an early age may have longer-lasting effects.

What's the magic in Mozart's flute? One theory is that the intricate musical structures may resonate in the brain's dense web, lubricating the flow of neurons. Gordon Shaw, a University of California, Irvine, physics professor involved in the research, says neural structure includes regular firing patterns that build along the surface of the brain like bridges. Mozart's musical architecture may evoke a sympathetic response from the brain the way one vibrating piano string can set another humming.

Shaw suspects that other music may have a similar effect, and he wants to take on genres like rock and roll and jazz. His guess is that Louis Armstrong and Axl Rose will fire up the intellect as well as the imagination. Both seem to move the hips.

EXERCISE THREE

For the article in this exercise, and for the articles in Part Two of this book, you will be given a preview question or statement to help guide your reading. Also, some of the difficult words in the article will be listed in the order they appear in the article. In the article, these words will be underlined. As you preview, look at the context in which the words are used.

STEPS TO FOLLOW:

1. **Preview question or statement.** Before reading "Wool…the Living Fiber," read and think about the title. Do you like to wear wool clothes or use wool blankets? If not, is it because you find it scratchy or too warm? If you do like this fabric, why?

2. **Scan the list of words and locate them in the article.**

> crossbreeding
> affinity
> nonflammable
> intricate
> follicles
> forages

3. **Read the article.**

4. **Divide the article into sections and label the sections.**

5. **Outline the article, including the topic, main idea, and major details.**

6. **Write a summary of the article from your outline.**

WOOL...THE LIVING FIBER
by Joseph Plaidly
from Pendleton Woolen Mills pamphlet

For centuries man has gratefully accepted the protective qualities of wool. By the careful <u>crossbreeding</u> of sheep, he has developed fibers of different lengths, diameters, and various degrees of softness and crispness.

Wool is almost custom-made by nature to fit the needs of man. In its processing and manufacture, man takes up where sheep left off. But while new processes and treatments have made wool more versatile in its uses, man has not improved the fiber itself. <u>Wool has a number of characteristics that make it an ideal material.</u>

Wool is the only fiber possessing a natural crimp, or wave. It is the crimp which gives wool its resiliency and vitality. Wool can be stretched to 50 percent of its length and returned to its original dimension without damage. It can be twisted out of shape and subjected to repeated strain under dry or wet conditions. The crimps will always return to their original positions.

The outer scaly covering of wool sheds water, making it naturally rain-resistant. The protein cortex, on the contrary, readily absorbs moisture. Like a sponge, wool can absorb up to 30 percent of its weight in water or body vapor without becoming damp. This quality also enables woolen clothing to absorb normal perspiration. Wool provides the most warmth with the least weight. This is due to the millions of air spaces enclosed within its compression-resistant structure. In clothing, wool acts as a shield against cold and hot air. It regulates the loss or gain of heat and keeps the body at its normal temperature.

Wool is the most naturally wrinkle-resistant of all fibers. Its spindle-shaped molecules have an <u>affinity</u> for one another and a determination to remain folded together in their normal arrangement. Wrinkles caused by body movements during wear or compression in a suitcase displace and stretch the material. When the wool relaxes, it corrects any displacement and returns to its original position, eliminating the wrinkle.

Wool takes dye completely, permanently, and beautifully. Striking evidence can be observed in the dye kettles. When wool is dyed, the dye in the liquid agent is completely absorbed, leaving behind only a clear solution in the kettles after the wool is removed.

Wool resists fading from sunlight, atmospheric impurities, and perspiration. It maintains its natural luster for years of service and wear. Even after wool has been worn for many years, it can be shredded back into fiber to be spun and woven into new fabrics. The recovery and re-use of wool in low-price fabrics is an industry of its own.

Wool is also <u>nonflammable</u>. Fire insurance companies recommend the use of wool blankets, rugs, or coats to extinguish flames. Practically all laboratory or industrial activity involving highly flammable materials requires that wool blankets be made available to extinguish small fires or ignited clothing. Wool, unless it is in continued direct contact with flame, will extinguish any fire. The denser the weave and the greater the weight of a wool fabric, the less likely it is even to char due to its smaller oxygen content.

Another property of wool is its lack of static. Static attracts dirt from the air and imbeds it in fabrics. This quality makes wool the easiest of all fabrics to keep clean. Freedom from static permits woolen fabrics to hang and drape in natural lines, unlike materials woven from artificial fabrics or blends.

Finally, wool is a living fiber, <u>intricate</u> in its chemical composition and physical structure. It is composed of cells that grow out of the inner <u>follicles</u> in the skin of sheep. Wool forms within the protection of a wax-like substance called "wool grease" which protects the fibers as the sheep <u>forages</u> for food. The fiber also contains suint, the salts of perspiration. In the first step of processing, the wool grease, or suint, and other foreign matter adhering to the fiber, are removed. Refinement of the wool grease produces lanolin, the base of beauty preparations and the perfect carrier for medicinal ointments. The lanolin and its by-products are also used as a rust preventive.

EXERCISE FOUR

In Chapter Three you chose two articles from Part Two of this book and wrote an outline of each. Now, use your outlines to write good summaries of the articles.

REMEMBER:

- A summary of an article is a condensed version of something you have read, written in your own words.

- To write a good summary:

  - Outline the article, including the topic, main idea, and major details.

  - Include the title, author, and main idea of the article in your opening sentence.

  - Write the major details in sentence form, adding minor details when necessary.

  - Write the summary in your own words; if you use the author's exact words, be sure to use quotation marks.

WRITING A RESPONSE

The models and exercises in this chapter will help you to

- Record your initial reactions to an article.
- Write a response to an article.

A response is an answer or reply. When you talk with others, you usually respond to their ideas in some fashion. Similarly, as an *active* reader, you react to the author's ideas by asking questions or perhaps agreeing or disagreeing. The author probably will not hear or read your response, but there is still some interaction between you (the reader) and the author. In fact, this interaction is what makes reading fun.

Your first reaction to something you have read is probably a combination of thoughts and feelings. Authors may present an opinion that bothers or pleases you, or they may just present you with new information. Your response to what you read is personal and unique and will be based on your education and life experiences, including your cultural heritage, ethnicity, gender, age, and political views.

RECORDING YOUR FIRST REACTIONS

Before you write a response to an article, record your first thoughts and feelings. This pre-writing or brainstorming activity allows you to organize your thinking before you write. To record your thoughts and feelings, ask yourself a series of questions about the article as well as your own feelings.

Questions about your **feelings**:
- Are my feelings positive or negative about this subject? Why?
- Are my feelings strong about this subject?

Questions about **the article**:

- What is it about the article that made me feel this way?
- Has the author presented mostly facts or opinions?
- Is the author qualified to write on this subject?
- In what kind of publication was this article printed?

Questions about **how this relates to you**:

- How does the information relate to my own knowledge of the subject?
- How can I use the information I have read?
- Can I add *my* experience and perspective on this subject to help others understand it?

Suggestions for Recording First Reactions

Listing: Identify your initial thoughts and feelings about the ideas and opinions you read without worrying about spelling, grammar, or punctuation. List your thoughts as quickly as you can; many times one idea will lead to another, so try to write without stopping.

If you can't think of anything to write, answer the preceding questions about your feelings, the article itself, and how the article relates to you. If your answers lead to other thoughts, list those as well. No idea is too unimportant or too silly to list in this brainstorm step. Try not to evaluate your responses as you write—just write.

MODEL ONE: Listing first reactions to an article

First Reactions List #1

These reactions were written by a student who read "The Myth of Romantic Love" by Scott Peck in Part Two of this book. The writer followed the categories of questions listed above. As he answered the questions, a personal experience came to mind, and he ended up writing about this experience in his response (see Model Three).

Feelings

Agree with Peck that most matches are not necessarily made in heaven

This myth is "a dreadful lie"? Not sure I think this romance stuff is __that__ bad

Thoughts about the article

Peck makes it sound like commitment is a fault, resulting from belief in the myth
   —couples sometimes ignore true feelings
   —I think this is what I did with my ex-girlfriend

Peck is a doctor and sounds like he has worked with a lot of married couples

How this relates to me

I think communication is one of the most important things in a relationship
    —by not being honest about falling out of love with my girlfriend, I probably hurt the relationship
    —I thought things would get better if I just went along
    —could have avoided a terrible fight that ruined our friendship as well as our relationship

First Reactions List #2

The following first reactions were written by a student who read "Marriages Made to Last" in Part Two of this book. "Marriage" is the focus of the student's initial reactions to the articles. Since she had many feelings and thoughts about the topic, she had no trouble listing several ideas and chose not to use the list of questions.

Marriage
—Not necessary for success

—Not like the fairy tales where everyone is a prince or princess who meets up with a person who is predestined to be a perfect match

—Loving marriages
    —I agree with Lauers that positive attitude towards your spouse is most important
    —Be interested in spouse; be patient; spend time together; be best friends

—Other aspects that make marriages last
    —Each partner should give more than 50%
    —I think females usually give 60-70% and men typically give 40% at the most!
    —I agree that although sex is important, it is not the most critical part of a good relationship

Mapping: Another way of brainstorming is called **mapping** or **clustering**. As you can see in Model Two, this method is quite different from listing. Mapping shows how ideas relate to each other, and the process helps one idea lead to another. Basically, you are drawing a map of your thoughts and reactions, letting the thoughts themselves determine the shape of the map.

How to map

1. Draw a circle or box in the center of a page. Write the subject of the article in the box.
2. Show related ideas in other circles or boxes. Draw lines to show how those ideas are related to the main idea or to each other.

3. Work quickly; don't stop to evaluate your ideas or worry about spelling.
4. When your map is finished, look at it. Is one part more detailed or more interesting to you than the rest? That may be the part you'll want to write about.

MODEL TWO: Mapping first reactions to an article

First Reactions Map #1: The following map contains the same information that is in the First Reactions List #1 in Model One.

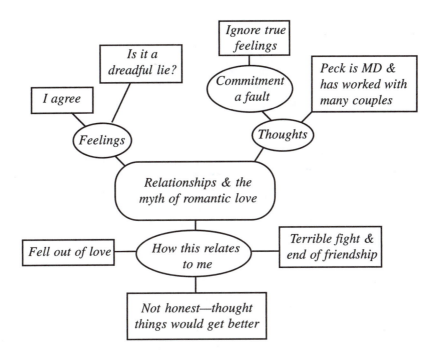

First Reactions Map #2: The following map contains the same information that is in the First Reactions List #2 in Model One.

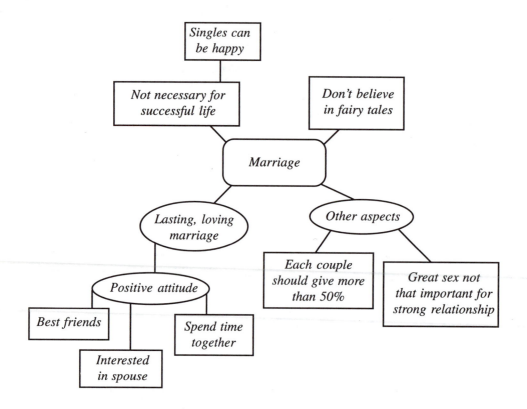

EXERCISE ONE

Read the following article, then write your initial reactions in the form of a list or a map.

MEN'S JOBS—WOMEN'S JOBS

by George Simpson
from *Cosmopolitan*

I heard a woman complain the other day that her new boyfriend never helps her with the laundry and that he'd rather buy new dishes than wash dirty ones. I said, "Sounds like you ought to trade the boyfriend in for a good maid. . . ." I was really thinking, Hey, wait a second! It seems to me there's a natural order to life—some things are simply *your* job. . .and some are simply mine. When was the last time you took a whitewall-tire brush to the grill? Or changed the oil in the car? Whose job is it to catch the bat that inadvertently flies in the window? Who *always* puts up the bookshelves? Changes the flat bike tire tubes? Unclogs the gutter?

It's not that I *can't* fold laundry. But you hate it when I don't turn the socks right side out or when I fold the towels into quarters instead of thirds. You have a vision of correctly folded laundry, I do not. It's Nature's way of assigning you that important task. Do you know how to replace the washers in the dripping faucet? I do. That's why it's my job. Seems like part of life's Great Plan.

Don't you agree that there's a pretty good balance between my jobs and yours? And although there's no law that says we can't help each other, let's not make it a skirmish in the battle of the sexes when we don't.

You might counter by saying, "Well, half the laundry is yours." My response: "You ride in the car. But I don't ask you to remember the date of the last tune-up or if it's time to rotate the tires." Because I know that's *my* job. Just like I know it's my job to mow the lawn and shovel the sidewalk.

And it's a good thing men are so compulsive about their jobs. Nobody else would notice that there are only *two* cans of beer left or that we're just about out of garlic-jalapeño-pepper-flavored chips or that the grill needs more propane. Your job, on the other hand, is to keep an eye on the toilet-paper supply and make sure the eggs are thrown out before they hatch.

It's a wonderful balance, don't you think? Isn't it a load off your mind *not* to have to worry about when the gym memberships expire or what time the Redskins game starts on Sunday? Isn't it reassuring to know that you *never* have to worry about cleaning the fish or moving the mulch pile? I know I sleep better not having to think about when the sheets were changed last, how many pints there are in a quart, and the date the new Mel Gibson picture opens. . . .

I don't think that all jobs should be classified as necessarily "women's work" or "a man's job." As a matter of fact, I can outcook and outclean most women I know (and most of them can walk all over me on the tennis court), but we should try to acknowledge the symmetry of having jobs that are ours alone, jobs that if done well—and cheerfully—benefit both of us. And that should be plenty of reward.

WRITING THE RESPONSE

The brainstorming you do by recording you initial reactions will help you determine your strongest reactions and interests relating to the article. Now, write a response paragraph that focuses on the key elements of your reactions. Here are some guidelines to help you.

1. Be clear about your opinion. Once you decide on the focus of your response (the topic), write a sentence that states the main point you want to make. In Chapters Two, Three, and Four, you practiced identifying authors' main ideas. Now you are the author, stating your main point in what is often called a **topic sentence**.

Here are some specific suggestions for helping you write a topic sentence:

■ Make a personal connection between what you've read and your own experience. Ask how this new information adds to or changes how you act and relate to your surroundings.

■ Your topic sentence should contain a judgement. A response *is* an opinion, so do not be afraid to clearly state your opinion.

For example, the following are topic sentences students have written for their responses to articles on relationships in the section entitled "The Sexes" in Part Two of this book.

> *In the articles I read and in my own experience, I realize that relationships are often jeopardized by lack of clear communication.*

> *I do not look at marriage as a step one should take in life in order to be considered successful; however, I do feel that loving marriages are possible.*

> *From my own experience I can say that if a marriage is not based on friendship, it is destined to fail.*

2. Explain your feelings and reactions. General terms such as "interesting," "helpful," or "frightening" may be appropriate, but try to explain how or why you used such a word to describe your feelings. In Chapter Three you identified the major and minor details that authors used to explain or clarify the main idea. As an author, you will want to include examples, facts, and other details to explain your main idea.

3. It is appropriate to use personal pronouns, such as "I," "me," "we," or "us" in this type of writing.

MODEL THREE: Two responses to articles

Response #1: The following response was written by the student who wrote the First Reactions List #1 and Map #1.

> *In the article I read and in my own experience, I realize that relationships are often jeopardized by the lack of clear communication. In "The Myth of Romantic Love," Scott Peck says that even when couples have fallen out of love, they tend to ignore that fact and hope that everything will work out all right. I had a similar experience with a girl I had been dating for about a year. I no longer had the feelings for her that I once did, and I wanted to change our relationship. However, I stifled my feelings and tried to go on. One day our relationship was destroyed in a terrible fight. It wasn't until two years later that we were able to sit down and talk it out. Since that experience, I have been trying to work on being honest and straight forward when I need to be.*

Michael "Cody" Brooks (student)

COMMENTS: Cody focuses on his own experience and the way that the information in the "The Myth of Romantic Love" relates to that experience. Notice that he begins his response with a clear topic sentence, then paraphrases one of the author's ideas before relating this idea to his own life.

Response #2: The following response was written by the student who wrote the First Reactions List #2 and Map #2.

> *I do not look at marriage as a step one should take in life in order to be considered successful; however, I do feel that loving marriages are possible. A loving marriage is not based on fairy tale ideas; instead, it involves having a positive attitude toward your mate. In fact, a positive attitude is the key to a lasting marriage.*
>
> *To have a positive attitude you need to find a person you find interesting. I believe that the more time you spend with your spouse, the more interesting he or she will become. According to a survey conducted by Robert and Jeanette Lauer of people married for many years, one man feels the same way I do. Married for 30 years, he says this about his wife: "I have watched her grow and shared with her both the pain and exhilaration of her journey. I find her more fascinating now than the day we were married." The Lauers also found that "the most frequently named reason for an enduring, happy marriage was having a generally positive attitude towards one's spouse: viewing one's partner as one's best friend and liking him or her 'as a person.'"*

Janette Lentes (student)

COMMENTS: Janette's response to the article has a different focus because her interests and background are different from Cody's. Notice that in this response the student relates her thoughts to specific quotes from one of the articles.

MODEL FOUR: Essay response to 'Your Child's Self-Esteem'

Sometimes you may find that you have an extended response to an author's ideas and your response may be several paragraphs long. This is the case with the following student response to an article in the section entitled "Parenting/Family" in Part Two of this book.

BUILDING SELF-ESTEEM IN CHILDREN
WITH LEARNING DISABILITIES

Trying to build self-esteem in children with learning disabilities is one of the hardest responsibilities for a parent. The reason I know this is because two of my children have learning disabilities. It has been tough to build up their self-esteem only to have someone else knock it back down.

Children with learning disabilities are constantly being rejected by their peers because they're perceived as being different. My daughter had a friend in grade school, and because of peer pressure in middle school, her friend dumped her just so the others would accept her. On my daughter's sixteenth birthday, nobody came to her party. Her self-esteem took a real beating that day, and I learned a valuable lesson. The two of us do something special together to celebrate her birthday from now on.

In "Your Child's Self-Esteem," Lilian G. Katz tells us that "Parents can help a child cope with occasions of rejection or indifference by reassuring her that Mom's and Dad's own acceptance of the youngster has not been shaken." I disagree that this is enough, especially with a learning-disabled child. Telling my children that I love them isn't what they want to hear; what matters to them is acceptance by their peers. I've tried to reinforce their good behavior and encourage them to see themselves as valuable human beings, but their peer acceptance means more than mine or their teachers'.

I have found that what works well with my children is explaining everything in detail and not talking down to them. It has taken me many years and mistakes to learn how to build their self-esteem. Although it's one of my responsibilities as a parent, I often wonder if I'll ever be finished with this part of my job.

Sandy Krepps (student)

EXERCISE TWO

On page 64 you read "Men's Jobs, Women's Jobs" and wrote your initial reactions. Now write a response that is at least one paragraph long and has a clear topic sentence.

EXERCISE THREE

On page 34 in Chapter Three, you read "The Importance of Childhood Memories" and saw a model which identified the major details. Now brainstorm your reactions and write a response.

REMEMBER:

■   A response is an answer or reply to what you have read which allows you to explore your feelings and thoughts about a subject and share them with others.

■   To write a response:

   •   Ask yourself questions about the topic and the author as well as your own feelings about the article and how it relates to you.

   •   Record your answers to these questions in the form of a list or a map.

   •   Using your list or map as a guide, write your opinion in a sentence which clearly expresses the main idea.

   •   Explain your opinion as clearly as you can.

Chapter Six

READING TEXTBOOKS

The models and exercises in this chapter will help you to

- Identify the main ideas and major details in textbook chapters.
- Use a study-reading system to learn and remember textbook material.

Textbooks present special reading challenges. Very often they include technical and specialized terms that are difficult to spell, pronounce, and remember. The chapters are sometimes lengthy, and the relationships between chapters may be unclear. Despite these difficulties, you have to remember much of the material at test time, sometimes weeks after you have read it.

However, there is good news! There are methods you can use to help you understand and remember information in textbooks better than you have before. Most students read a textbook just as they would a novel or magazine article. However, viewing a textbook as a source of information, much like a dictionary or encyclopedia, will lead to other approaches that are more effective. The basic rule to remember is this: Do not *read* your textbooks—*study* them.

BECOMING FAMILIAR WITH YOUR TEXTBOOK

Use Textbook Aids

Most textbooks have special features such as headings (sometimes in different-sized type and color), pictures, charts, graphs, study questions, and glossaries to help you understand and remember the subject matter. In some cases, you gain a better understanding of a concept by studying a picture or graph than by just reading an explanation.

Preview the Entire Textbook

When you first get a textbook, spend some time *previewing* or looking over the entire book to get the an overall idea of the subject you will be studying. Take a few minutes to examine any of the following features that your textbook contains:

- The *preface* (sometimes titled "To the Student" or "Foreword") is found before the table of contents and provides you with the author's perspective on the subject. In this section, authors often explain their philosophy about the subject as well as the way the book is organized. Reread the "To the Student" section in this book as an example of this feature.

- The *table of contents*, found at the front of the book, lists the book's chapters. By studying the chapter titles, you can get an idea of what each section of the book is about and how the topics relate to each other.

- The *index*, located at the end of the book, is an alphabetical listing of the topics, terms, and names mentioned in the book. Use this section to find the page where a particular concept or a person is discussed.

- The *glossary* is a list of technical and specialized words and their definitions. In a textbook, a glossary may be found at the end of a chapter or at the end of the book. Sometimes glossary entries appear in the margins of the text, near where the words they refer to are used.

- The *appendix* presents additional information that can be helpful to your understanding of the book's subject matter. Found near the back of the book, an appendix may include charts, graphs, special documents, or alternate views and approaches to the subject.

- *Questions, problems, or exercises*, typically found at the end of a chapter, provide practical application of the ideas in the chapter or things to look for as you read.

STUDYING A TEXTBOOK CHAPTER

Let's suppose you are assigned Chapter One in your biology text. If you are like most students, you will probably open the book to page 1 (or the first page of the chapter) and start reading. But there is a better way. If you apply one of a number of textbook reading strategies (including the method you have been using in this book to read and understand articles), you will be able to read the chapter faster, and, better yet, you will **understand** and **remember** the material better. Reading for understanding leads to better grades.

What Is a Study-Reading System?

A study-reading system is a step-by-step procedure for reading a textbook chapter. Using such a system will help you concentrate on, understand, and remember what you read. Keep in mind that textbooks should not simply be read—they are to be studied as well.

Study-reading systems work. Research studies show that students who are taught to use a study-reading system understand and remember what they read much better than do students who have not been taught to use such a system.

The next few pages will explain strategies for each of three stages involved in the process of studying textbook chapters: **before you read, as you read, and after you read**. Following the explanation is a sample chapter from a biology textbook which provides models of how to mark a textbook and opportunities for you to practice these strategies on a college-level textbook.

BEFORE YOU READ

Preview

The preview step of studying a textbook chapter is more extensive than the preview step before reading an article, but in the long run, it will save you a great deal of time and help you remember the information in the chapter. It is critical that you recall what you already know about the topic and get a clear overview of the whole chapter **before** reading individual sections of the chapter.

Step One: Warm up your thinking.

Information and ideas you already have about a topic are called **prior knowledge** or **background knowledge**. This knowledge is as significant as what is written in the chapter, so it is very important to bring it to your conscious mind before you begin reading.

How do you do this? As you read the title and headings in bold type, jot down things you already know about the topic (or topics) in the chapter. You might do this in the form of a freewrite—writing down whatever comes to your mind without worrying about grammar, punctuation, or paragraphing—or you might just make a list of your thoughts. Another possibility is to put your thoughts in the form of a chart or a map.

Any of these formats will help you recall what you already know about the topic. This preview "brainstorming" is very similar to the "first reaction" step you did before writing your response in Chapter Five. The obvious difference in this case is that you are writing your ideas and thoughts *before* you read the author's ideas.

Continue this "warm up" step by determining how many pages there are in the chapter and how many major topics are covered. Major topics are usually indicated by the headings in the largest and darkest type. Read the summary if there is one; the summary usually contains the author's most important points. Also glance at any illustrations, graphs, charts, or other special features in the chapter. If you know very little about the topic, continue with the rest of the steps in the preview, then come back to this step and try freewriting again.

If the material you are reading is extremely difficult or has a lot of new terminology, you may want to try an additional strategy before before going on to Step Two. Try "playing with the text"* by letting your eyes skip over the columns of print without really reading the words. Stop on whatever catches your interest, but if you find yourself actually reading, quickly move your eyes further down or to the next column. Do this two or three times on the whole chapter—no one time should take more than four or five minutes. This added step will help you become a little bit familiar with the vocabulary and some of the ideas so that reading the chapter will be easier.

EXERCISE ONE

Preview the sample chapter entitled "Introduction to Biology" from a biology textbook, which appears on pages 82-94.

1. Which of the following special features does the chapter have? Give a page number for each feature you locate.

    boldface headings
    preview questions
    main ideas of the chapter
    pictures
    graphs
    charts
    vocabulary words
    summary
    other (write the feature and the page number)

2. Read the "Key Concepts" on page 82. What is the author's purpose in listing these key concepts?

3. The author has included "Bio-Bits" in boxes on pages 83, 87, and 92. Read these. Why do you think the author included these?

4. The sample text chapter provides several questions in a box labelled "Curiosity Questions." Thinking about these questions as you read will help you relate the information in the chapter to your own life. This will help you to understand the material better and remember it longer.

*This technique was developed by Roberta Kern, an educational specialist in Seattle, Washington. She talks more about how to get comfortable with difficult textbook material in her book *The Experience of Learning*.

Step Two: Anticipate what the chapter might contain.

As you think about the title and headings, make either written or mental notes about what you think the author will discuss.

EXERCISE TWO

Complete your preview of "Introduction to Biology" by answering the following questions.

1. Reread the chapter title, headings, and introduction (pages 82-83). What is the **general topic** of this chapter? What is the **specific topic** of the chapter?

2. What do you already know about this topic? Write any information in the form of a list, a map, or a freewrite.

3. How many pages are there in this chapter? How many major topics?

4. Read the summary and the captions under the pictures and charts.

5. If you know very little about this topic, look over the chapter quickly two or three times. Then write any additional information that you now have in response to question #2.

Step Three: Make a survey map.

In addition to identifying the major topics in the chapter, it is important to understand the relationships between those topics. To do this you can create a **"survey map"** like the one in Model One.

What is a survey map?

A survey map is a two-dimensional picture that connects the chapter headings and subheadings with lines and shapes to show the relationships between them.

How to make a survey map

First, draw a box or a circle in the middle of a piece of paper and in it write the title or main topic of the chapter. (Use a whole piece of paper so that you have plenty of room.) Next, write down the major headings and indicate their relationship to the chapter title. Usually, this is done by putting the headings in boxes or circles that are somewhat smaller than the one for the chapter title and connecting them to the title with lines. Finally, draw lines from the figures containing the major headings to each of the subheadings. On the following page is an example of what a survey map for this chapter might look like.

MODEL ONE: Survey Map of Chapter Six of *Read and Respond*

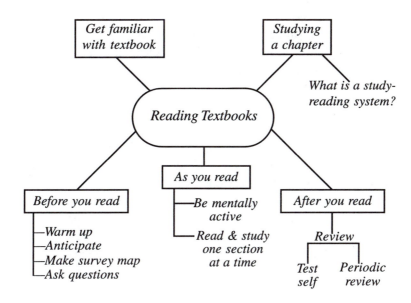

COMMENTS: When you make a survey map, be sure that all the words run in the same direction so that they will be easy to read and follow. Students often find it helpful to use different colors of pencil or ink to distinguish major headings and sub-headings. You may need to try a couple of different drawings before you find a layout that works well. Like any technique, this one will be easier to do after you practice it a few times. There is **no one way** to do a survey map; use your own ideas and creativity to create a map that is meaningful to you. The important thing is to clearly show all of the topics in the chapter and how they are related to each other.

EXERCISE THREE

Begin a survey map for the biology chapter on pages 82-94 by putting the chapter title ("Introduction to Biology") in a box or circle in the middle of a piece of paper. Next, look at the main headings; the sample chapter has only three: "Biology: A More Complete Picture"; "Biology: Saving Your Life and Preserving the Earth"; and "Life: Only on Earth." Write these headings in boxes or circles and add them to your map, connecting them with lines to the chapter title.

Now look at the chart on page 89. Prominent graphic aids such as this also have a topic and main idea. By reading the title and the items in bold print in the column entitled "Problem," we know that the topic of this chart is *current environmental problems*. Since the topic "current global environmental problems" is also mentioned in both the the summary and in the "Curiosity Questions," it is clearly an important topic in the chapter. Therefore, it would be a good idea to add it to your survey map.

This may seem like a lot of things do to **before** reading, but remember: the more you do before you begin, the easier and better your reading will be. You will also remember the information better.

Step Four: Ask questions.

Frank Smith, a reading expert, says that reading involves "getting answers to questions."* The preview step will generate a lot of questions; you can create additional questions by **turning headings into questions.**

Major headings in a chapter are answers to specific questions. Use the headings to figure out what the question is for each section. Often, the chapter will also have subheadings which divide the material under a major heading into sections. If subheadings are provided, ask questions for them as well. Always try to determine how the sections and sub-sections relate to each other.

MODEL TWO: Creating questions for chapter headings

The first major heading of the biology chapter is "Biology: A More Complete Picture." An appropriate question for this section would be, "What makes the picture more complete?" or "What do I need to know to have a more complete picture of biology?"

EXERCISE FOUR

Write two questions for the major heading on page 86 and two questions for the major heading on page 90 .

AS YOU READ

Read actively.

The suggestions in Steps One and Two of the "Before You Read" section will help you read actively; by previewing, you *get your mind focused*; by asking questions and looking for answers to those questions, you *keep your mind focused.*

As you read, the important thing is to make sense of the material, so you will probably need to read a textbook more slowly than you read other kinds of books.

---

*Frank Smith writes about the reading process in his book *Reading Without Nonsense.*

Tackle the chapter one major section at a time.

You have already discovered how the chapter is organized by creating a survey map. Keep your survey map in front of you to help keep track of the "big picture" of the chapter and focus on one major section at a time.

Here are some additional suggestions to help you read actively:

1. **Look for the answers to the questions you asked in Steps Two and Four**. When you feel you have found an answer, write it down on a piece of notebook paper or in the margin of your textbook.

2. **Look for other questions to be answered**. Write down answers as you find them.

3. **Look for main ideas** of paragraphs and sections under each heading and sub-heading.

4. **Think about important points or sections that do not make sense**. You may need to look up certain words in the glossary or a dictionary, refer to your lecture notes and/or talk to a study partner to help clarify the meaning of a paragraph or section.

5. **Mark the text as you read** (with a pencil or an ink pen—**not** a highlighter pen; marking with a highlighter is *passive*, and you are working to become an *active* reader).

   a. Divide sections into sub-sections. When there are no boldface headings in a chapter, as is the case on pages 82-89 of the sample chapter, you will need to divide the section into sub-sections and identify the topic of each section in the margin. Basically, you will be doing the same thing you did with longer articles in Chapter Four.

   b. Draw lines between sections.

   c. Label the sections. Sometimes the heading will work; other times you will need to write a new heading for a section and/or divide it into smaller sections, writing a heading for each sub-section.

   d. Put a check mark or an X in the margin beside any new or special words you want to understand and remember.

   e. Underline the main idea of the paragraphs or sections, BUT underline no more than 10 to 20 percent of a page.

MODEL THREE: Markings and notes in a sample biology textbook chapter

Turn to pages 82-86 of the sample text chapter. Notice that key points have been underlined and that Section 1-A has been divided into sub-sections and labelled. Also pay attention to other notes in the margins.

EXERCISE FIVE

Read section 1-B, "Biology: Saving Your Life and Preserving the Earth" on page 86. Divide it into sub-sections and label the topic of each sub-section in the margin. Underline the main idea of paragraphs and/or sub-sections and make any other margin notes that you think might be helpful for studying the chapter. Compare your sections and margin notes with a classmate's or discuss them with your instructor.

AFTER YOU READ

Study the information in the chapter you have just read.

Earlier in this chapter you read that a basic rule of textbook reading is to *study* textbooks, not just *read* them. Previewing and asking questions are a part of "studying." Equally important is what you do after you finish reading each section.

There are many ways to study the information after you have read it. The strategy demonstrated here is an extension of the strategy you practiced in Chapter Three—making a **summary outline** of what you read.

MODEL FOUR: Summary outline of a sample biology textbook chapter

Topic: Advances in biology and new understandings about living things

Main Idea: Scientific investigations have led to new advances and understandings about living things.

Major Details:
Advances
    –greater knowledge of the biology of cells because of more powerful microscopes and biochemical techniques
    –more knowledge in many areas of biology, all arrived at via the scientific method
New understandings based on combining new knowledge with previously known information
    –**continental drift** thought of as a fairy tale until further investigations of sediments of ocean floor
    –**theory of evolution of species by natural selection** is the basis for all biological study

COMMENTS: Sometimes, if the material you are reading is very difficult for you, you will need to do a summary outline on each section of the chapter. Other times, the notes you write in the margin of your text will be all that is necessary to help you understand and remember the information.

EXERCISE SIX

For sections 1-B and 1-C of the sample biology textbook chapter, write a main idea statement in your own words. As was suggested in the "As You Read" stage, you have already identified (or stated in your own words) the **topic** of each section. Now simply write the main point the authors are making about the topic of that section. Then, write the major details in that section that explain or support the authors' main point.

Other strategies for studying the chapter

1. Write out your questions and answers (as always, in your own words). This strategy is known as the SQ3R—Survey, Question, Read, Recite, and Review. While it is time-consuming to do an SQ3R, it is a very thorough process, and some students like doing it because they feel that they learn the material thoroughly.

2. Make a more detailed map of the entire chapter. After completing a survey map, make a map of **each major section of the chapter**. Students who learn best visually prefer this method.

3. Create a chart of the information. Some information is easier to study in this format.

4. Make flashcards of key terms and special vocabulary that you are unfamiliar with.

5. Answer questions from a study guide. Some instructors make up study guides to help you identify the most important information in the chapter; other times, a study guide is available when you buy your textbook.

Your instructor may have other suggestions for methods of studying information from your textbook. The important thing is to condense the material and put it into your own words without changing the original meaning.

Review

To review, go over what you have read. Recite margin labels. Cover up your written answers to questions and/or major details in your summary outline, and **test yourself** to see if you can recall them.

It is also a good idea to refer to your Survey Map at this point to see how much you can recall about each major heading without looking at your margin or written notes. Turn to Model One on page 75. Test yourself on the ideas in this chapter by looking only at the information in boxes. Cover up the information beneath each box, and recall as much of the information as you can about each phase of textbook reading.

The **first** review should take place when you finish the entire chapter. This will help you remember the material very well for approximately one day. You need to do a **second** review within one day. It can be as short as five to ten minutes. This review will probably help you remember the information for a week. A **third** review should take place within a week (again, five minutes will probably be enough time). A **fourth** review should come after one month. This should help you retain the information permanently in your long-term memory.

Periodic reviews will help prevent forgetting what you learn. Before a test you will just need to **review, not re-learn**, the material.

EXERCISE SEVEN

Look at the survey map that you made for the sample biology textbook chapter (Exercise Three). Test yourself on this information by looking at the major headings and recalling as much information as you can about this "introductory journey into biology."

REMEMBER:

- Preview the entire textbook to become familiar with its contents and special features.

- Use a study-reading system to understand and remember the information in a textbook chapter.

- Before you read, preview by:
  - Warming up your thinking
  - Anticipating what the chapter will be about
  - Making a survey map
  - Asking questions

- As you read
  - Read actively
  - Tackle the chapter one major section at a time

- After you read
  - Study the information by completing a summary outline or using one of a number of other study strategies
  - Review

Introduction to Biology

(Intro. to whole text as well as to this chapter)

You are about to embark upon a journey that will take you to strange and wondrous places—places as exotic as the treetop pools in tropical rain forests and as remote as snow-swept penguin rookeries in Antarctica. We will travel to spaces as small as the nuclear landscape within a single ✓ nerve cell and as large as the **biosphere**: the entire fabric of life that covers the planet we call home. The purpose of our journey is to show you the diversity of living creatures and to help you to understand how they go about the business of life. You will learn how life on Earth is organized at many different levels: subcellular, cellular, and all the various layers of complexity that culminate in a living **organism**: an individual living creature. Along the way you will learn much about the workings of your own body and how it is similar to and different from those of other animals. You will study the lives of plants, fungi, bacteria, and single-celled organisms called **protists**. We shall discuss the history of life on Earth, how we think it

Definitions of key terms

originated more than 4 billion years ago, and the ways living things have changed in that time. You will learn about **natural selection**, the major evolutionary mechanism that has produced the variety of living organisms, and **ecology**, the study of interactions of living things with one another and with their environment. The overall plan of our journey is to travel from small to large: we will begin at the subcel-

KEY CONCEPTS

- Recent advances in technology have led to a better understanding of many aspects of biology.
- The theory of evolution is the central principle unifying all biology.
- Using the scientific method, biologists are currently working on many problems of great human importance. These include the AIDS epidemic, loss of biodiversity, and the global environmental impact of the expanding human population.

Curiosity Questions
- What evidence do we have that evolution occurs in living organisms?
- Why do current global environmental problems require the immediate attention of your generation?
- How can we tell whether something is alive?

lular level with biological chemistry and work toward the most-encompassing level, ecology and conservation biology.

In the days when steamships were the mode of overseas travel, it was widely recognized that travel teaches you things. While on a trip, chaperones would typically murmur, "Travel is so broadening," as they watched their teenaged charges play shuffleboard. Similarly, the main goal of our journey into life is to display the entire field of biology before you, introducing you to the broad concepts of the science of life, as well as embroidering on much of the detail that makes living things so fascinating. In this introductory chapter, we will discuss why biology has recently moved from merely a broadening educational experience—a discipline full of facts that every literate citizen should understand—to a science that is crucial to the continued existence of all forms of life on Earth, including humans. Biology has become more than just another part of a good education; today's biology class might save your life and, through you, it will have an impact upon future generations of all living things as well.

Reasons for studying biology

I-A BIOLOGY: A MORE COMPLETE PICTURE

(First subsection) Right now is an exciting time to be making this journey into biology. For one thing, knowledge of living processes and their interactions has greatly expanded. Today we know more than ever about the biological world, and, because we know more, we can form a better, more integrated picture of how living things operate and relate to one another. Through the hard work of biologists all over the world, new pieces

of the biological puzzle continue to fall into place and, although there is still much to learn, the scope of our knowledge steadily increases. Recently we have learned much about the biology of cells. For example, in your laboratory classes you will probably study the protist, *Amoeba*. Fifty years ago, the outer edge of *Amoeba* was merely a dark line in images seen through the most powerful microscopes. Today, improved technologies in the form of electron microscopes and intricate biochemical techniques have shown us that this line is actually a complicated, chemical sandwich, studded with molecules that control the movement of substances into and out of *Amoeba*.

Advances in cell biology

The advances in cell biology are only a beginning. We now have a better grasp of how heredity works and how cells make the proteins needed for life and growth. We know more about the biochemistry of processes like respiration and photosynthesis and understand more of the interlocking functions of digestion, respiration, circulation, excretion, movement, nerve activity, and hormonal control. We are beginning to understand how the brain works, how predators and prey interact, what birds hear, and how dinosaur societies might have been organized. We have better ideas of what caused the massive die-offs of many forms of life that appear in the fossil record. We have glimmerings of how complex the relationships are between plants and insects, and between

Other advances in biology

BIO-BIT

An adult human typically has more than 50 trillion cells (=50,000 billion)!

plants and fungi. We are beginning to appreciate the central role that bacteria play in the operation of the biosphere. Finally, we have a better understanding of the complex web of relationships that links all life on our planet.

Common thread to all advances

All of the investigations that have resulted in this explosion of biological knowledge have had one thing in common: they all have used the scientific method to arrive at their conclusions. Most people have only a hazy idea of the scientific method and mentally connect the phrase with images of white-coated, wild-eyed, bespectacled eggheads peering into test tubes in dim and faintly sinister laboratories. To make your journey into life more meaningful, you will need a thorough understanding of this method for attacking problems, answering questions, and making decisions.

. . . .

(Second sub-section)

New information isn't the only reason that your journey will be more meaningful than ever. Older pieces of the biological puzzle have been incorporated with new information to yield a fuller picture of life on Earth. For example, 50 years ago the theory of **continental drift** (Figure 1-1) was mainly a geographical and geological fairy tale. Then, people viewed continental drift with the bemused scorn that we have toward unicorns, sirens, and

New under-standings based on ✓ old and new information Ex: contin-ental drift

Theory of Continental Drift

(a) Pangaea: Late Paleozoic Era, 230 million years ago

(b) Laurasia and Gondwanaland: Mesozoic Era, 180 million years ago

(c) Modern continents (with minor exceptions) had formed by the end of the Mesozoic Era, 110 million years ago

(d) Present day

FIGURE 1-1

The continents of today resulted from the gradual break-up of the super-continent Pangaea.
Arrows indicate the direction of land mass movement.

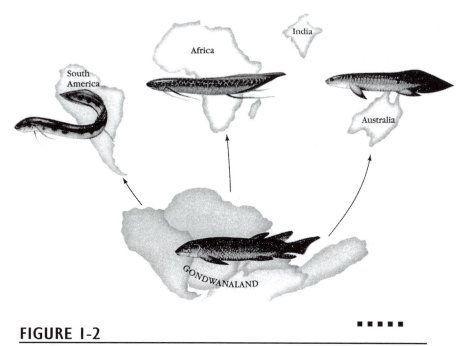

FIGURE 1-2

Continental drift and the geographical distribution of lungfishes. The separation of
continents by continental drift divided many populations of living organisms, resulting in new
species as genetic changes were no longer shared. As Gondwanaland became subdivided,
ancient populations of lungfish evolved into different forms on three continents.

other fantastic mythological creatures.
Today, explorations of the sediments of
the ocean floor have demonstrated that
continental drift is a reality that helps to
explain the present geographical distribution of many groups of plants and animals (Figure 1-2).

Basis for all bio. study

    The **theory of evolution of species as
directed by the process of natural selection**, jointly proposed by two Englishmen,
Charles Darwin and Alfred Russet Wallace
in 1858, provides the theoretical foundation for all biological studies. For nearly
150 years this theory has been tested by
observation and experimentation, and it
remains a central and viable idea in biology today. The relationship that the theory
of evolution of species by means of natural selection has to biology is similar to
the relationship that gravity has to physics. Like gravity, evolution of species by
means of natural selection is a basic, natural phenomenon. But, unlike gravity, which
is more or less intuitively understood by
anyone who has ever learned to walk, evolution of species by means of natural selection is widely *misunderstood*. Before
you begin your journey into life, you

should familiarize yourself with the process of natural selection and its relationship to evolution, presented in *A Journey into Evolution*: Natural Selection. Natural selection and evolution are such important topics that we will devote a full chapter to them.

Author's summary of this section

The scientific method is the basic process by which scientists investigate the world around us. In recent years, great advances have been made in understanding cellular and molecular biology, ecological relationships, geological events, and how organisms change over time. The theory of evolution is central to all of biology and is supported by a wide variety of scientific experiments and observations.

I-B BIOLOGY: SAVING YOUR LIFE AND PRESERVING THE EARTH

No one needs to tell you that we live in precarious times. AIDS (autoimmune deficiency syndrome) threatens the entire human population, and a host of ecological disasters looms larger with each passing year. On our journey into life we will review the known biology of HIV, the virus that causes AIDS, and view the current crisis in the biological framework of host-parasite relationships (Chapter 25). Until a cure is found, your knowledge of the biology of AIDS and the HIV virus that causes it may save your life. When a cure is found for AIDS, it will be biologists who find it, even though they may call themselves by a specialist's title. Immunologists, oncologists, even cytologists are all biologists.

AIDS is a grave health problem: a fast-spreading, incurable disease that usually kills within ten years. We are, however, faced with even more serious problems that are the result of the accumulated neglect and exploitation of the biosphere. After 100 years of abuse, these problems are now beginning to have a serious impact. These environmental problems will take perhaps 200 years to become critical, but, by that time, it will be too late to fix many of them: the biosphere will have been irreparably damaged. Life will go on and the mechanism of natural selection will still oper-

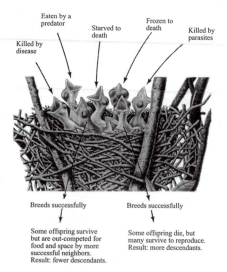

FIGURE I-3

Selection against young. Many factors select against the numerous offspring that most animals produce. Those babies that do survive to reproductive age must still find a mate, prepare and defend a breeding site, and guard and provide for their young.

ate; species will still evolve, but many individuals of our own species will have been selected *against* (Figure 1-3). Many familiar and charismatic species such as elephants, mountain gorillas, and Bengal tigers will have disappeared. If present trends continue, the atmosphere may be radically different, and life for humans may be quite unpleasant.

■ ■ ■ ■ ■

One of the main goals of this journey into life is to alert you to the existence, causes, and far-reaching effects of the ten worst environmental problems, and to suggest ways that you can help rescue yourself, your children, and their grandchildren—as well as the biosphere. We emphasize environmental problems in our journey into life because they have already had, and will continue to have, a grave impact upon the biological world. Refer to Table 1-1 for a summary of causes, potential and realized negative effects, suggested solutions, and references to fuller discussion in subsequent Journey Boxes.

We are now nearly ready to embark upon this journey. You know our itinerary and you have packed two essential understandings into your mental suitcase: the scientific method of inquiry and the theory of evolution by means of natural selection. But before we depart, it would be good to more fully define what we mean by "life." What are the major features of living organisms?

1. *Living things are organized into units called cells, the units of structure, function, and reproduc-*

BIO-BIT

AIDS is the leading cause of death of adults living in some cities in Africa.

---

tion in organisms. Most cells are so small that we must use a microscope to see them. Many small organisms, such as bacteria and protists, consist of one cell each, while larger organisms, such as grasses and humans, contain up to hundreds of millions of cells. Each cell is a discrete packet of living material, a biochemical factory that shows all the features of life listed below.

2. *Living things are highly ordered.* All organisms contain very similar kinds of chemicals, and the proportions of these chemical elements in living things are very different from those in the nonliving environment. A living organism's chemical composition, structure, and function are all more complex and more highly organized than those of nonliving things.

3. *Living things obtain and use energy from their environments to grow, to reproduce, and to maintain and increase the high degree of orderliness of their bodies.* Most organisms depend, directly or indirectly, on energy from the sun. Green plants use solar energy to make food. This supports the plants themselves and is also used by all organisms that eat plants, and even-

tually by those that eat the plant-eaters.

4. *Living organisms respond to stimuli from their environments.* Most animals respond rapidly to environmental changes by making some sort of movement—exploring, fleeing, or even rolling into a ball. Plants respond more slowly, but still actively: stems and leaves bend toward light, and roots grow downward. The capacity to respond to environmental stimuli is universal among living things.

5. *Living things develop.* Everything changes with time, but living organisms change in particularly complex ways called development. A nonliving crystal grows by addition of identical or similar units, but during its life cycle a plant or animal develops new structures, such as leaves or teeth, that differ in chemistry and organization from the structures that produced them.

6. *Living things reproduce themselves.* New organisms arise only from the reproduction of other, similar organisms. New cells arise only from the subdivision of other cells.

7. *The information each organism needs to survive, develop, and reproduce is segregated within the organism and passed from each organism to its offspring.* This information is contained in the organism's genetic material—its chromosomes and genes—and it specifies the possible range of the organism's physical, bio-chemical, and behavioral features. An organism passes genetic information to its offspring, and this is why offspring are similar to their parents. Genetic information does vary somewhat, though, so parents and offspring are usually similar, but not identical.

8. *Living things evolve and are adapted to their environments.* Today's organisms have arisen by evolution, the descent and modification of organisms from more ancient forms of life. Evolution proceeds by way of natural selection, the differential survival and reproduction of those organisms that carry the genes best suited to their environment. This process of adaptation works so well that we can predict roughly how a given organism lives merely by examining its structure.

Although we intuitively think that we can tell if something is alive or not, it is often difficult to do so. It is important to emphasize that *all* of these characteristics *taken together* define life.

AIDS and environmental exploitation of the biosphere are just two of the many serious biological problems facing humans today. Addressing these problems will require broad education, serious investigations, and coordinated efforts to change human behavior. There are at least eight characteristics that collectively help us to define life.

Table I-I
Our Current Environmental Problems

Problem	Cause	Potential Negative Effects	Realized Negative Effects	Solutions
Overpopulation	too many people having too many babies	stress, disease, conflict, death, pollution, environmental destruction, starvation, war	stress, disease, conflict, death, pollution, environmental destruction, starvation, war	education, increase in the status of women, population control
Global warming	greenhouse gases, primarily CO_2	climatic disruptions, rise in sea levels	0.5 degree rise in temperature	decrease emissions of CO_2 and methane
Acid rain	SO_2 and NO_2 emissions	forest collapse and acidified lakes and ponds, loss of aquatic species	loss of forest trees, frog and fish populations down	clean up emissions, reduce population
Ozone hole	chlorofluorocarbons	skin cancers increase, death up food chain in Antarctic waters	ozone holes over Arctic and Antarctic, ozone thinning elsewhere	cease manufacture and use of CFCs, reduce population
Deforestation	clear-cutting, greed, people trying to feed and support their families	loss of species, climatic disruptions	loss of species, climatic disruptions	habitat protection, population control
Loss of species	habitat loss in forests and wetlands, competition from introduced species, over-hunting	impoverished biosphere	impoverished biosphere	habitat protection, population control
Loss of topsoil	careless farming and irrigation	loss of soil fertility	loss of crops, siltation of estuaries, death of reefs	better farming practices, population control
Loss of water	overpopulation	increased desertification, war, economic strife	water shortages, desertification, economic strife	population control
Polluted water	toxic metals, toxic landfill leachate, careless farming, inadequate sewage treatment	water shortages, illness, death	illness, death water shortages	remodeling factory and waste-disposal practices, population control
Over-farming	poor education, greed, desperation	loss of soil fertility, food shortages, hunger	loss of soil fertility, food shortages, hunger	better education, population control

I-C LIFE: ONLY ON EARTH

Surrounded by life, we seldom stop to consider how remarkable it is. Not only does the beauty in living organisms outshine any human works of art, but living things move and act independently. Busy on their own errands, they live their lives in ways that we fail to understand. Think for a moment what life must be like for a dragonfly. Don't just imagine yourself as a human encased inside an armor-plated, winged, dragonfly suit, but instead try to imagine how the big insect perceives the world. What does it see or smell as it flies above the pond? Does it have thoughts? How do the insects it snatches out of the air taste to it? How does it recognize prey? How does it recognize members of its own species? How does it learn to fly? Does it sleep at night? If you're like most of us, you will have no answers for these questions and you will appreciate the limitations of our current knowledge.

Except for the handful of domesticated creatures that rely upon humans in one way or another, the vast majority of living organisms that share our world lead lives as remote from ours as we are from the mountains of the moon. Blind and deaf to the textures of the lives of most other organisms, we coexist in connected, but separate, spheres. Civilization further disconnects us from nature. Our meats, fruits, and vegetables come not from animals and plants, but in plastic-wrapped packages from the supermarket. Experiences with "wild" animals are limited to those on display at zoological parks and captured on nature specials we watch on television. If people think of plants at all, it is as outdoor decoration, and trees are confined to street margins or parklands. In the last 5000 years—equivalent to the blink of an eye in geological time—the human relationship with living creatures has changed from worship and reverence to exploitation and eradication.

This careless attitude is especially strange when you remember that there is no evidence that living things exist anywhere else in the universe. Conditions are too fiery on Mercury, too poisonous on Venus, and too cold on the rest of the planets of our solar system for life to thrive. Only Earth's unique oceans fostered the earliest living organisms. Furthermore, each species is the current product of millions of years of evolution. The chemical products made by each species' genes have been fine-tuned by natural selection so that it can cope with the normal range of fluctuations in its environment. Although there are many species called living fossils because apparently identical representatives have been found preserved in rocks that are tens, even hundreds of millions of years old, most species don't last that long. Paleontologists—scientists who study fossils— have estimated that the life span of a typical species ranges between one and ten million years. And they further speculate that between one to ten species naturally go extinct each year. Yet, humans have so little regard for other forms of life that it is estimated that *each day between 10 and 100 more species are forced into extinction.* Loss of habitat to the demands of an ever-expanding human population is the most common, but not the only, reason for this tragic occurrence. If we allow it to continue, this daily erosion of life (estimates vary from 4000 to 90,000 species per year) will result in a biological impoverishment of unparalleled proportions. Soon we will be left with only those species that are tough enough to coexist in the margins of human society.

A species is an irreplaceable thing, the culmination of millions of years of evolution, an object of fascination and wonder even if it is physically unattractive. Moreover, each species is a piece of the biological puzzle. Each has an ecological role, each is full of history and information, and each has a separate way of life. When the European colonists first came to America, the trees were full of strange, colorful birds. Recorded by explorers as early as 1588, the Carolina Parakeets were well described by the ornithologist Alexander Wilson in 1828:

> At Big Bone Lick, thirty miles above the mouth of the Kentucky River, I saw them in great numbers. They came screaming through the woods in the morning, about an hour after sunrise, to drink the salt water, of which they, as well as the Pigeons [Passenger Pigeons, another species that is now extinct], are remarkably fond. When they alighted on the ground, it appeared at a distance as if covered by a carpet of richest green, orange, and yellow: they afterward settled, in one body, on a neighboring tree, which stood detached from any other, covering almost every twig of it, and the sun, shining strongly on their gay and glossy plumage, produced a very beautiful and splendid appearance. Here I had an opportunity of observing some very particular traits of their character: Having shot down a number, some of which were only wounded, the whole flock swept repeatedly around their prostrate companions,

> and again settled on a low tree, within twenty yards of the spot where I stood. At each successive discharge, though showers of them fell, yet the affection of the survivors seemed rather to increase, for after a few circuits around the place, they again alighted near me, looking down upon their slaughtered companions with such manifest symptoms of sympathy and concern, as entirely disarmed me.

Although Wilson's account is sentimental, it is accurate. And, because of their habits, it is little wonder that millions of the small, gregarious, green and yellow parrots were shot for food, for feathers to decorate women's hats, and for "sport." Farmers killed Carolina Parakeets because they attacked grain and fruit crops, and professional bird-catchers captured and sold many thousands as cage birds. By the 1880s, the parakeets were extremely rare and the last wild specimen was shot in 1901. The Carolina Parakeet had been bred successfully in captivity, but unfortunately the last captive bird died in 1914. There are too many similar stories that detail the demise of too many species.

Loss of a single species is not a huge ecological disaster, but the current relentless loss of species pulls strands from the fabric of life that supports us all. Perhaps the zoologist and explorer William Beebe stated the importance of a species best:

> The beauty and genius of a work of art may be reconceived, though its first material expression be destroyed; a vanished harmony may yet again inspire the composer; but when the last individual of a race of living things breathes no more, another heaven and another earth must pass before such a one can be again.

BIO-BIT _____

Over 99 percent of all of the species of
life that ever existed are now extinct.

We hope that humans are becoming
more concerned over the future of this
planet. Although we often act as though
only *Homo sapiens* matter, we do not in-
habit this planet alone. Every species of
animal, plant, fungus, and bacterium has
a role to play. In India this lesson is beginning to be better understood. Two species of Indian bullfrogs are currently
threatened with extinction because, each
year, tons of frozen frogs' legs are ex-
ported to the dinner tables of Western Europe. But the frogs are worth more alive
than dead, because an adult bullfrog usually eats its weight in insects *each day*.
India's vanishing bullfrogs are linked to
higher rates of malaria and greater losses
of crops to insects. Malaria is a poten-
tially lethal disease carried by mosquitoes
that is the leading cause of death worldwide. Although there are medicines to
prevent malaria, few Indians can afford
them. And in its struggle to feed its huge
population, India cannot afford to lose
any food crops to insect pests.

From the 1930s to the 1950s, before
space exploration became a reality, there
was a common perception, rooted in the
American immigrant and frontier heritage, that one day, when this planet became uninhabitable because of pollution,
we would all put on silver space suits and
climb into needle-nosed ships that would

take us off to colonize brave, new planets. Interestingly, our space program
showed us a very different scenario—the
view of Earth from the moon. We learned
that we live on a lovely blue and white
planet. Veiled with swirling clouds, it
floats in isolated grandeur—a tiny sap-
phire against the velvet blackness of space.
From this vantage point we can see no national boundaries, no sign of humanity.
Even more important: as far as we know,
we are alone in space.

This image has begun to change the
way we think of Earth. Many now realize
that we all *are* space travelers, and that
this unique and fragile planet is our space-
ship. Like all our fellow earthlings, we
were born on board. Although a handful
of us will become astronauts, most will
never climb into that needle-nosed ship to
escape a polluted Earth. We are only beginning to comprehend how complicated,
interconnected, and irreplaceable our home
planet is.

Today, our environmental problems
have reached the stage at which we're
nearly out of time. We have only a few
years to change the habits that worsen global warming—to rein in the human population explosion. Our highest task is to edu-
cate ourselves and new generations. We
must become convinced that all life—not
only human life—is unique and valuable.
We must learn that our own species has
special responsibilities not to scuttle the
ship that carries all of us through space,
because there is nowhere else to go.

With these ideas in mind, our journey
begins.

Human disregard and neglect have resulted in monumental increases in the number of species of life forced into extinction. The loss of a single species can have disastrous, unforeseeable effects. A dramatic change in human attitudes and behaviors will be necessary to reduce the impact that we humans have on other life forms.

SUMMARY

1. Scientists rely upon the scientific method to investigate the world around us.

2. Knowledge of the biological world has expanded greatly in the last 50 years. This is due primarily to advanced technology.

3. The theory of evolution of species as directed by natural selection is the central concept in all of biology.

4. Biological education can help address serious problems such as the AIDS epidemic and the global impact of humans on the environment.

5. All living organisms:
    a. are organized into units called cells,
    b. keep their internal environments fairly constant,
    c. obtain and use energy from their environments to grow, to reproduce, and to maintain and increase the high degree of orderliness of their bodies,
    d. respond to stimuli,
    e. develop,
    f. reproduce themselves,
    g. pass the information to survive, develop, and reproduce to their offspring, and
    h. evolve and adapt to their environments.

6. Humans have seriously affected other life forms by destroying or altering their habitats. As a result, the rate of extinction has increased dramatically.

THINKING CRITICALLY

1. After every hard rain you find dead earthworms lying on the sidewalk. What experiments would you perform to show the cause of death?

2. To what extent should scientists be held responsible for the social and moral consequences of their discoveries?

3. Many professional scientific societies have adopted ethical conduct guidelines for their members and have pledged legal aid to members who "blow the whistle" on employers who make dangerous products or dispose of hazardous materials unsafely. Nevertheless, employees who bring valid protests often find themselves out of a job (management can always find an excuse to eliminate a person's position, or a way to make an employee so uncomfortable that he or she resigns). Why do company managers act this way? What might our society do to ensure its own safety by guaranteeing security to these whistle-blowers?

4. Is some scientific information too dangerous to know?

5. Many characteristics of life can be found in some nonliving things. Can you think of examples of these?

6. What might you expect was the selective pressure that resulted in each of the following adaptations?

    an elephant's trunk
    the scent of honeysuckle
    a leopard's spots
    the bark of a tree
    human language

SELECTED KEY TERMS

biosphere, *p. 82*

continental drift, *p. 84*

ecology, *p. 82*

evolution, theory of, *p. 85*

natural selection, *p. 85*

organism, *p. 82*

protists, *p. 82*

PART TWO

Part Two contains 33 articles grouped in 5 sections according to theme. Reading individual articles can provide insight and entertainment, but reading several articles on a general theme allows for in-depth analysis and critical thinking about a topic. The articles provide a wealth of material for practice in writing a summary and response.

For each of the articles in Part Two, follow these steps in order:

1. *Preview the article*
2. *Study the vocabulary*
3. *Read the article*
4. *Write a summary*
5. *Write your personal response*

1. Preview: Before reading the article, think about the title. Then read the questions or statements preceding the article. Thinking about these ideas for a few moments will help you focus on the subject of the article. In your reading outside this book, try to ask your own questions or think briefly about the subject before you begin reading. Reading "actively" will help you read for comprehension.

2. Study the vocabulary: In the short introduction to each article, note the list of vocabulary words. The words are listed in the order that they appear and are underlined in the article. It would be a good idea to see how the word is used by looking at those words "in context" before you read the article.

If these or other words are keeping you from understanding the article, stop and look the word or words up. If there are words you don't know, but they **do not** keep you from understanding the article, try to get the meaning of the word from the context rather than stopping to look it up. If you do need to look up a word, make a flashcard to help you learn the word permanently. (See Appendix B for more information on learning new vocabulary words).

3.   Read the article: Remember to read for the main idea and the major details which support the main idea. Try not to get bogged down with details, facts, and figures. Notice the details, but realize that you are trying to understand the author's main points so you can summarize and respond to them. When you read textbooks for a different purpose, such as taking a multiple choice test, you need to study and memorize details; however, for much of your reading, you gain more from understanding the main points.

4.   Write a summary: Summaries will vary in length. Remember, a summary is written mostly in your own words and is generally no longer than one-fourth the length of the article. Rather than count the words, ask your teacher to help you determine if you have included the main idea and major details.

5.   Write your personal response: The response is one of the most rewarding parts of the reading process. You get a chance to talk back, in effect, to the author. Once you have understood the author's point and the support for the point, you can get in your "two cents'" worth.

From time to time you may want to reread these directions for review and to make sure you are following all the steps.

LEARNING STRATEGIES

The articles in this section, listed below, can help you become a better learner—in or out of school.

- **STEPS TO BETTER LISTENING**
- **HOW TO SPELL**
- **LISTEN CAREFULLY**
- **HOW TO IMPROVE YOUR VOCABULARY**
- **TEST DE-STRESS**
- **BLOCK THAT MENTAL BLOCK**

Steps to Better Listening

by Cynthia Hamilton and Brian H. Kleiner, Ph.D.
from *Personnel Journal*

Some of the difficult words in the article are listed below in the order in which they appear. In the text, these words are underlined. As you preview, look at the context in which the words are used.

condemn	**cushion**	**steepled**
interrogated	**gestures**	**intonation**
curb		

Almost half of our waking day is spent listening. Yet we forget most of what we hear within one hour! These authors identify some things that interfere with our listening and provide some suggestions for improvement.

Most people operate at only 25-30% of their listening efficiency.

Because listening plays a vital role in our everyday communications, and consequently affects everything we do and expect done, this inefficiency is a constant cause of problems.

The principles and rules necessary for effective listening include overcoming major stumbling blocks, learning listening techniques, watching speakers' nonverbal actions, and listening for emphasis within the message.

With a little knowledge and practice, people can double their listening ability.

Larry L. Barker reports in "Listening Behavior" that 70-75% of our waking day is spent in one of the four types of communication: listening, 42% of the time; talking, 32%; reading, 15%; and writing, 11%.

Throughout our formal education, however, reading and writing skills are emphasized, but the skills of speaking and, especially, listening remain in the background.

Many people don't want to, or won't, listen, and when people fail to hear and understand each other the results are costly.

But listening is not as simple as might be expected. Tests have shown that after a 10-minute oral presentation, the average listener hears, receives, comprehends, and retains only about 50% of any given message.

After 48 hours, most listeners only remember about 25% of what they heard.[1]

To improve listening skills, one must identify and overcome certain barriers.[2]

■ Don't let your eyes wander or your head turn aimlessly about. Keep from drumming your fingers, snapping gum, or mindlessly handling pens, pencils, and so on.

■ Facts are important, but only as stepping stones to ideas leading to a major point.

Don't keep your mind so occupied with bits of information that you miss the speaker's overall message.

■ The burden of listening is on the listener. Don't automatically <u>condemn</u> a speaker or the subject as uninteresting.

Also, don't prejudice your listening because you don't like the speaker's looks, hairdo, voice, race, sex or other facts irrelevant to the message.

■ Don't pretend to be receiving the message while your mind has made a mental detour and is busy with different ideas.

If the speaker tries to interact with you at this point, you'll find yourself completely lost.

■ Whatever you feel about the speaker or his or her subject, hear the speaker out first.

Don't allow yourself to become irritated or overexcited by what is said or how it is said. Otherwise, the message gets lost in a flash of emotion.

■ You can't try to write everything a speaker is saying, word for word, and expect to hear the message.

Just jot down highlights or key ideas and pay more attention to hearing the message than to writing everything down.

■ Don't waste listening time.

You can listen faster than the speaker can speak. The average speaking rate is about 125 words per minute; your capacity to listen is about 400-600 words a minute.

Therefore, while you are listening you have about 75% of your time free.[3]

You can use this extra time not only to improve your understanding of what is being said but to think up answers, make decisions, and plan suggestions.

At times you can deliberately ask questions to stall for time to think.

Listening Guidelines Focus on Common Sense and Courtesy

In addition to identifying and overcoming obstacles to effective listening, following these six guidelines can improve listening efficiency.[4]

Look at the Person Speaking

Looking at the person talking shows interest. Don't stare. Rather, look at the speaker's hairline, neck, or mouth.

Even notice eye color, but don't look at the floor, ceiling, or out the window.

Many people won't trust a person who won't look at them; distrust blocks communication.

Ask Questions

This is the best way for someone to become a better listener quickly.

This is a necessity for parents, teachers, managers, and salespeople.

There are two types of questions. Closed-ended questions discover facts that give specific, concise answers, i.e., "How old are you?"

The other type of questions are open-ended questions. You can find out most of your required information by using these questions.

For example, "How did you get into the line of work you're in now?"

In addition, although asking questions is important to listening, have a purpose to each question. Nobody likes to feel they're being <u>interrogated</u>.

Don't Interrupt

There is a tendency to want to jump into the middle of a conversation when one gets an idea or is reminded of something by someone else's words.

But that presents problems. We need to practice letting other people finish their sentence or ideas before butting in.

Most of us go out of our way to avoid interrupters because we don't like getting cut off while speaking. Therefore, let others finish what they are saying.

Don't Change the Subject

Interrupting is bad enough, but going on and changing the subject at the same time adds insult to injury.

The person who was cut off may not offer any more ideas and will probably find a reason to get out of the presence of the rude interrupter who also changed the subject.

Emotions

Some people get angry or excited about certain words, i.e., taxes, abortion, communism, Reagan.

It isn't wise to over react to words and ideas from someone. <u>Curb</u> your emotions and control your urge to interrupt and express your opinion.

Try to understand the speaker first and then present your ideas in a controlled manner.

Also, too much excitement causes us to mentally debate or fight any idea that differs from our own personal view, experience, or bias.

Responsiveness

Let your speaker know you are interested.

Show signs of understanding. An occasional "uh-huh" will help. Most people won't talk long unless we are responsive and offer some sign of understanding.

Occasionally, an interruption used to clarify a point not only shows attentiveness and responsiveness, it ensures you're receiving the message as its sender intended.

In addition, clarification helps you focus on the rest of what is being said.

<u>Cushion</u> the interruption with an, "excuse me," or an inquiry that asks for an elaboration, such as, "how many?" or "what was the date?"

Body Language Underscores or Undermines Verbal Messages

Many people communicate by their non-verbal actions. Often the voice, facial expressions, <u>gestures</u>, or body movements and positions reveal much more than words.

The things to look for are presented below. Remember, however, it normally takes a cluster of body expressions to indicate a true attitude or feeling.

A single movement may be something the person does all the time, and you may interpret the message to be something other than what is intended.

Open hands and an unbuttoned coat indicate an *openness* about a person.

On the other hand, *defensiveness* is indicated by arms crossed over the chest; crossed legs; an index finger pointed at others while talking; karate chops; and fisted gestures.

Suspicion is indicated by crossed arms; glancing sideways; touching or rubbing the nose or eyes; buttoning the coat; and drawing away.

With a little knowledge and practice, people can double their listening ability.

Cooperation is shown with open hands; sitting on the edge of the chair; unbuttoning the coat; tilting the head; and hand-to-face gestures.

Frustration can be noted in those who breathe or speak in short breaths; wring their hands; rub the back of their neck; rub their hands through their hair; use fisted gestures; or point the index finger.

Insecurity is indicated by pinching the skin; chewing on a pen or pencil; rubbing one thumb over the other; biting finger-nails; or keeping hands in pockets.

Nervousness can be detected by those who openly clear their throat; smoke; whistle; cover the mouth with the hand while speaking; tug at the pants while seated; jingle money in one's pockets; tug at the ear; wring the hands; fidget in the chair; and don't look at the other person.

Confidence is shown by sitting up straight; hands steepled or behind the back.

Body movements that indicate *reflection* include: stroking the chin; tilting the head; peering over one's glasses; taking one's glasses off or cleaning them; pipe-smoking gestures; biting on the end of one's glasses; and putting one's hand on the bridge of the nose.

In addition, facial expressions are important in determining a person's feelings.

A smile, a frown, a puzzled look are some of the expressions that communicate feelings of fear, anger, surprise, and boredom.

But some people are so serious when they speak that others misinterpret their feelings as unfriendly or unhappy.

Intonation and accent also play a critical role in interpreting messages.

Word Count: 1385

NOTES

[1]Lyman K. Steil. *Effective Listening* (Massachusetts: Addison-Wesley Publishing Company, 1983), p. 51.
[2]Robert L. Montgomery. *Listening Made Easy* (New York: AMACOM, 1981), p. 31.
[3]Lyman K. Steil. *Listening: It Can Change Your Life* (New York: John Wiley and Sons, 1983), p. 45.
[4]Montgomery, op. cit., p. 65.

How to Spell

by John Irving
from 'Power of the Printed Word' Program
International Paper Company

Some of the difficult words in the article are listed below in the order in which they appear. In the text, these words are underlined. As you preview, look at the context in which the words are used.

intimidate **bugbear** **permissible**
synonym

Are you a good speller? Chances are your answer is "no." For many people, spelling is not easy, so if you answered "no," you have plenty of company. In the following article, the novelist John Irving offers some advice for you.

Let's begin with the bad news.

If you're a bad speller, you probably think you always will be. There are exceptions to every spelling rule, and the rules themselves are easy to forget. George Bernard Shaw demonstrated how ridiculous some rules are. By following the rules, he said, we could spell *fish* this way: *ghoti*. The "f" as it sounds in enou*gh*, the "i" as it sounds in w*o*men, and the "sh" as it sounds in fic*ti*on.

With such rules to follow, no one should feel stupid for being a bad speller. But there are ways to improve. Start by acknowledging the mess that English spelling is in—but have sympathy: English spelling changed with foreign influ-ences. Chaucer wrote "geese," but "guess," imported earlier by the Norman invaders, finally replaced it . Most early printers in England came from Holland; they brought "ghost" and "gherkin" with them.

If you'd like to <u>intimidate</u> yourself—and remain a bad speller forever—just try to remember the 13 different ways the sound "sh" can be written.

*sh*oe	suspi*ci*on
*s*ugar	naus*e*ous
o*c*ean	con*sci*ous
i*ss*ue	*ch*aperone
na*ti*on	man*si*on
s*ch*ist	fu*ch*sia

Now the Good News

The good news is that 90 percent of all writing consists of 1,000 basic words. There is, also, a method to most English spelling and a great number of how-to-spell books. Remarkably, all these books propose learning the same rules! Not surprisingly, most of these books are humorless.

Just keep this in mind: If you're familiar with the words you use, you'll probably spell them correctly—and you shouldn't be writing words you're unfamiliar with anyway. Use a word—out loud, and more than once— before you try writing it, and make sure that you know what it means before you use it. This means you'll have to look it up in a dictionary, where you'll not only learn what it means, but you'll see how it's spelled. Choose a dictionary you enjoy browsing in, and guard it as you would a diary. You wouldn't lend a diary, would you?

A Tip on Looking It Up

Beside every word I look up in my dictionary, I make a mark. Beside every word I look up more than once, I write a note to myself—about WHY I looked it up. I have looked up "strictly" 14 times since 1965. I prefer to spell it with a K—as in "stric*k*tly." I have looked up "ubiquitous" a dozen times. I can't remember what it means.

Another good way to use your dictionary: When you have to look up a word, for any reason, learn—and learn to *spell*— a *new* word at the same time. It can be any useful word on the same page as the word you looked up. Put the date beside this new word and see how quickly, or in what way, you forget it. Eventually, you'll learn it.

Almost as important as knowing what a word means (in order to spell it) is knowing how it's pronounced. It's gover*n*ment, not gov*er*ment. It's Feb*ru*ary, not Feb*u*ary. And if you know that *anti-* means against, you should know how to spell *anti*dote and *anti*biotic and *anti*freeze. If you know that *ante-* means before, you shouldn't have trouble spelling *ante*chamber or *ante*cedent.

Some Rules, Exceptions and Two Tricks

I don't have room to touch on *all* the rules here. It would take a book to do that. But I can share a few rules that help me most. Some spelling problems that seem hard are really easy. What about *-ary* or *-ery*? Just remember that there are only six common words in English that end in *-ery*. Memorize them, and feel fairly secure that all the rest end in *-ary*:

cemetery	monastery
millinery	confectionery
distillery	stationery (as in paper)

Here's another easy rule. Only four words end in *-efy*. Most people misspell them with *-ify*, which is usually correct. Just memorize these too, and use *-ify* for all the rest:

stupefy	putrefy
liquefy	rarefy

As a former bad speller, I have learned a few valuable tricks. Any good how-to-spell book will teach you more than these two, but these two are my favorites. Of the 800,000 words in the English language, the most frequently misspelled is *alright*; just remember that *alright* is *all*

When you have trouble, think of poor Andrew Jackson and know that you're not alone.

wrong, would you? That's how you know you should write *all* right.

The other trick is for the truly worst spellers. I mean those of you who spell so badly that you can't get close enough to the right way to spell a word in order to even FIND it in the dictionary. The word you're looking up is there, of course, but you won't find it the way you're trying to spell it. What to do is look up a synonym—another word that means the same thing. Chances are good that you'll find the word you're looking for under the definition of the synonym.

Demon Words and Bugbears

Everyone has a few demon words— words that never look right, even when they're spelled correctly. Three of my demons are *medieval, ecstasy,* and *rhythm.* I have learned to hate these words, but I have not learned to spell them; I have to look them up every time.

And everyone has a spelling rule that's a bugbear—it's either too difficult to learn or it's impossible to remember. My per-

sonal bugbear among the rules is the one governing whether you add *-able* or *-ible*. I can teach it to you, but I can't remember it myself.

You add *-able* to a full word: adapt, adaptable; work, workable. You add *-able* to words that end in *e*—just remember to drop the final *e*: love, lovable. But if the word ends in two *e*'s, like agree, you keep them both: agreeable.

You add *-ible* if the base is not a full word that can stand on its own: credible, tangible, horrible, terrible. You add *-ible* if the root ends in *-ns*: responsible. You add *-ible* if the root word ends in *-miss*: permissible. You add *-ible* if the root word ends in a soft *c* (but remember to drop the final *e*!): force, forcible.

Got that? I don't have it, and I was introduced to that rule in prep school; with that rule, I still learn one word at a time.

Poor President Jackson

You must remember that it is permissible for spelling to drive you crazy. Spelling had this effect on Andrew Jackson, who once blew his stack while trying to write a Presidential paper. "It's a damn poor mind that can think of only one way to spell a word!" the President cried.

When you have trouble, think of poor Andrew Jackson and know that you're not alone.

What's Really Important

And remember what's really important about good writing is not good spelling. If you spell badly but write well, you should hold your head up. As the poet T.S. Eliot recommended, "Write for as large

and miscellaneous an audience as possible—and don't be overly concerned if
you can't spell 'miscellaneous.' " Also
remember that you can spell correctly
and write well and still be misunderstood. Hold your head up about that,
too. As good old G.C. Lichtenberg said,
"A book is a mirror: if an ass peers into
it, you can't expect an apostle to look
out"—whether you spell "apostle" correctly or not.

Word count: 1228

Listen Carefully

by Tom W. Harris
from *Nation's Business*

Some of the difficult words in the article are listed below in the order in which they appear. In the text, these words are underlined. As you preview, look at the context in which the words are used.

morale	**gestures**	**habitually**
enterprises	**maximize**	**diligence**

Effective listening can be used in business as well as in school to boost morale, improve productivity, sell, teach, inform, or achieve other goals.

Consultant Germaine Knapp wants you to hear something. "Effective listening—we call it power listening—is one of the strongest assets in professional life today," she says. "Too few of us take advantage of it, but all of us could. There are dozens of field-proven techniques and tactics for applying the power of listening, and they get results."

Knapp is president of Wordsmart Inc., a consulting and training firm in Rochester, N.Y. Her clients include Xerox and Eastman Kodak as well as banks, hospitals, manufacturers, and colleges. Training in listening skills is one of Knapp's specialties.

Knapp cites observations by Lyman K. Steil, a former University of Minnesota professor who is president of Communication Development Inc., a consulting firm in St. Paul, Minn. He has developed and carried out programs designed to improve employees' listening skills. His programs have ranged from a multimillion-dollar, listening-oriented advertising campaign some years ago for Sperry Corp.—now Unisys—to training for countless small and midsized enterprises.

"Overall," Steil says, "if each of America's more than 100 million workers prevented just one $10 mistake by better listening, their organizations would gain over $1 billion in profits. A $10 mistake is as simple as a few minutes' error in the time of a meeting, putting an item of stock in the wrong place, or having to retype a letter."

Knapp says that effective listening—or power listening—can be used to help persuade, motivate, improve productivity, boost morale, obtain cooperation, sell, teach, inform, or achieve other goals.

"Effective listening is continually active, not passive," she says. "For example, to draw out information from the other person and get the whole story, actively show that you're listening. We train people in a number of techniques that are very simple—and very effective," such as gestures and comments.

Gestures and mannerisms can communicate interest. Lean forward rather than back while listening, Knapp suggests. Nod occasionally to show comprehension. Smile. Look directly at the person speaking. Comments such as "I see" and "Go on" can show that you are attuned to what the speaker is saying. When used with sincerity, these tactics can pay dividends.

Another way to improve listening is to take notes, Knapp says. "It helps make you focus on the highlights of what's being said. And the other person, seeing you write things down, will usually try to maximize accuracy and clarity. One word of caution: Too much note-taking may make some people angry or nervous and uncommunicative."

Consultant Steil has found that note-taking also works in phone conversations. He cites the example of a salesman who habitually made comments such as, "Just a second—could you mention that again—I want to write it down." In the salesman's view, "better listening made better sales." Customers became more precise in explaining their needs, he said, and they were favorably impressed with his diligence for detail.

Business people in various fields have adopted effective-listening tactics. For example, Dan Fazenden, president of Roger Fazenden Realty Inc., a real estate company near Minneapolis, says: "I use the 'plan to report' principle. When someone tells you something, listen so intently that you could report it all to someone else."

...if each of America's more than 100 million workers prevented just one $10 mistake by better listening, their organizations would gain over $1 billion in profits.

It is important to "listen for what isn't said," Knapp says, as well as to ask questions. She stresses two important rules:

"*Never* end a conversation without being sure what was said—and why. Furthermore, don't pretend you understand when you don't. Chances are the speaker, not you, caused the confusion. So don't walk away and later make mistakes that you, not the speaker, will be held responsible for."

Once your employees become good listeners, it will pay you in turn to listen to those listeners, says auto dealer John Zimbrick of Madison, Wis. Zimbrick's employees listen to customers to determine their attitudes, and management keeps current on the employees' findings. "It can be even more effective than customer-research projects," says Zimbrick. "Many firms can't afford specialized customer research. This can do the job better."

The other side of power listening is the power to make other people listen. Knapp explains: "One of the most skillful communicators I know of has an office position in a medium-sized business. When she senses somebody isn't listening, she stops talking. She lets two or three seconds tick away. The other person 'hears' this pause and gets back to listening." Other effective tactics, she says, include leaning forward, standing up, gesturing, asking a question.

For a typical employee, Knapp says, time spent communicating during the workday may be as high as 50 percent, and for top managers, the figure can reach 75 percent. "An average 45 percent of this time is spent listening," she says. "So, either for an individual or an organization, when you polish up listening skills, you may well be tapping into your greatest undeveloped success resources."

Word Count: 807

How to Improve your Vocabulary

by Tony Randall
from 'Power of the Printed Word' Program
International Paper Company

Some of the difficult words in the article are listed below in the order in which they appear. In the text, these words are underlined. As you preview, look at the context in which the words are used.

manacle **innocuous** **Aristophanes**
corroborate **stuffed shirt**

How often are you puzzled by the meaning of words when you try to read? When you write, do you sometimes struggle to come up with just the right word to express your thoughts? Tony Randall, an actor and comedian, offers some hints to improve your vocabulary.

Words can make us laugh, cry, go to war, fall in love. Rudyard Kipling called words the most powerful drug of mankind. If they are, I'm a hopeless addict—and I hope to get you hooked, too!

Whether you're still in school or you head up a corporation, the better command you have of words, the better chance you have of saying exactly what you mean, of understanding what others mean—and of getting what you want in the world.

English is the richest language—with the largest vocabulary on earth. Over 1,000,000 words!

You can express shades of meaning that aren't even *possible* in other languages. (For example, you can differentiate between "sky" and "heaven." The French, Italians and Spanish cannot.)

Yet, the average adult has a vocabulary of only 30,000 to 60,000 words. Imagine what we're missing!

Here are five pointers that help me learn—and remember—whole *families* of words at a time.

They may not *look* easy—and won't be at first. But, if you stick with them, you'll find they *work*!

What's the first thing to do when you see a word you don't know?

1. Try to guess the meaning of the word from the way it's used.

You can often get at least *part* of a meaning—just from how it's used in a sentence.

That's why it's so important to read as much as you can—different *kinds* of

Rudyard Kipling called words the most powerful drug of mankind. If they are, I'm a hopeless addict— and I hope to get you hooked, too!

things, magazines, books, newspapers you don't normally read. The more you *expose* yourself to new words, the more words you'll pick up *just by seeing how they're used.*

For instance, say you run across the word "manacle": "The manacles had been on John's wrists for 30 years. Only one person had a key—his wife." You have a good *idea* of what "manacles" are—just from the context of the sentence.

But let's find out *exactly* what the word means and where it comes from. The only way to do this, and to build an extensive vocabulary *fast*, is to go to the dictionary.

(How lucky, you *can*—Shakespeare *couldn't*. There *wasn't* an English dictionary in his day!)

So you go to the dictionary. (NOTE: Don't let dictionary abbreviations put you off. The front tells you what they mean, and even has a guide to pronunciation.)

2. Look it up.

Here's the definition for "manacle" in *The American Heritage Dictionary of the English Language.*

man-a-cle n. Usually plural. 1. A device for confining the hands, usually consisting of two metal rings that are fastened about the wrists and joined by a metal chain; a handcuff. 2. Anything that confines or restrains. -*tr.v.* **manacled, -cling, -cles**. 1. To restrain with manacles. 2. To confine or restrain as if with manacles; shackle; fetter. (*Middle English manicle,* from Old French, from Latin *manicula,* little hand, handle, diminutive of *manus,* hand.)

The first definition fits here: A device for confining the hands, usually consisting of two metal rings that are fastened about the wrists and joined by a metal chain; a handcuff.

Well, that's what you *thought* it meant. But what's the idea *behind* the word? What are the roots? To really understand a word, you need to know.

Here's where the detective work—and the *fun*—begins.

3. Dig the meaning out by the roots.

The root is the basic part of the word— its heritage, its origin. (Most of our roots come from Latin and Greek words at least 2,000 years old—which come from even earlier Indo-European tongues!)

Learning the roots 1) helps us *remember* words, 2) gives us a deeper understanding of the words we *already know*, and 3) allows us to pick up whole families of *new* words at a time. That's why learning the root is the *most important part of going to the dictionary.*

Notice the root of "manacle" is *manus* (Latin) meaning "hand."

Well, that makes sense. Now, other words with this root, *man*, start to make sense too.

Take *man*ual—something done "by hand" (*man*ual labor) or a "handbook." And *man*age—to "handle" something (as a *man*ager). When you e*man*cipate someone, you're taking him "from the hands of" someone else.

When you *man*ufacture something, you "make it by hand" (in its original meaning).

And when you finish your first novel, your publisher will see your—originally "handwritten"—*man*uscript.

Imagine! A whole new world opens up—just from one simple root!

The root gives the *basic* clue to the meaning of a word. But there's another important clue that runs a close second—the *prefix.*

4. Get the powerful prefixes under your belt.

A prefix is the part that's sometimes attached to the front of a word. Like—well, *pre*fix! There aren't many—less than 100 major prefixes—and you'll learn them in no time at all just by becoming more aware of the meanings of words you already know. Here are a few. (Some of the "How-to" vocabulary-building books will give you the others.)

PREFIX		**MEANING**	**EXAMPLES**	
(Latin)	(Greek)			(Literal Sense)
com	sym, syn	with, very	conform	(form with)
co, col, cor	syl	together	sympathy	(feeling with)
in, im	a, an	not,	innocent	(not wicked)
il, ir		without	amorphous	(without form)
contra	anti	against	contravene	(come against)
counter	ant	opposite	antidote	(give against)

Now, see how the *prefix* (along with the context) helps you get the meaning of the italicized words:

- "If you're going to be my witness, your story must <u>cor</u>roborate my story." (The literal meaning of *corroborate* is "strength together.")
- "You told me one thing—now you tell me another. Don't *con*tradict yourself." (The literal meaning of *contradict* is "say against.")
- "Oh, that snake's not poisonous. It's a completely <u>in</u>no<u>c</u>uous little garden snake." (The literal meaning of *innocuous* is "not harmful.")

Now you've got some new words. What are you going to do with them?

5. Put your new words to work at once.

Use them several times the first day you learn them. Say them out loud! Write them in sentences.

Should you "use" them on *friends*? Careful—you don't want them to think you're a <u>stuffed shirt</u>. (It depends on the situation. You *know* when a word sounds natural—and when it sounds stuffy.)

How about your *enemies*? You have my blessing. Ask one of them if he's read that article on pneumonoultramicroscopicsilicovolcanoconiosis. (You really can find it in the dictionary.) Now, you're one up on him.

So what do you do to improve you vocabulary?

Remember: 1) Try to guess the meaning of the word from the way it's used. 2) Look it up. 3) Dig the meaning out by the roots. 4) Get the powerful prefixes under your belt. 5) Put your new words to work at once.

That's all there is to it—you're off on your treasure hunt.

Now, do you see why I love words so much?

<u>Aristophanes</u> said, "By words, the mind is excited and the spirit elated." It's as true today as it was when he said it in Athens—*2,400 years ago!*

I hope you're now like me—hooked on words forever.

Word count: 1163

TEST DE-STRESS

by Keith Blanchard
from *Young & Modern (YM)*

Some of the difficult words in the article are listed below in the order in which they appear. In the text, these words are underlined. As you preview, look at the context in which the words are used.

adrenalin	**nausea**	**deprivation**
subconsiously	**diarrhea**	**hilarious**
nausea	**carbohydrates**	**doofus**

It's exam period, and you feel as if you're in a movie: The Exams That Ate My Life. *You can't even read the back of a cereal box without highlighting the salient points. Are you going insane? More important, are you going to pass? Here's a handy guide to get through exams with your mind—and GPA—intact.*

Emotions in Motion

While a little anxiety can be good for you (it pumps up your adrenaline and helps focus your attention), when stress starts to interfere with studying or with taking an exam, it's time to take action.

Pre-test Stress

Feeling angry, depressed, restless, or nervous around test time can be a result of negative self-instructions. According to Linda Locher, Ph.D., director of Counseling and Psychological Services for the University of Rochester, "We all have self-image messages we subconsciously play in our head. I call them 'muzak tapes.' At exam time they're usually along the lines of 'I hope I do well.' But for the highly stressed person, the messages become 'I'm stupid,' or 'I'm going to fail.' The key is to recognize these negative messages and replace them with coping ones. Whenever you think, 'This is too hard,' or 'I'll never get through this,' counter these thoughts with, 'This may be hard, but I didn't get here by luck,' or 'I may not be a genius, but I can pass a calculus test.'"

Mid-test Stress

"If you don't manage your stress well *during* an exam, it can build until you really can't perform at all," claims Dr. Locher. And that makes you susceptible to "dumb errors," like leaving out parts of an answer or misreading a question. To combat mid-test stress, stop and close your eyes for a second between questions, blank your mind, and you'll be more receptive to the new question. Try to focus on a pleasant image: You're lying on a beach in Mazatlan with a diploma curled between your toes. "Sometimes it helps just to rephrase the question in your own words," claims Pam Reynolds,* a senior at Spencer-Van Etten High School in New York. "Teachers and professors try to make the questions sound tougher than they are."

Physical Stress Busters

Many students mistakenly view the physical symptoms of stress, which range from sweaty palms to headaches, nausea, and diarrhea, as unrelated to the stress itself. "As if I didn't have enough on my mind with this Pig Latin 201 exam, now I have to get sick, too!" But if exams make you barf, it may be because you're giving your mind a workout but neglecting your body. In other words, you can't just sit in your room with your eyelids stapled up, highlighting textbooks and shoveling pizza into your mouth. Larry Merkel, M.D., staff psychiatrist, Student Health Service at the University of Pennsylvania, offers some tips for keeping your body from falling apart during exams:

Brain Food

Try eating six mini meals instead of three large ones, since big meals make you sleepy. In terms of *what* to eat, protein (yogurt, peanut butter, cheese) is your best bet because it gives you longterm energy.

Sugar (Ding Dongs, chocolate bunnies) gives you energy, but the "sugar high" is deceptive because you crash soon after-

> *...you can't just sit in your room with your eyelids stapled up, highlighting textbooks and shoveling pizza into your mouth.*

ward. You should also avoid OD-ing on carbohydrates, such as pasta and bread. They bog you down, making sleep more attractive than studying. And speaking of sleep, caffeine does help you stay up late, but unfortunately, large amounts affect your cognitive ability, making it harder to learn new things—so if you absolutely need coffee to stay awake, drink no more than three or four cups in a 24-hour period, and wait an hour or two between "doses."

Mental Floss

There are two types of study breaks—short ones and long ones—and you need both for efficient studying. Short breaks let your mind take a breath and should be taken often. "Find out your study attention span (usually 45-60 minutes)," advises Dr. Merkel, "and take a two- to five-minute break ten or 15 minutes short of that. Waiting until you're exhausted wears down your system and builds up

*Name has been changed

frustration." You should also take slightly longer breaks, say 15 to 20 minutes, every three hours.

Let's Get Physical

Jogging your memory isn't enough. It's also important to get regular exercise during exam time. According to Dr. Merkel, a quick 20-minute workout every day or so will keep your body in tune and keep anxiety tuned out. And it will help you sleep better.

Stay Up or Hit the Sack?

You can't stay up three nights before the exam and expect to do well. "Sleep <u>deprivation</u> really takes its toll," claims Dr. Merkel. "Some sleep is always better than none." There's no minimum requirement of sleep, though you should try to maintain your normal sleeping habits. And if you *are* forced to pull an all-nighter, don't do it more than one night in a row and try to work in at least a two-hour nap the next day.

Practical Tips for the Practically Ready (and the Hopelessly Unprepared)

Before the Exam:

1. *Know your exam schedule.* This will help you spot scheduling problems and give you an idea of when to do your studying. Claims Dr. Merkel, "Some students spend all their energy studying for their first exam and find they're too exhausted afterward to continue at the same pace."

2. *Find out what you can about each exam.* How long is it? Can you bring a calculator? Is it multiple choice, fill in the blanks, or essay? Consult old tests (if available), talk to people who've taken the course, or ask the professor. It will help you organize your studying and make you more confident.

3. *Make up study cards.* Summarize the important points from lectures, readings, and old tests into a few study sheets organized so you can quiz yourself. Just making up the cards lets you run through the stuff once, plus you won't have to lug books around to study.

4. *Choose study partners carefully.* Study groups are helpful if you have a fairly good grasp of the material. They're a waste of time if you haven't even begun to study.

5. *Set your alarm clock.* Every school counselor tells the <u>hilarious</u> story about the student who stayed up all week and then slept through the test. Nobody ever laughs.

On Exam Day:

1. *Eat light.* The old advice about eating a big breakfast before an exam is wrong, according to experts: It sends blood to your stomach instead of to your head, where you really need it. You should eat a moderate-sized breakfast a few hours before the test, so you can have time to digest your meal.

2. *Relax.* Take a deep breath, let your heart slow down. You have plenty of time. You know this stuff. Look at the <u>doofus</u> over there *still* cramming. Thank heaven you're not him.

3. *Do what you know first.* Get all the guaranteed points you can, then come back to the difficult questions. It builds confidence and opens up the right sections

of your mind, which will help you remember things you think you don't know.

4. ***If you have a question, ask.*** Your professor or teacher might be able to rephrase the question in a way that makes more sense.

Word Count: 1177

[Keith Blanchard is a freelance writer/editor living in Summit, NJ.]

Block that Mental Block

by Catherine Black
from *Cosmopolitan*

Some of the difficult words in the article are listed below in the order in which they appear. In the text, these words are underlined. As you preview, look at the context in which the words are used.

acrimonious	sabotage	exacerbates
sidle up	phenomenon	preened

Fear of forgetting freezes the best of us at the worst of times—here's how to whisk those words off the tip of your tongue!

Several years ago, while my parents were in the midst of an acrimonious divorce and not speaking to each other, my father went to a bar with a client. As soon as he sat down, he spotted one of his firm's most important investors, Tom Smith, standing across the room. The man was with his wife, whom my father had met socially a number of times. In vain, he tried to recall her first name. Then he broke into a sweat.

My father is terrible at remembering names, and helping him had always been my mother's job. At parties, they used a sort of code: He'd sidle up to her and mutter, "The guy with the silver hair, we met him at the Blooms'. . . ."

"Ed Potter," my mother would murmur. "His wife is Gail." That said, my father would glide back in the direction of Ed and Gail Potter, ready to greet them with a hearty handshake and introduce them around.

Now, however, there was no help in sight. It was essential that he say hello to the Smiths and introduce his client, but without Mrs. Smith's name, he couldn't do it. Excusing himself, he slunk off to the phone booth and dialed my mother, praying she'd be there.

"Barbara," he said when she finally answered. "Listen, I need to ask a favor."

"Are you joking?" my mother demanded, having just returned from a meeting with her lawyer.

"Please," my father begged. "I'm desperate."

He must have sounded awful, because my mother stayed on the line. "Tom

Smith's wife," he hissed, "brown hair, kind of kinky? You met her at the . . ."

In spite of herself, my mother burst out laughing. "It's Gloria," she said. "Honestly!"

What's amazing is that we don't forget more often.

He nervously thanked her, then rushed back to the bar just in time to say hello to Tom and Gloria Smith before they left.

It would make a better story if the incident had spurred a reconciliation between my parents, but this was not to be. They're long divorced now, friendly again, and occasionally, one or the other will tell that story and laugh. Not that my father's problem is unusual—a tendency to forget people's names is just one of many common mental blocks. But whether it's a name, movie title, speech, even your own telephone number, at the very least, such blocks are embarrassing. At their worst, they can <u>sabotage</u> your performance.

No one is exactly sure how memory works. We understand that the mind can store a tremendous amount of information—far more than any of us is capable of thinking about in a given moment. Having information *in our minds*, however, doesn't always mean having *access* to it. We've all experienced moments when we're certain we know something

but are unable to remember it. Scientists have given the sensation a name: Tip-of-the Tongue <u>phenomenon</u>. It's in this category—things we know but can't remember—that mental blocks originate.

Our daily lives are filled with routines that require the continual use of memory. We drive cars, operate computers and calculators. We produce the addresses and telephone numbers of friends, our social-security and bank-account numbers, access codes to answering machines. We hardly need to concentrate—our memories do the work automatically. But at times, these routines become *so* automatic that we fail to concentrate at all—and then we slip up: We walk into a room and forget why we came; leave keys in the front door; make a call and draw a blank on the person we've dialed.

None of this is unusual. According to Judith Beck, a psychologist at the Center for Cognitive Therapy at the University of Pennsylvania, "Most of us—women especially—are trying to juggle so much; it's no surprise that we become confused. What's amazing is that we don't forget more often."

Trying to remember something we normally do by rote often <u>exacerbates</u> the problem. My friend Carol opened the door to her apartment one night, punched in the code to her burglar alarm, and was startled when the warning signal remained on. Normally, she pressed the numbers without thinking; now, suddenly, she couldn't recall the code. The signal continued, and Carol was aware that in less than a minute the alarm would go off. Frantically, she began hitting random numbers, but to no avail. Later, she wondered how she could possibly have forgotten the code—it was the second half of her telephone number!

A lack of concentration probably caused Carol to punch the wrong code in the first place, but it was her sudden *anxiety* that caused the block.

"How can we explain why a particular skill that is taken for granted, and is applied smoothly and automatically under normal circumstances, can suddenly be disrupted in the face of a threat, especially when that skill is most needed?" write Aaron T. Beck and Gary Emery in *Anxiety Disorders and Phobias: A Cognitive Perspective.* The answer, according to Aaron Beck, is that "a person feels vulnerable if she believes she lacks the skills necessary to cope with a particular threat." Not only are we less able to remember under pressure, but our fear of what will happen if we *don't* remember actually distracts us from whatever we're trying to recollect. Mental blocks are self-perpetuating: The block triggers fear; the fear stalls memory; we then become more nervous and remember even less.

Few people are lucky enough *not* to have a personal example of this experience. Heidi, a painter, was overjoyed to reach the finals of a competition for a prestigious art scholarship. During her interview, the panel of judges asked her to assemble a hypothetical dinner party, including her favorite living artists. Her mind went completely blank. "I'd been going to art galleries every week," Heidi says, "but I couldn't come up with the name of a single living artist. Not one!" The judges waited patiently, but the more frightened she became, the less able she

was to focus. In desperation, she asked to come back to the question later, but the panel was unimpressed—Heidi did not win the scholarship.

Perhaps the most famous kind of mental block is writer's block. Stories of writers staring for weeks at a blank page, unable to write a word, are legion. A former colleague of mine was halfway through her first novel when a publisher bought it for a generous advance—with a deadline. Overjoyed, Virginia now had the chance to quit her job and write full-time. But the moment the contract was signed, she, too, froze. "I sat there all summer, writing sentences, then tearing the page out of my typewriter and throwing it away," she says. "Under the pressure of that deadline, I just could not write." In despair, she told her agent that she wanted to break her contract. Instead, the agent negotiated a later deadline with the publisher. Only then was Virginia able to relax and finish her book.

Since mental blocks are caused by tension and anxiety, the key to overcoming them is relaxation. But "Hey, relax!" isn't always such easy advice to follow. Here, some expert counsel on coping with the three biggest blocks.

Public Speaking

Fear of humiliation is the prime cause of this type of block—the speaker is petrified that those listening are just waiting to put her down publicly. What she must begin to realize is that the audience isn't looking for mistakes or signs of nervousness—*it just wants to hear the speech!* "Sometimes I ask people with public-speaking anxiety to make a list of all the speakers they've thought were incompetent," says Robert Leahy, a psychologist at and director of the Center for Cognitive Therapy of New York City. "More often than not, they're unable to name a single one."

A few short-term preventive measures *can* reduce the risk of a mental block while speaking in public. Judith Beck sometimes recommends telling the audience that you're nervous, and then using notes. "In general, people are sympathetic," she says. Occasionally, speakers are afraid that during question-and-answer sessions they'll be stumped. "When that happens, turn the question back on the audience, ask what they think," Leahy advises. Just keeping these strategies in mind will often lessen terror and thereby reduce the risk of blocking.

Test Anxiety

The first step toward coping with anxiety during an exam is anticipating it. "Prepare yourself mentally beforehand," says Judith Beck. "When you accept panic, it's less likely to happen." If a block still occurs once the test has begun, she has this suggestion: "Read through the whole exam, find something you do know, and begin there. As you build up confidence, your memory will come back."

Remembering Names

Judith Beck, who admits that she herself has a tendency to forget names, often eases the tension by making a joke of it. "If I can't remember someone's name, I'll say, 'Look at me: I'm getting more and more like my father.'" After laughing with

her, there's little chance that the person whose name she blanked out on will be insulted.

Certainly, accepting your tendency toward mental blocks is the first step in reducing the fear that causes them. For that reason, it's wise to be prepared with coping strategies in case a block occurs. But the *heart* of the problem lies in the unrealistic expectations that so many people have of themselves. "Someone who expects to do a reasonable job most of the time is much less likely to experience a mental block than someone who expects to do a perfect job all the time," says Judith Beck. In other words, perfectionism can be destructive. If we tell ourselves that we can't make mistakes, we create anxiety that may completely ruin our performance. What anyone plagued by mental blocks *must* remember is that *everybody* messes up—it's part of the human condition. Knowing that we're not alone can only help.

Excruciating as mental blocks are for those who suffer from them, occasionally they're not such a bad thing. I never fail to laugh when I think of the time I interviewed my university's star quarterback—a handsome guy with a neck the size of my leg and an ego too big to measure—for the college TV station. It was the day after his team had won the championship, and he couldn't wait to get in front of the camera. While I interviewed the other players, he preened, rearranging his hair and pumping out his chest like a turkey. When it was his turn, I asked him why the team had been so successful that year. To my amazement, he elbowed me to one side and grabbed the microphone from my hand.

"Well, Cathy," he said, tossing his head back and flashing his perfect teeth, "here's what it all comes down to." He paused and gazed at the camera. "What it all comes down to is . . ." He faltered and blushed, then began again. "It comes down to . . . I mean it all . . . wait a minute, cut! *Cut!*" But the camera kept rolling. He finally just gave up and hid his face in his hands. The entire crew was hysterical, and even I found it hard not to laugh. It took that quarterback nine more tries before he could speak coherently, and by that time, he was humbler than anyone—

including himself, I imagine—would have dreamed possible. Still, the producer could not resist including one of his goofs in the final show, simply to show his fans that, godlike though he might seem on the field, he was as human as anyone else.

Word Count: 1939

HEALTH AND FITNESS

The articles in this section, listed below, explore different opinions on how to achieve and maintain good health.

- **DIET AND EXERCISE DANGERS**

- **MORE THAN THE RDAS**

- **WHEN STAYING THIN IS A SICKNESS**

- **HOW TO KEEP YOUR LEGS YOUNG**

- **SPEEDWALK**

- **FACING THE TEST**

- **THE TWO MOST DANGEROUS HOURS OF YOUR DAY**

Diet and Exercise Dangers

by Anastasis Toufexis

from *Time*

Some of the difficult words in the article are listed below in the order in which they appear. In the text, these words are underlined. As you preview, look at the context in which the words are used.

ligaments	**neophyte**	**fallacy**
metabolism	**bizarre**	**devotees**

Have you thought carefully about your diet and exercise habits? What works best for you and what hasn't seemed to work? Note that the title mentions the dangers of both diet and exercise. Both are considered necessary to good health but must be done correctly.

All the instruments and experts agree that there are often painful pitfalls on the rigorous road to glowing health. Pick up a racket, and you run the risk of a sprained ankle, twisted knee or tennis elbow. Condition your heart by pumping over hill and dale on a racing bike with low-slung handle bars, and you can come up with chronic low back pain. Play softball and be prepared for torn knee ligaments and broken fingers.

Though many different sports put a strain on the same parts of the body and result in the same injuries, some produce their own peculiar ills. Golfers get twinges of golfer's elbow. Swimmer's shoulder may catch up with anybody who favors the butterfly stroke. There is even some-thing known as "duck laceration syndrome" that strikes high-flyers who slam the ball through the basket, hitting their hands against the hoop.

At its best, exercise—particularly regular exercise—is good for the heart rate, blood pressure, respiration and metabolism. Says Jim Barnard, research cardiologist at UCLA: "It's similar to tuning up your car's engine to make the car run more efficiently." Vigorous physical effort helps release tension too. But it can also do a lot of damage, especially if the athlete is a neophyte or weekend warrior, both of whom tend to try to do too much too soon.

The trouble usually starts when sudden demands are made on an unconditioned body. In tennis and basketball, the knees and ankles must accommodate quick stops and starts and lightning changes of direction. In jogging, the athlete's feet typically strike the ground 800 to 1,000 times a mile, with an impact equivalent to about three times the body's weight. The shock jolts the entire skeleton. Statistically, at least, everyone of the nearly 30 million runners in the United States can expect some ailment.

Besides forcing their bodies to perform beyond their capabilities, many people have the Spartan belief that exercise will do no good unless it is pursued until the

Fads fail because they do not offer a diet people can live with.

body aches. Says Gilbert Gleim of Lenox Hill Hospital's Institute of Sports Medicine in Manhattan: "If you're training to be healthy, exercise should never hurt." A few simple precautions, sports specialists point out, can prevent many injuries. Choose an appropriate sport for your weight and body build and always do warming-up and cooling-down exercises.

Diet poses a whole set of different hazards, especially the quickie weight-losing schemes that separate United States dieters from a few pounds each year. Among the current "in" diets are the Pritikin, the Atkins, and the Beverly Hills Diet. Nutrition experts insist that many fad diets

are not really diets at all but bizarre and temporary ways of depriving the subject of adequate nutrition.

The problem, of course, is that nobody can (or should) stick to such diets for a long time. Fads fail because they do not offer a diet people can live with. And that, actually, is a blessing. Most people do not stay on such diets long enough to do themselves any physical damage. But more than 80% of people who do lose weight by dieting tend to gain it back within a year.

Fad diets are usually based on some nutritional fallacy. Of the current popular regimes, the one that comes closest to being nutritionally acceptable is a low-fat diet recommended by Nathan Pritikin, somewhat similar to the one that people in underdeveloped countries follow out of necessity. Pritikin, 66, founder of the Pritikin Longevity Center in Santa Monica, California, is a self-taught nutritionist.* He forbids all fats, salt and sugar, oils, most processed foods and dairy products, and discourages the use of tobacco, caffeine, sugar and salt substitutes and even vitamins. Devotees eat mainly fresh fruits, vegetables and whole-grain breads, hoping Pritikin is correct when he claims that the diet curbs heart disease, diabetes, and hypertension. Doctors say more testing is needed to substantiate such claims. They also say the Pritikin Diet is unnecessarily restrictive, especially for healthy people. Says nutritionist Myron Winick of the Institute of Human Nutrition at Columbia University: "If you follow it, you almost can't eat in a restaurant."

The diets that get the poorest medical marks are two very popular ones—Atkins and Beverly Hills. The first, conceived by Dr. Robert Atkins, 51, restricts carbohydrates but allows unlimited consumption of meat and fat. Says nutritionist Nancy Tiger of Boston's Beth Israel Hospital: "You can eat as much bacon, fresh sausage and those kinds of things as you want. They're high in cholesterol and saturated fat. Not good in terms of heart disease."

The Beverly Hills Diet is the creation of Californian Judy Mazel, 37, an aspiring actress until she became a nutritional guru. Mazel allows only fruit the first ten days—as much as five pounds of grapes a day—and no meat, poultry or fish until day 19. Some doctors say the book should be listed under fiction. A leading nutrition expert says, "If you went to a bookstore and bought a history book that said the Declaration of Independence was signed in 1827 or World War I began in 1095, you'd be pretty angry." If fol-lowed too long, the Beverly Hills Diet may lead to diarrhea, and although medical evidence is scant, doctors warn of other complications.

Many physicians shake their heads at the public's gullibility about diets. As Psychiatrist Albert Stunkard of the University of Pennsylvania points out, "The only way to lose weight is to make really big changes in your life-style."

*Editor's Note: Nathan Pritikin died in 1985. The Pritikin Longevity Center is still in existence.

Word count: 925

COPYRIGHT NOTICE

MORE THAN THE RDAS

by Elizabeth Somer, M.A., R.D.

from *Shape*

Some of the difficult words in the article are listed below in the order in which they appear. In the text, these words are underlined. As you preview, look at the context in which the words are used.

scurvy	**dermatitis**	**suboptimal**
beriberi	**osteoporosis**	**provocative**
pellagra	**depletion**	**antioxidants**
complacent	**folic acid**	**atherosclerosis**
marginal deficiencies		

Feeling sub-par, irritable or anxious? Maybe you're still not getting all of the nutrients you need.

You probably think serious nutritional deficiencies are a thing of the past, at least for those of us living in modern societies. Indeed, diseases such as scurvy, beriberi and pellagra have receded into history along with smallpox, yellow fever and the plague.

But don't get too complacent. There's a whole category of nutritional shortcomings that scientists are now talking about: marginal deficiencies.

As science develops more sensitive tests for nutritional status, researchers are challenging long-cherished beliefs about nutritional adequacy. The amounts of nutrients known to prevent outright deficiency diseases, such as beriberi and scurvy, are not necessarily adequate to maintain optimal health or prevent chronic disease, according to a stockpile of new research.

On-Sight Evaluation

Just a few years ago, physicians judged their patients' nutritional status primarily by looking at them. You were considered to be nutritionally healthy if your gums didn't bleed, if your growth during childhood hadn't been stunted, if your red blood cells were normal and if you didn't suffer from severe dermatitis or hair loss. The recommended dietary allowances (RDAs) and the four food groups were our guide.

"The RDAs were derived by asking how much of a nutrient will prevent a clinical deficiency then adding an extra amount as a margin of safety," says Jeffrey B. Blumberg, Ph.D., a nutrition professor at Tufts University. "But how much calcium prevents osteoporosis, how much

Vitamin and mineral deficiencies also can wreak havoc on your immune system, your body's natural defense against everything from the common cold to cancer.

vitamin E prevents heart disease, or how much zinc strengthens the immune system are very different questions."

For years, many of nutrition's profound yet subtle effects on health went unnoticed. Today, experts recognize that nutritional depletion can progress from mild to severe over the course of days, weeks, months or years, much like other disorders, from the common cold to heart disease.

The Symptoms

The problem with marginal deficiencies is that the symptoms, if they exist,

are vague. "The definition is still very imprecise," says Douglas Heimburger, M.D., director of the Division of Clinical Nutrition at the University of Alabama at Birmingham. "Often, the effects of a marginal deficiency have nothing to do with how a person looks or feels." For example, tissue levels of folic acid or vitamin C often are low in smokers who appear healthy; these deficiencies may place smokers at higher risk for oral and lung cancers.

If there *are* symptoms, they may be something as vague as "feeling under the weather" or "not up to par." A marginally nourished person may feel tired, stressed or irritable or be more prone to colds and the flu. Complications following an illness or surgery also are more common.

Insomnia, poor memory, irritability or mood swings are common signs as well. For example, suboptimal intake of vitamin B_1 can produce feelings of depression or anxiety even in otherwise healthy people. In studies conducted at the University of Giessen in Germany, marginally deficient yet otherwise healthy subjects tended to be more nervous and depressed than their well-nourished counterparts, and they performed worse on memory tests.

Vitamin and mineral deficiencies also can wreak havoc on your immune system, your body's natural defense against everything from the common cold to cancer. Diminishing resistance to conditions associated with aging—such as memory loss, cataracts and osteoporosis—may be more a result of poor diet than aging genes, several studies show.

Common Ground

How common are marginal deficiencies? Repeatedly, national diet surveys report that people in the United States consume suboptimal amounts of several vitamins and minerals. Nine out of 10 people in this country consume less than the lowest recommended intake for chromium, according to Richard Anderson, Ph.D., a research chemist at the USDA Human Nutrition Research Center in Beltsville, Maryland. Folic acid, iron and magnesium intakes average less than half of what most women need.

Only one person in five consumes recommended levels of vitamin B_6. Many don't consume even the daily recommended amount of vitamin C, obtainable from one orange, half a cup of cooked broccoli or one kiwi.

Even if your nutrient intake is within current recommended levels, you can still develop a marginal deficiency. The new USDA Food Guide Pyramid recommends six to 11 servings of grains and five to nine servings of fruits and vegetables, but only 9 percent of the U.S. population actually eats this way, according to Blumberg. "Even if a person achieved these dietary guidelines to reduce fat and increase fiber," he says, "there are provocative data that for some nutrients and some disease states, we can do even better."

The antioxidants are a case in point. The tidal wave of research on beta carotene, vitamin C and vitamin E suggests that current recommended levels are below the amounts necessary to maintain optimal health and a strong defense against disease. Of the 87,245 women in Harvard Medical School's ongoing Nurses Health Study, those who consumed several times the current recommended dietary allowance of vitamin E, or more than 100 IU (international units), had a 40 percent reduction in the risk of developing heart disease in comparison with women whose intakes were at or below the recommended level of 12 IU. Risk continued to decrease as vitamin E intake increased.

"These findings are consistent with the emerging body of research suggesting that high levels of antioxidant nutrients reduce the risk of atherosclerosis," says James E. Enstrom, Ph. D., M.P.H., an associate research professor at the UCLA School of Public Health at the University of California, Los Angeles. Enstrom's research on vitamin C intake and heart disease shows that people who consume 300 mg of vitamin C or more daily have a 42 percent lower risk of dying from heart disease than people who consume 50 mg or less.

A number of other life situations, including stress, smoking, medication use and exposure to air pollution, might increase nutrient needs. For example, studies on women who use birth control pills show that blood levels of several nutrients, including the B vitamins such as vitamin B_6, are low even when dietary intakes fall within recommended levels.

Don't Take It Lying Down

Your best bet is to prevent a deficiency or at least treat it in the early stages. While there aren't inexpensive and reliable tests to assess nutritional status for most vitamins and minerals, practicing a few dietary and lifestyle habits will improve your chances of getting everything you need to feel your best. (See "Beating the Odds," below.)

The vague symptoms attributed to marginal deficiencies also can result from a host of other factors, from the genes you were born with to an argument with your boss to a serious illness. But setting your nutritional sights on optimum levels of vitamins and minerals can improve your stamina and well-being. Consuming enough, not just a little, of all nutrients could make the difference between feeling under the weather and at your best.

Beating the Odds

Do you have a marginal deficiency? Answer the following questions yes or no to assess your diet and prevent a nutritional slip from progressing into a full-blown deficiency.

1. Do you consume six to 11 servings of whole-grain breads and cereals daily? If not, your diet may be low in the B vitamins and some trace minerals, such as chromium.

2. Do you consume five to nine servings of fresh fruits and vegetables daily, with at least one of vitamin C-rich foods (such as citrus fruits) and two of dark green leafy vegetables? If not, your diet could be low in vitamin C, beta carotene, magnesium and folic acid.

3. Do you consume at least three servings a day of low-fat dairy products daily? If not, your diet could be low in magnesium, calcium, vitamin B_2 and vitamin D.

4. Do you eat at least two to four servings of cooked dried beans and peas, lean meat, chicken or fish daily? If not, your diet may be low in B vitamins, iron, selenium and zinc.

5. Do you consume at least 2,000 calories daily from the above nutrient-packed foods? If not, consider a low-dose multiple vitamin and mineral supplement with extra vitamin C, beta carotene and vitamin E.

6. Do you take any medications, including birth control pills, aspirin or antacids? If you do, be aware that these and other medications can increase the need for certain vitamins or minerals, such as B vitamins, vitamin C and iron.

7. Do you smoke or are you around smokers? If the answer is yes, your daily need for vitamin C, beta carotene and folic acid may be above average. Consume an extra citrus fruit and dark green vegetable every day.

8. Do you exercise vigorously or are you under chronic stress? If so, your daily requirements for vitamin C, magnesium, the trace minerals and the B vitamins might be slightly above average. Consume extra servings of citrus fruits, nuts, extra-lean meats and cooked dried beans and peas.

9. Do you live in an area with air pollution? If you do, your need for the antioxidant nutrients, especially vitamin E, might be above average. Consider taking a low-dose multiple that contains extra vitamin E.

Word Count: 1503

WHEN STAYING THIN IS A SICKNESS

by Earl Ubell

from *Parade*

Some of the difficult words in the article are listed below in the order in which they appear. In the text, these words are underlined. As you preview, look at the context in which the words are used.

binge	**prone to**	**kleptomania**
purge		

Most of us know or have heard of someone who has an eating disorder. What are the causes and symptoms? How are they cured? What are your thoughts about these dangerous disorders?

She could be your closest friend. Your co-worker. Even your wife or your sister. And you wouldn't know that a terrible disease had gripped both her mind and body, threatening her very life.

But she would know.

Gayle Cappelluti, 29, of Brooklyn, New York, knew that something was terribly wrong with her each time she shut herself away in her room to eat.

"I'd have a whole pizza—one of the big ones. And a couple of pounds of candy and more cookies," recalls Gayle, an elementary school teacher. "Then I'd telephone a Chinese take-out restaurant and order $30 worth of food.

"It was like being in a dream. I didn't think of anything. I'd just eat all night long."

Yet Gayle never gained much weight. At 5 feet 4½ inches, she weighed 109 pounds. And that was the second part of her guilty secret: Gayle vomited all of the food she ate.

"I'd do it many times a day," she says. "I'd try not to think about what I was doing. But when I did, I hated myself. 'Ugh,' I'd think, how could you do a thing like this?"

Until recently, few doctors considered it an illness when people like Gayle would <u>binge</u> on food and then throw it up or take laxatives. Today, the affliction is called bulimia (from the Greek word meaning "ox hunger") or, simply, the "binge-<u>purge</u> disease."

Physicians and psychologists now rank bulimia as a major physical and mental health problem. Studies reveal bulimia in five to 20 percent of female students aged 13 to 23. Dr. Harrison G. Pope Jr. of McLean Hospital in Belmont, Massachusetts, says estimates show that only one man in 20 is bulimic

It was like being in a dream. I didn't think of anything. I'd just eat all night long.

but as many as 7 million women, aged 10 to 52, are trapped at some point in their lives in the binge-purge syndrome. Jane Fonda says she was bulimic as a teenager.

You may be bulimic and hide it from yourself. Here are some of the signs: 1) eating huge amounts of food; 2) vomiting or using laxatives to purge; 3) hiding your binges from others; 4) trying to control your weight by binging and purging; and 5) feeling out of control once you start eating.

Bulimics may maintain normal body weight and look healthy, but they are prone to such ailments as swollen salivary glands, an inflamed pancreas and gallbladder problems. Constant vomiting harms the stomach and food pipe, or esophagus. Stomach acid coming up into the mouth erodes tooth enamel. I saw a bulimic with so much enamel gone, only tiny stubs of teeth remained.

At its worst bulimia can kill. Purging empties the body of potassium; this makes the heart irritable and prone to stop. Estimated death rate for severe bulimics is one to 10 percent. Some bulimics spend up to $300 a week on food. They isolate themselves at work and at home, even from their spouses. Sometimes they cannot work and lose their jobs.

Bulimia is related to anorexia nervosa, a condition in which patients refuse to eat anything at all and waste away.

Dr. C. Phillip Wilson of Columbia University's College of Physicians and Surgeons in New York City calls anorexia nervosa and bulimia two sides of the same coin because both are rooted in the fear of becoming fat. Every bulimic I spoke to confessed that fear. "Even at 100 pounds, I felt fat," Gayle Cappelluti said. She weighs 120 now.

Nobody knows why the binge-purge syndrome snares mostly women. Dr. Pope and Dr. James I. Hudson, also of McLean Hospital, call bulimia a form of a major depressive disorder. Says Dr. Pope, "Among our bulimic patients, 80 percent suffer from major depressive or manic depressive illnesses."

Dr. B. Timothy Walsh of Columbia University's College of Physicians and Surgeons reports success with anti-depressant drugs. "Bulimics not only stop binging and purging," he says. "For the first time, they feel better."

One of Pope's patients, Sheri Swanson, 34, bulimic since she was 18, says she hid the problem from everyone: "It's so shameful." All treatments failed until Pope prescribed an anti-depressant drug, desipramine. Sheri noticed a difference right away. She says, "This oppressive cloud was lifted. Within a matter of weeks, the binging was gone. It was astonishing."

Studies also show that bulimic women have other psychological disturbances. Up to a third have attempted suicide. Bulimics tend to abuse alcohol and street drugs. "We think a third of our patients have <u>kleptomania</u> too," says Pope. "Imagine a middle-class woman who can buy anything she wants yet steals a bottle of perfume."

Treatment for bulimia varies. Daniel Baker, Ph.D., director of the eating disorder program at University Hospital of the University of Nebraska Medical Center, Omaha, trains bulimics to turn away from food and to build self-esteem.

Associates for Bulimia and Related Disorders, a group of psychologists in New York City, teaches clients to turn to other people rather than to food. Says Ellen Schor, Ph.D., a co-director, "We tell them: 'You have a food addiction. Food has been your secret lover, your confidant and worst enemy. If you go on like this you will never get close to people.' " In groups, patients are taught the facts about bulimia, urged to keep diaries and to make contracts with themselves to change. Co-

director Judith Brisman, Ph.D., reports that every year, a third of the group no longer binges and another third cut their gorging by half.

When all else fails, Dr. Katherine Halmi of Cornell University Medical College in White Plains, New York, hospitalizes her patients for an average of three months. Hospitalization keeps the bulimic away from food; in serious cases, it can save the person's life. Step by step, patients are taught to eat normally. At $370 a day, the cost for three months would come to about $33,000.

Aided by group meetings at the American Anorexia/Bulimia Association in Teaneck, New Jersey, Gayle Cappelluti today is a recovered bulimic. She has remarried and expects a second child.

Word count: 987

How to Keep Your Legs Young

by Joann Rodgers

from *Parade*

Some of the difficult words in the article are listed below in the order in which they appear. In the text, these words are underlined. As you preview, look at the context in which the words are used.

nethermost	**heft**	**mania**
apparatus	**culled**	**regimen**
balk		

Our legs are something we take for granted, but they could be the first parts of our bodies to give us problems as we get older. Read this article to find ways to keep this from happening.

Legs, darn them, are the first of our equipment to outlive our fantasies of youthful vigor. At the very time when wisdom, wit and experience peak, our <u>nethermost</u> <u>apparatus</u> begins to fail, giving the lie to our prowess and the wobbles to our will.

As both men and women round the young-adult bend and head toward middle age, the legs <u>balk</u>. Knees lock, thighs slump, joints stiffen and muscles ache in mute protest.

"No question about it, the legs go first," complains Gabe Mirkin, 47, a physician, author, competitive runner and world class expert on legs. "Twenty years ago, I could easily run 100 miles a week, and now I'm happy if I can do 25. The coordination is still there. The brain sends the right signals. But the legs don't listen as well."

We can't, of course, stop the march of time. But the good news is that regular and rigorous exercise begun at any age can mount an impressive holding action.

Why do the legs go first? Legs are the body's major weight-bearing organs. Housing the largest, longest and strongest of the adult's joints and 206 bones, they must withstand forces many times the body's <u>heft</u> for hours at a time.

In youth, the thigh bone alone can support a compact car. Cable-like muscles that allow us to leap stairs or turn on a dime are always tensed to fight gravity and maintain tone. But for each decade over 20, if we are inactive, we can expect to lose up to five percent of the muscle tissue. Beyond 30, the heart's blood-pumping ability may decline, cutting oxy-

In a healthy adult, almost-daily leg exercises will begin to strengthen and tighten the super-structure within weeks.

gen supply to muscles of the calves and feet. At the same time, a reduced supply of calcium softens and shrinks bones, diminishing toughness and range of motion. By 80, says Dr. Nathan Shock, a government specialist on aging, muscle strength may fall to about 55 percent of what it was at age 25.

Yet experts insist the situation isn't hopeless. "It's something of a fallacy to say the legs go first," says Robert Porter, the head of the sports medicine clinic at Dartmouth College in Hanover, New Hampshire, a hot-bed of running in the East. "With exercise, your endurance and ability to perform decline noticeably less per decade. If we maintain muscle tone and fitness, our legs should be able to perform 80 percent of the capability we had at age 20 as we enter middle age."

And it's never too late to start. Studies of elderly people show that exercise

significantly increases their muscle and bone strength and slows the loss of muscle tissue. Exercise that emphasizes motion can prevent the locking of even the worst arthritic joints that normally occurs through disuse.

So begin today. Some tips on leg exercises, culled from the advice of specialists and their patients, follow. A word of caution, however: The exercises will not make lean, mean marathon runners out of potbellied desk pilots or give slack-thighed matrons pin-up limbs.

What they will do is tone and strengthen your personal transportation; help ward off the complications of arthritis; and fight fat, cramps, sprains, breaks, aches and other ills of middle-aged hips, thighs, calves, ankles, feet and toes. Not least of all, they will extend your enjoyment of sports, dancing and the out doors to the end of your life.

Getting started. If you are launching a first or new assault on what Shakespeare called the "decreasing legs" of age, have a checkup that includes hips, knees and feet as well as the heart and lungs. Then, buy the right sport shoes—at least $35 to $45 in a reputable specialty store.

Which exercise is best? The answer will vary with individual interests, climate, time and resources.

Many sports—and even common activities like walking up steps, two at a time—offer excellent conditioning. Jogging, walking and running increase lung power and lower-body strength while reducing fat and blood pressure. But don't overdo it. "Running," says Dr. Mirkin, "is the most dangerous sport known for legs. You quickly build tolerance and need more distance to get the high it produces." Such mileage <u>mania</u> often leads to injury, he adds.

Handball, tennis (singles), squash, racquetball and skiing (downhill and cross-country) can be part of your <u>regimen</u> into the 50s and beyond, but only if you are one of the long-term fit. "I play a lot more doubles than I used to," says a 60-year-old bank officer. "I get as much kick out of the mental game now as I used to get out of the tougher physical game. And the running I do during matches keeps my legs as strong."

Of all solid exercise, swimming is probably the safest, especially for arthritis victims and those with foot problems. Arthritis puts unusual stress on joints, so even walking may put too much strain on them. For almost everyone else, however, experts agree that brisk walking is the best overall leg-strengthening exercise. In addition to being safe, it offers aerobic benefits to the heart and lungs and gets the walker out of doors for at least part of the year. "Anything you can accomplish running you can accomplish walking," says Dr. Saul Haskell, a sports medicine specialist in Chicago. "It just takes a little longer."

How much exercise how often? Injuries to the knee and other parts of the leg almost always occur in men and women who overtrain, skip warm-ups or try to "play through" pain.

A hard workout often causes a certain amount of muscle swelling and microscopic damage, and healing takes 48 hours even in those who are fit. Never,

therefore, use the same muscle groups hard every day. Specialists advise even professional athletes to follow a "hard-easy-hard-easy" workout schedule. Alternate running days, for instance, with cycling or swimming. Stretch muscles gently between workouts. If you bicycle, stretch the muscles above the knee and at the calf. If you run, stretch the calf, hamstring (at the back of the upper leg), inner thigh and lower back muscles. If you jog, do a two-minute jog-walk routine, increasing the running time week by week. Jog no more than three days a week.

Pay strict attention to warm-ups and cool-downs. Thomas Jefferson advised "not less than two hours a day" devoted to exercise. To keep legs fit, however, 45 minutes to an hour a day will do, not including warm-up periods.

Protect the back and knee. Always include lower back stretching exercises before tennis, skiing and racquetball. Sit-ups, which develop abdominal muscles, will help the back and legs too.

To strengthen knees, work on the muscles that pull them, especially if the foot rolls inward. (The lower legs may then twist one way, forcing the knee joint in the opposite direction.) Wearing shoes with good arch support, stand straight, pull the kneecap up an inch or so, hold the position for a 10-count and relax. Repeat several times a day.

Don't cramp your style. Learn to distinguish the types of leg cramps. Those that strike the calf muscle in the middle of the night are exaggerated muscle tendon reflexes. Stretching and massage will work these out. Cramps that begin soon after you start exercise may be serious. Have a checkup before continuing. Cramps after an hour of exercise, especially in heat, usually mean dehydration. Drink a cup of cool water every 15 minutes during exertion.

For women only. Women are more vulnerable to knee and foot injuries, in part because of ill-fitting shoes, but also because of their wider pelvic bones and stance. Building up thigh and calf muscles is an excellent preventive measure.

Dr. Stanley Cohen, who plans physical therapy for disabled patients at Sinai Hospital in Baltimore, says the combination of bad arches, pointy-toed shoes, and high heels can strain the knees, aggravate arthritis and make it too painful to exercise. Women who wear high heels often have Achilles' tendons that are never stretched enough for running in flat shoes. Try foam wedges in sport shoes to slightly elevate the heels.

Exercise those veins away. Varicose veins, a painful swelling in leg veins, occur when flow valves in the circulatory system allow blood to pool there. Standing still encourages the process. To prevent them, "move, move, move," advises Mirkin. "Leg muscles can function as a second heart. When you relax the muscles, the veins fill. When you con-tract or move them, they empty." Thus, running, walking, skating and cycling are also therapeutic.

How long before results? In a healthy adult, almost-daily leg exercises will begin to strengthen and tighten the superstructure within weeks. Noticeable differences can be expected after several months. Within a year, you are on your way to maximum strength.

A few months ago, a friend and I watched our teenage sons working out before a soccer match. Their legs pumped tirelessly up and down the field for half-an-hour without a break. Running with them was their coach, a man in his mid-50s and a grandfather. "No problem," he shrugged when asked how he kept up with youths a quarter his age. "I just keep the legs moving, and they take care of the rest of me."

Word count: 1537

SPEEDWALK

by Pat Smith

from *Mirabella*

Some of the difficult words in the article are listed below in the order in which they appear. In the text, these words are underlined. As you preview, look at the context in which the words are used.

simultaneously   **synchronization**   **reluctant**

Today many people want to keep fit, but what exercise is best? For some of us, walking, not running, may be the answer.

I may never walk the same way again and for good reason. Since I met Casey Meyers, the former runner and author of *Aerobic Walking* (Random House), walking has become more than a way of getting there; it's now a way of exercising.

I've always wanted to believe that walking ten minutes could be just as beneficial as running ten minutes and that for overall muscle toning, there was no better way to invest thirty minutes than walking. I wanted to believe that the most natural of human activities was also the best.

Casey Meyers told me what I wanted to hear and more. In 1984, Meyers, a fitness runner, suffered severe knee damage. Recently retired and with time to spare, he began a quest for an alternative to running.

"I was looking for an exercise that was highly effective, injury free, natural, and sustainable," he says. So he started walking in the rolling countryside surrounding his home near St. Joseph, Missouri. He read works by physical anthropologist C. Owen Lovejoy, who says we are physiologically programmed to walk as much as our prehistoric ancestors did. Meyers also interviewed race walkers, including the only American ever to win an Olympic medal in the 50-kilometer (31.1 miles) event. He talked with doctors, trainers, zoologists; studied college physiology textbooks and popular running magazines. And he kept walking, faster and faster. And the faster he walked, the easier it became to sustain the pace.

After a year, Meyer's treadmill stress tests, performed at the famed Cooper

Clinic in Dallas, charted him as superior for a male thirty years of age or younger. He was fifty-nine at the time.

Meyers came to the conclusion that there isn't any other single exercise, not even cross-country skiing, that uses more muscles <u>simultaneously</u> in a rhythmic movement, is so injury free, and can burn more energy at a higher rate than walking. He's convinced that walking as an aerobic exercise has been grossly underrated and underutilized when compared to running. "We've been brainwashed and oversold a bill of goods about running, a track and field event that has turned into a mass exercise. But our bodies just can't take running over the long term. They break down," he says.

Now Meyers walks three miles in thirty-three minutes, five days a week. He holds monthly clinics at the Cooper Center In-Residence Program and teaches the gospel at other clinics around the country.

"Walking is posture, technique, rhythm, and speed. If you lose the first three, you should reduce your speed and get back into <u>synchronization</u>."

The use of speed is what makes aerobic walking more effective than running. A person moving at twelve to thirteen minutes per mile burns more calories walking than running because at that speed running is the more efficient gait.

"If a walker and a jogger exercise side-by-side at an eleven-minute-per-mile pace, the walker will burn more calories, use more oxygen, and have a higher heart rate than the jogger," Meyers says.

I fit the stereotype of most people at his clinics. A former <u>reluctant</u> runner with bad knees, I have tried most everything aerobic, sometimes only once. I told Meyers I wanted to get fit but I didn't want it to take much of my time.

He told me to walk, but not the way I was used to walking. All my life people have said I walk too fast, but Meyers

...walking as an aerobic exercise has been grossly underrated and underutilized when compared to running.

called my normal walk, about a twenty-minute mile, a stroll. He proceeded to show me how to get a lot for my investment. His rules are simple.

Stand straight up, shoulders back, head level, and chin up. The shoulders should be directly over the hips.

■ Bend arms to form 90-degree angles at the elbows. This shortens the pendulum of the arm swing so you can increase the frequency of the swing. Vigorous arm swinging is essential to increase your pace.

■ Walk loosely and rhythmically. I did. My arm on the forward swing crossed the center of my rib cage, while the arm on the backswing came back to where my wrist brushed the side seams of my shorts. When I moved my arms faster, I walked faster. When I broke the angle of my arms, I slowed down. When I looked down, I didn't walk as straight and my shoulders felt stiff. The more I thought about what I was doing, the better I did, and the faster I walked.

Although Meyers said I would need to increase my intensity level to receive optimum aerobic benefit, I felt good in this natural, rhythmic gait. I wasn't pounding the ground as I did when I jogged (or lumbering, as I sometimes did when I got tired), but rather mechanically, methodically picking up my feet and placing them down, one by one. It wasn't difficult.

His other words of wisdom were to monitor my heart rate and work to be in aerobic training range (65 to 85 percent of maximum heart rate for most people). "Just listen to your heart. It will tell you if you are walking too slowly or too fast."

Word count: 857

COPYRIGHT NOTICE

FACING THE TEST

by Laura Fraser

from *Vogue*

Some of the difficult words in the article are listed below in the order in which they appear. In the text, these words are underlined. As you preview, look at the context in which the words are used.

bolt   **discreet**   **coercion**
anonymous   **subtle**

AIDS is certainly frightening, but so is AIDS testing—even if the test is negative. Who will see the results? What are your options concerning testing sites? These questions are addressed in this article.

The thought of having an HIV test hadn't crossed my mind until my new boyfriend suggested, or rather, insisted, I get myself checked out. I was surprised, and even offended. People like me don't get AIDS, I argued. But he knew better; he'd watched a dear friend slowly waste away from AIDS and understood that no one who has sex is safe from the virus.

I agreed to the test—what could it hurt?—and made an appointment at Planned Parenthood, the first place I could think of. Before the test, the counselor assured me that given my history (more than one relationship, but no needle users or bisexuals in the bunch as far as I knew), there wasn't much likelihood I was positive. I was probably one of the worried well who regularly troop through Planned Parenthood for their peace of mind. I

rolled up my sleeve to have my blood drawn.

The days waiting for results were filled with nagging memories of what I'd done in the late seventies. What if I *was* positive? Would my individual health insurance policy cover the cost of my treatment? I had no idea. How would I support myself if I was sick? Could I tell my friends? Could I handle the news?

Three days later, my counselor walked me into her office, sat down slowly, and said, "You're negative." It was all over. I prepared to bolt.

But not so fast. First, she wanted to make sure I understood exactly what the results meant. No HIV antibodies had shown up in my blood, but that didn't mean I hadn't been exposed—it takes around six months for antibodies to appear. In other words, I shouldn't have unprotected sex with my partner until we had another round of tests in six months— until we knew that neither of us had had unsafe sex in the past half year. The counselor pressed me further. If I was planning on having unprotected sex with my partner, was I sure I could trust him not to have any flings? She kept me there until she seemed sure that I wouldn't do anything foolish because of my HIV-negative status.

I walked out of the clinic lucky—and not just because I was HIV negative. Unwittingly, I'd chosen a good testing center, one that provided sensitive thorough counseling before and after the test. And had I been positive, the Planned Parenthood in my state would have kept my results <u>anonymous</u> and given me referrals for treatment. As uncomfortable as the experience was, it was a best-case scenario.

Being tested for HIV makes more sense than ever before; new drug treatments are helping people with AIDS live longer, fuller lives, and the earlier the treatment is started, the better. With women now the fastest-growing segment of the population diagnosed with AIDS, doctors and public health officials are urging more and more women to consider testing.

The official message is that HIV testing is easy, confidential, and necessary. But it's not that simple. Not all testing situations include counseling and follow up care. Not all tests are anonymous—or even voluntary. Finding out your HIV status before you are prepared can be devastating; having someone else find out can be much worse.

Consider these cases:

Sandra*, a professional in her thirties, decided to be tested and made an appointment with her private physician. She was accustomed to dealing with her own doctor, and she didn't believe the care would be as good at an anonymous-testing site. Sandra was assured that the test result would be confidential. But *confidential* doesn't mean *secret*. Her test, which was positive, was billed to her insurance company. Then the results made their way to her employer's desk. She wasn't fired, but she suffered great anxiety over the fact that her employer—and who else?—knew about her HIV status.

Beth*, who was married, applied for health insurance and was told she had to take an HIV test first. She tested positive and was denied coverage.

Charlene*, a twenty-nine-year-old Washington, D.C., woman, went to her obstetrician for a pregnancy test and was told that an HIV test was standard procedure. A nurse called her later to say she was pregnant *and* HIV positive. Her physician advised her to have an abortion but didn't tell her that the chances of her baby being infected with HIV were between 25 and 30 percent. Charlene agreed to end the pregnancy, but it took her several weeks to find a clinic willing to perform an abortion on an HIV-positive woman.

In Florida, Katherine* donated blood, unaware that it would be tested for HIV and traced back to her. She opened a letter from the blood bank while driving her car; she was positive.

*These names have been changed.

Every one of these women needed to know her HIV status in order to get the best possible treatment. But testing—particularly involuntary testing—can have serious implications. Women have lost jobs, partners, housing, and employment when the results of their HIV tests were revealed.

"There's a balancing act going on here," says Leslie Wolfe, executive director of the Center for Women Policy Studies in Washington, D.C. "You have to go into testing with your eyes open about the fact that society isn't as advanced as we'd like it to be."

For now, AIDS experts say, the only sure way women can avoid these problems is with anonymous testing. Many women feel reassured when a doctor says their test results will be kept confidential. But *anonymous* and *confidential* can be misleading terms, and in this case they aren't the same. *Confidential* information can be shared with insurers, employers, other doctors, and sometimes partners. "We all know that medical records are of limited confidentiality," says Anke Erhardt, a psychologist and director of the HIV Center for Clinical and Behavioral Studies in New York City. Talk things over with your physician to be sure he or she will be <u>discreet</u>—some will bill an HIV test simply as a diagnostic test, for example—or find an anonymous-testing site. *Anonymous* means that your results will be filed only under a number, not your name; no one will be able to trace results back to you.

Anonymous testing is not always easy to find, however. Fifteen states guarantee your anonymity and hold doctors crimi-nally and civilly liable for revealing test results. Seven states have no such requirements, and policies vary among hospitals and clinics. Four states require testing centers to report some names to health officials (for example, those of infected nurses and doctors); seventeen states report

Finding out your HIV status before you are prepared can be devastating; having someone else find out can be much worse.

names to the health department but have at least one anonymous-testing site available. In Alabama, Alaska, Arizona, Idaho, Minnesota, North Dakota, South Carolina, and South Dakota, the results of all HIV tests are reported, by name, to the health department. Some of these states merely keep statistics; others trace and notify partners. In twenty-seven states, the results of your test may be given to a partner without your permission or notification. With all the variation, it's important to understand the ground rules before you have blood drawn.

Some AIDS tests are hard to avoid; many hospitals and clinics routinely run an HIV test whenever a patient has other blood work done.

Many more test newborns for HIV (if a baby is HIV positive, the mother is sure to be). A study of hospital HIV-testing policies conducted by Charles E. Lewis of the University of California in Los Angeles and sociologist Kathleen Montgomery of the University of California in Riverside found that of 471 hospitals with a testing policy, 12 percent require HIV tests on some or all patients, 69 percent require that test results appear in patients' records, and 17 percent allow HIV testing without a patient-consent form. "It would be nice if you could ask what your blood is going to be tested for," says Leslie Wolfe, "but often you're not in a position to do that."

Sometimes HIV testing is done with a patient's consent but under subtle coercion. When Robin*, a thirty-four-year-old San Francisco woman, went to her obstetrician for prenatal care, she was told an HIV test was routine. "The nurse practitioner urged me to have the test; she said everyone did it," recalls Robin, whose results were negative. "No one counseled me about it at all. It was coercive because it was all so casual."

AIDS experts recommend that no HIV test ever be given without counseling. "Testing without it is virtually useless," says Elizabeth Cooper of the American Civil Liberties Union AIDS Project. "One of the most important things about being tested is finding out not if you're positive or negative but what those results really mean."

A woman who tests negative but isn't counseled is likely to walk out the door assuming that she no longer needs to practice safer sex. A pregnant woman who tests positive may not be given enough information to make a decision about abortion. A woman who tests positive and isn't referred to a treatment program or a support group may assume that there's no hope for her. S. Denise Rouse of the DC Women's Council on AIDS says too many women are "dumped"— given only a phone number of a public hospital—after testing. "HIV-positive women die faster than HIV-positive men," she says, "because they're not getting the care they need."

HIV-positive women also die faster because they don't find out about their infection soon enough to get early treatment. The only way to find out is to be tested.

But you shouldn't just walk into a clinic and rely on luck, as I did. And you can't assume that you'll be able to avoid a test indefinitely. Before you roll up your sleeve, you have to know what the consequences of an HIV test will be for you— positive or negative.

Word count: 1662

THE TWO MOST DANGEROUS HOURS OF YOUR DAY

by Lowell Ponte

from *Reader's Digest*

Some of the difficult words in the article are listed below in the order in which they appear. In the text, these words are underlined. As you preview, look at the context in which the words are used.

cardiovascular	**excitation**	**myocardial infarction**
ischemic heart disease	**catecholamines**	**electrolytes**
homeostasis	**ischemia**	**ethanol susceptibility**
circadian	**angina**	**beta endorphins**

Your internal clock has far-reaching effects on your health.

You awaken after a good night's sleep and start to climb out of bed. Take care! You are beginning the most dangerous time of your day. For the next two hours or so, you are two to three times more likely to suffer a heart attack or a stroke than you are in the late evening, the safest cardiovascular time of your day. According to a study headed by Merrill Mitler of Scripps Clinic and Research Foundation in La Jolla, Calif., 6 a.m. to 10 a.m. is the average peak time for many other major causes of death: ischemic heart disease, cancer, bronchitis, emphysema and asthma.

Until recently doctors were taught that the human body lives in homeostasis, changing little during the day. The science of chronobiology—the study of how time affects life—is sparking a medical revolution by revealing how much our bodies change through circadian (daily) rhythms.

"These natural biological rhythms are as vital as our heart beat," says Lawrence E. Scheving of the University of Arkansas for Medical Sciences in Little Rock. "By learning their secrets, we are discovering new ways to prevent and cure illness. There isn't a function in your body that doesn't have its own rhythm. The absence of rhythm is death."

While you sleep, your blood pressure falls, your temperature drops more than a degree from its daily afternoon high, and some blood pools in your body's

> ## By understanding our body clocks, we can improve our health and continue to foster our survival.

extremities. Come morning, the body has to "jump start" itself from its sleeping to waking stages with a surge of excitation chemicals called catecholamines. Heart rate increases and blood vessels constrict, raising blood pressure and reducing blood flow to heart muscle; this might cause ischemia, or angina, as well as sudden death from myocardial infarction. If hardened plaques of cholesterol coat arteries, fragments may break loose, causing the clots that lead to heart attacks.

Also, your blood swims with cell granules called platelets that are most likely to stick together during these morning hours. When a leap from bed and a surge of catecholamines combine to "get your blood moving," your blood is near its daily peak in thickness and tendency to clot. Packing kids off to school and rushing to get ready for work

add emotional tension to the physical stress.

This circadian cardiovascular risk comes not from your bedside clock but from your interior biological clock. "Whatever hour you get up," says Dr. James Muller, chief of cardiology for New England Deaconess Hospital in Boston, "your peak risk of myocardial infarction will come within two to three hours after awakening."

The master timekeepers in our bodies help synchronize us with such outside cycles as day and night. Like orchestra conductors, they coordinate hundreds of functions inside us. Our body dances through the day to complex inner rhythms of rising and falling tides of hormones, immune cells, electrolytes and amino acids.

The long-held belief that some of us are "larks," or morning people, and others are "owls," or evening people, has now been confirmed. Measurements of circadian rhythms in morning people show heart rates peaking between 1 and 2 p.m., while evening people peak between 5 and 6:30 p.m. Larks produce more of the stimulating hormone adrenaline during the morning hours, followed by decreasing levels of performance through the day. Owls start the day more slowly, produce more nearly level amounts of adrenaline, and improve performance through the day and into early evening.

Most people enjoy a peak in short-term memory and mental quickness in the late-morning hours until shortly after noon. Then a measurable dip in energy and efficiency begins around 1 p.m. In some Mediterranean cultures, shops close during the afternoon for a period of siesta.

In the afternoon, exercise endurance, reaction time and manual dexterity are at their highest. Some research indicates that from then until early evening, athletes put in their best performances. From 6:30 p.m. until 8:30 p.m. is the sharpest time of day for long-term memory, an optimal time to study.

Our daily rhythms can bring a dark side to the early evening, however. These hours include a second daily peak in heart attacks, although smaller than the morning's. Around 7 p.m., alcohol takes longer to be cleared by your liver, and hence can be more intoxicating and performance-impairing than at other times of day—except 11 p.m., which brings a second peak of high ethanol susceptibility.

Students often cram during late-night and early-morning hours. Research, however, shows this is the time of the circadian cycle when long-term memory, comprehension and learning are at their worst.

Sensitivity to pain has generally increased throughout the day; it reaches its peak late at night. But by early morning the body may have almost doubled its nighttime levels of beta endorphins, which help relieve pain. Researchers theorize that this is what increases the body's pain tolerance during the hours after awakening.

For most of us, sleep is a time of life's renewal. Within the first 90 minutes or so of sleep, we reach our daily peak of growth hormone, which may help regenerate our bodies. And among pregnant women, the hours between midnight and 4 a.m. most commonly mark the start of labor. "Early-morning labor and birth may be part of our genetic inheritance and may have had some survival value for the species," speculates chronobiologist Michael Smolensky of the University of Texas Health Science Center in Houston.

By understanding our body clocks, we can improve our health and continue to foster our survival. Without grasping, for instance, that our natural temperature rises one to two degrees from morning until evening, we could misjudge thermometer readings. A temperature of 99 degrees might signal perfect health at 5 p.m. but augur illness at 7 a.m.

The effects of drugs are also subject to our rhythms. For instance, many doctors are learning to give powerful cancer drugs with the patient's biological clocks in mind. A given chemotherapy drug may be highly toxic to the kidneys at one time of day, for example, and far less harmful at another. "For every one of more than 20 anti-cancer drugs, there is an optimal time of day," says Dr. William Hrushesky of the Stratton Veterans Administration Medical Center in Albany, N.Y.

Some prescription drugs can reduce morning heart-attack risk, as can aspirin. One major study found that taking an aspirin *every other day* reduced overall incidence of heart attack in men by almost 45 percent and morning risk by more than 59 percent. You should, of course, consult your doctor about the use of aspirin.

Aside from using medicine, there are ways to make your mornings less stressful and, perhaps, less risky. Set the alarm clock a bit earlier to give yourself time to stretch arms and legs slowly while still lying down, the way your dog or cat does. This gets the pooled blood in your extremities moving. Move slowly. Don't subject yourself to the thermal shock of a very hot or cold shower, which could boost blood pressure. Then eat breakfast. Dr. Renata Cifkova at Memorial University of Newfoundland at St. John's says, "Skipping breakfast apparently increases platelet activity and might contribute to heart attacks and stroke during morning hours."

To avoid the "Monday morning blues," don't change your schedule on weekends. Your body's clock naturally runs on a cycle of about 25 hours. During the week your body uses mechanical clocks, mealtimes, work schedules and other cues to reset itself to 24 hours each day. On week-

ends it is tempting to let the clock "free run" forward by staying up late Friday and Saturday, then sleeping late Saturday and Sunday. This action will leave you "jetlagged," an unnecessary stress.

By turning the cycles of your biological clock in your favor, you may reduce your daily danger and increase your days of life.

Word Count: 1302

COPYRIGHT NOTICE

PARENTING/FAMILY

The articles in this section, listed below, deal with contemporary parenting and family issues.

Preschool Bully

by Lawrence Balter, Ph. D.

from *Sesame Street Parents' Guide*

Some of the difficult words in the article are listed below in the order in which they appear. In the text, these words are underlined. As you preview, look at the context in which the words are used.

vulnerability　　　　**apprehensive**　　　　**demeanor**

What can you do if your child is being bullied? How can you help your child stand up for himself?

My four-year-old is being bullied by another child in his preschool class. I've talked to the teacher and she has taken steps to separate them, but I'm not sure how to discuss the issue with my son. He's somewhat timid and doesn't seem to be able to stand up for himself.

Young bullies are usually children who are poorly treated by their families. Because these children feel pushed around and unappreciated, they try to establish a sense of themselves by putting down someone else. It is as if they believe that making another person feel powerless (as they often do) will make them more powerful.

Bullies pick on children whom they view as weak. Some psychologists suggest that when a bully senses <u>vulnerability</u> in another child, it makes him feel <u>apprehensive</u> because it reminds him of his own insecurity. To ward off such anxiety, a bully goes on the offensive. His nasty behavior is actually a cover for underlying feelings of defenselessness and fear.

Explain to your son that he can take steps to counteract the bully's attacks. Because a child's attitude and <u>demeanor</u>

Bullies pick on children whom they view as weak.

are important aspects of fending off a bully, it's a good idea to help your son practice assertiveness.

Through role-playing at home, teach your son to say in a loud voice, "You quit that. I don't like that." Let him know that even though it may not be polite to shout, it is acceptable in particular situations, such as in school when he is being picked on. Also tell him that he should let his nursery school teacher know when he cannot handle a situation by himself.

It might be helpful for your son to develop a circle of friends so that he feels supported in school. Invite several of his classmates to your home for after-school or weekend playdates. Your son will feel more protected if he is part of a group, and it is more difficult for a bully to attack a child who is among friends.

Word count: 337

Why You Must Listen

by Bernice Weissbourd

from *Parents*

Some of the difficult words in the article are listed below in the order in which they appear. In the text, these words are underlined. As you preview, look at the context in which the words are used.

undoubtedly   **realms**   **spur**
thwarted

By tuning in to your youngster, you stimulate and explore her mind.

Your two-year-old may be trying new words daily or already speaking in complete sentences. Either way, one of the exciting aspects of being a parent is observing your child's language unfold. Your youngster's speech is a window to her mind: It allows you to know beyond gestures and behavior what she is thinking and how she is feeling. That is why listening to what she says is so important.

Listening to your youngster even when she is talking to herself during play can give you a sense of how she views her world. She may be saying no to herself in the same tone that you tend to use; or perhaps she is telling her imaginary friend that the doctor is going to give her a shot that will hurt "for only a minute."

Another reason listening to your child is important is that it tells her that you value what she has to say and, therefore, value her. Furthermore, the respect you show by listening to her makes her feel good about herself and builds her self-confidence.

By listening to your child, you convey the message that you are pleased that she is talking to you, which encourages her to communicate even more. Her conversations with you help her become aware of new words, new views, and of the give-and-take of sharing thoughts.

The relationship between you and your child is enhanced when she communicates in words. Many parents express their enthusiasm about this new development by making such comments as "Now we can really have a conversation!" By listening and talking to your toddler, you lay the foundation for the open communication between the two of you that you will value so much later on.

Stay Tuned

When your two-year-old reaches the point where she is bursting with language and talks constantly, there may be moments when you <u>undoubtedly</u> will tune her out or answer her automatically. "My child demands so much of my attention," parents often say. It is understandable that sometimes you simply will not be able to stop what you are doing, bend down, and listen attentively to your youngster. At these times you can say, "I'm very busy right now, dear. I will be able to listen in one minute."

Bringing yourself back from an activity or from your own thoughts to listen to your child is, however, well worth the effort. A child whose parents regularly ignore her will likely feel that she doesn't matter to them and that talking isn't very important anyway. Her desire to achieve greater use of language will be <u>thwarted</u>, and with it, new <u>realms</u> of discovery. Learning becomes less exciting if no one encourages it.

These days, listening to children is especially important because of the growing concern over the number of them who are entering school unprepared to learn. You may not realize it, but when you listen to your child, you are encouraging essential elements of learning: self-confidence, communication skills, and social ease. By letting her know that you are pleased by, and proud of, her developing language, you <u>spur</u> her on to further growth and achievement.

Word Count: 807

Stepfamilies: A Family by Any Other Name

by John K. Rosemond

from *Hemispheres*

Some of the difficult words in the article are listed below in the order in which they appear. In the text, these words are underlined. As you preview, look at the context in which the words are used.

uni-polar	presumptuous	travails
bi-polar	vignette	pseudo
monogamous	aforementioned	

Terms like "bi-polar blended," "secondary step," or "double step" worry some people about to start a second family. Sometimes complex terms can make a family situation more confusing than is necessary.

I must admit, I have a little trouble keeping all these new names for families straight. Let's see, a stepfamily is one in which there is a stepparent. That's easy enough. But a stepfamily becomes a blended family when the stepparent and the biological parent conspire to have a child in common. Actually, that's a <u>uni-polar</u> blended family, since the blended-ness comes from only one previous marriage. But if both adults bring children from previous marriages to their union, then the family is a <u>bi-polar</u> blended family. Unless one parent's children do not live with the new family, in which case the family is a secondary-step,

bi-polar blended family. Then there's the double-step family, in which one parent brings children from not one, but two previous marriages. And it goes on from there, all the way up through uni-secondary, triple-step, bi-polar blended family, and that's not even taking adopted children into consideration.

Actually, a family by any other name is still a family. These different categories for families—whatever they are—have legal significance only. In fact, it generally takes a lawyer to untangle their meaning. Knowing whose kids are whose, who begot with whom, comes in handy at the reading of the will, but not before.

Otherwise, all this blended and stepfamily terminology is nothing but confusing. In the first place, the types of families to which these terms refer are nothing new. They've been with us since humans began getting together in long-term, monogamous relationships. Until recently, no one thought to categorize families like one might different species of butterflies. Families were families.

As far as I can tell, problems started to mount when people began not only thinking in these different terms but taking them seriously, as if being a blended family (or whatever) meant you had to operate according to a different set of rules than did a "normal" family.

To cite an example: A woman recently asked me if I could recommend any good books on blended families. I held up one of my own, saying, "I would hope this is good enough."

She laughed and said, "No, seriously, I'm looking for a book on blended families. Actually, I've read your books, and they're all about, well, normal families."

"What's abnormal about being a so-called blended family?" I asked, acting as naive as possible.

"Well," she began, "it's just that, ummmm, well, my husband is my children's stepfather, except we have one child—15 months old—in common. And my children, from my first marriage, that is, well I think they're somewhat confused about things, what with the new baby and all. After all, he's their brother. But then again, I mean, do they think we're two families living under one roof, or what?"

"I don't think your kids are confused," I said.

"You don't?" she said, incredulously.

"Nope. I think you're confused."

Boy, was she ever!

This woman was all tangled up in words over the simplest of matters: She married, had two children. She divorced, taking custody of the two children. She remarried, and she and her second husband have brought a third child into their family. As my stepuncle used to say, "Whatsa da bigga deal?"

In the first place, the similarities of families always outweigh their differences. So, a so-called blended family is probably 90 percent the same as any other family by any other name. Second, there's only one set of rules for family living. They are:

Rule 1:

Two married people should always pay more attention to their marriage than they do any children who live with them, whether full-time or part-time.

Rule 2:

By the time they are 3 years old, children should be paying more attention to their parents (including stepparents) than their parents are paying to them. (Fact: The more attention you pay to a child, the less the child will pay to you.)

Rule 3:

Both parties to the marriage have equal authority over every child in the household, regardless of how much time any given child spends in the household.

Rule 4:

Parents make decisions, and children—while they may, on selective occasions, be given a voice in matters—are to do what they are told, because they are told.

Rule 5:

Every child age 3 and older should be expected to perform a daily routine of chores around the home—not for payment, but because the child is a member of the family, period.

Rule 6:

Children should be expected to occupy their own time, do their own homework, resolve their own disputes with friends, and sleep in their own beds.

Rule 7:

Parents should hire baby sitters often. God made baby sitters so parents could take breaks on a regular basis.

Now I ask: Which of these rules does not apply to blended families, even triple-step, bi-polar ones? The answer: None. They all apply. Therefore, any good book on "normal" families is good for blended ones as well. And rules for rearing one's biological children apply just as well to rearing one's stepchildren.

Unfortunately, a lot of people today don't see it that way. They think blended and step-this or step-that means parents have to act differently, that expectations for children must change and normal rules go out the window. As a result, they become confused, and completely unnecessary problems ensue.

One of these problems results from what I call the separate-checking-accounts approach to blendedness in a family. I'm referring here to when the two adults agree that each will confine his or her discipline to his or her children only. In effect, this

> *These different categories for families—whatever they are—have legal significance only. In fact, it generally takes a lawyer to untangle their meaning.*

creates three separate families, all living under the same roof: his family, her family, and their family. At any given moment in time, it will be impossible for everyone to agree on which of these families they are operating within. The adult male of this human zoo may, for example, think that when he asks his stepson to hang up his coat he is simply asking a member of the family to perform a simple courtesy. Ah, but the adult female may see it differently, especially if her own flesh-and-blood offspring acts as if his self-esteem has been damaged by the adult male's <u>presumptuous</u> request. It will take lawyers to figure this out, and to the offices of various lawyers is probably where this brood will be headed.

A second completely unnecessary problem results because the adults forming the whatever-it-is family aren't proactive. They don't understand that precedents set before their marriage are going to either help the family or haunt the family. As my once-removed step grandmother used to say, "They go into it with their eyes closed."

Example: Our vignette stars a single parent and two relatively young children. This threesome (or whateversome) has become inseparable. They do everything together. Understandably, the children have become quite comfortable having a doting adult at their beck and call and see no reason why the arrangement should ever change.

Enter a potential spouse/stepparent who quickly (and correctly) realizes the strength of the aforementioned bond and adopts an "if you can't beat 'em, join 'em" strategy. To win over the children, this second party becomes their friend, their good buddy. At this point, one needs a playbill to tell the children from the adults.

Fast forward through a wedding (in which the children play principal roles, thus symbolizing the union of one to all), a honeymoon (the children come along), and the setting up of a new household. Not surprisingly, we find everyone clinging to old habits that, unfortunately, no longer work (if they ever did). Our formerly single parent has difficulty moving out of a primary relationship with the children and into a real, true-to-life marriage with his or her new spouse. As a result, the stepparent begins to feel like the proverbial third wheel.

Making matters worse, when the stepparent tries to shift gears from good buddy to authority figure, chaos breaks loose. The children act like any attempt on the part of the stepparent to discipline amounts to victimization. On such occasions, the children run to their "real" parent, complaining that the interloper is being mean. At this point, things really get interesting. Sometimes the children are told to obey, sometimes the stepparent is accused of over-reacting and/or being jealous of the kids. And round and round they go, and where they stop, heaven only knows.

An ounce of prevention is all that's needed to avoid the trials and travails of either of these soap operas.

Before forming a double-blended, triple-dip family, sit down and anticipate the kinds of problems you might encounter once you're all living together and how you're going to handle them when and if they come up. Any proactive solution you devise must, if it's going to work, be consistent with the first four rules enumerated earlier:

1. The marriage comes first.
2. Both adults have equal authority over all of the children.
3. Children (age 3 and older) pay more attention to parents than parents pay to children.
4. Children do as they are told, regardless of which parent is doing the telling.

There is no problem that cannot be solved in a family as long as everyone understands those four cardinal precepts.

For that reason, I've thought for a long time that they should be worked into any remarriage ceremony, as in, "Do you, Dorothy, promise to take Walter as your lawfully wedded husband and to be more wife to him than mother to any children who live with you, no matter their biology, and do you also promise to recognize that in consenting to marry Walter you have given him as much authority over your children as you yourself have, and that you will expect them to obey him as if he were their own flesh and blood, and do you Walter promise exactly the same, because let me tell you, if you don't, then I don't want to be any part of this, so help me God."

I know that's complicated, but after all, we're talking about a double-backflip with a full-gainer blended <u>pseudo</u>-stepfamily, right?

Word Count: 1702

HITTING THE ROAD

by David Elkind, Ph.D.

from *Parents*

Some of the difficult words in the article are listed below in the order in which they appear. In the text, these words are underlined. As you preview, look at the context in which the words are used.

bar (bas) mitzvah   **drastically**   **chauffeuring**

It is every teenager's dream and most parents' nightmare: getting a driver's license. What should parents and teens discuss about this important matter? It is a serious concern, and you may find this author's advice helpful.

Getting a driver's license is an important milestone of maturity for a teenager. Along with confirmation or a bar or bas mitzvah, a sweet-sixteen party, and a work permit, a driver's license signals that the teenager has taken a major step toward adulthood. Such markers give young people a sense of direction—of where they have been, where they are now, and where they are going.

Preliminary Talks

Even before a teenager applies for his driver's license, you should discuss a number of practical considerations associated with driving. Perhaps most important is finances. Teenagers need to be reminded that when a young person is listed on an insurance plan as a driver of the family car, the insurance rates go up quite drastically. They also must realize that if they get a ticket for a moving violation, insurance costs will rise even more steeply. If a young person is going to use the car regularly, particularly to go to and from a job, he should be expected to contribute to the car's upkeep and insurance. Even if the teen uses the car only on a limited basis, you should agree about who is to pay for the gas, oil, car wash, and so on. (This sort of discussion is especially important if the teenager is given a hand-me-down car or purchases one on his own.)

Establish Guidelines

It is also important for you to set general guidelines for the use of the family car. Teenagers must be told to plan for when they wish to use the car. They cannot expect to have it available at a moment's notice. They should also be

> ## *Teenagers must learn that along with the freedom to drive comes responsibility.*

expected to assume some family driving chores: for example, chauffeuring their younger brothers and sisters, shopping, and picking up elderly relatives. Parents, on the other hand, must be sensitive to teenagers' needs and obligations. They should try not to go back on a promise made to the teenager about when he can use the car.

Most teenagers *are* responsible drivers. The formation of SADD (Students Against Driving Drunk) is just one example of their sense of responsibility. Nevertheless, a few kids do abuse their driving privileges. They may take too many other young people in the car, drive recklessly, or drink and drive. If a teen-

ager abuses the right to drive, he should be grounded, quickly and firmly. How long a young person's driving privileges are suspended will depend upon just how reckless he has been. Teenagers must learn that along with the freedom to drive comes responsibility.

On the other hand, it is important for us as parents not to overreact if a responsible teenager gets a ticket or has a minor accident. More often than not, this is much more frightening to the youngster than to us and will teach him to be more cautious in the future. Driving a car is part of modern adult life, and teenagers who drive responsibly are accepting some of the conditions of being an adult. Although it may be sad for us to see them grow up so soon, it is also a relief to surrender the job of chauffeuring them around.

Word count: 527

THIS IS YOUR BRAIN ON TV

by Tommy Denton

from *Fort Worth Star Telegram*

Some of the difficult words in the article are listed below in the order in which they appear. In the text, these words are underlined. As you preview, look at the context in which the words are used.

relented	susceptible	arduous
zillionth	mesmerized	fathom
admonition	Cyclops	cathode ray tube
exasperation	Polyphemus	languor
demise	Odysseus	

TV wages war on our children's minds. It devours their attention and ability to think and make judgements for themselves. In the author's house, the parents are fighting back. Read to find out how.

Probably the most tiresome parental refrain my children have had to endure in their young lives—besides "Clean up your room!"—has been: "No, you can't cook your brains out in front of the TV."

My wife and I didn't even own a television set until our third child was born. While I was visiting the maternity ward before bringing mother and baby home, my own mother called a local dealer and had a set delivered to our house. Grandmothers can be that way.

At any rate, our family finally joined the TV age.

That was more than 11 years ago, and fighting the great American instinct to flip on the switch seems to have been almost incessant. Although we have <u>relented</u> and allowed rather liberal viewing privileges on Friday nights and Saturday mornings, weekdays and nights are basically off limits for the kids. We make occasional exceptions for particularly informative or otherwise special programs and some family viewing on non-school nights.

This oppressive restriction has met with plenty of resistance from our children and no small measure of comparison with the more beneficent generosity of their friends' parents.

Which, of course, leads to the <u>zillionth</u> version of our loving <u>admonition</u> that we are not other people's parents, and we care that the children not cook their brains out.

Eyes roll, gasps of <u>exasperation</u> issue forth and young feet shuffle—they have been known to stomp—off to respective bedrooms to while away the remaining hour or so with the obligatory book.

If this is a war being waged for our children's mind, it is a war worth fighting and winning, even thought much of American society at times seems to have blissfully surrendered.

In an essay appearing in an edition of the Hillsdale College publication Imprimis, best-selling author Larry Woiwode places television at the core of the <u>demise</u> of one of the essential skills in a republic: the capacity to think.

"Television, in fact, has greater power over the lives of most Americans than any educational system or government or church," Woiwode wrote. "Children are particularly <u>susceptible</u>. They are <u>mesmerized</u>, hypnotized and tranquilized by TV. No wonder, then, that as adults they are not prepared for the front line of life; they simply have no mental defenses to confront the reality of the world."

Woiwode compares TV with the mythical <u>Cyclops</u>, <u>Polyphemus</u>, encountered by <u>Odysseus</u> in his journeys after the Trojan War. After the war party was trapped in the giant's cave, Polyphemus seized two of Odysseus' men, bashed out their brains and devoured them.

"What I find particularly appropriate about this myth as it applies today is that, first, the Cyclops imprisons these men in darkness, and that, second, he beats their brains out before he devours them," Woiwode wrote. "It doesn't take much

imagination to apply this to the effects of TV on us and our children."

> *Children...are mesmerized, hypnotized and tranquilized by TV. No wonder, then, that as adults they are not prepared for the front line of life....*

The ultimate result, he said, is a destructive erosion of human critical faculties.

"TV eats books. It eats academic skills. It eats positive character traits. It even eats family relationships. TV eats out our substance."

Woiwode referred to observations by Jerry Mander, who wrote the 1978 book *Four Arguments for the Elimination of Television*, citing the numbing effect of television on the ability to differentiate between the real and the unreal.

"(With TV) what we see, hear, touch, smell, feel and understand about the world has been processed for us," Mander wrote. And when people "cannot distinguish with certainty the natural from the interpreted, or the artificial from the organic, then all theories of the ideal organization of life become equal."

In other words, all images being equal, value judgments about what is good or bad, right or wrong, become irrelevant. That may have some bearing on the results of numerous scientific studies showing a direct relationship between excessive TV viewing and the rising incidence of crime and violence in American society.

The relatively <u>arduous</u> task of reading Dostoevski's *Crime and Punishment*—with its fascinating plot structure, description, character development and the struggle to <u>fathom</u> the complexities of the human psyche in conflict—is no match for the passive absorption of "Dirty Harry" or "The Terminator."

Once life has been limited to the comfortable, glowing margins of a <u>cathode ray tube</u> and submerged in a pool of hypnotic <u>languor</u>, making sense of life's difficulties, perplexities, joys and pains hardly seems worth the effort.

In our house, we call that cooking your brains out.

Word count: 751

Your Child's Self-Esteem

by Lilian G. Katz

from *Parents*

Self-esteem, the liking or acceptance of ourselves as we are, is recognized today as extremely important for mental health and achievement. The author of this article suggests some ways to develop and improve self-esteem in children.

The idea that children should feel good about themselves is, remarkably, a relatively modern one. Only one or two generations ago, praise was withheld from children for fear that youngsters might become conceited or "swell-headed." These days, however, it often seems that we err to the other extreme, and many children are in danger of becoming too self-conscious and eager for praise.

It's not so difficult to understand how praising a child's efforts can positively affect his self-esteem, and parents may need little guidance in this regard. But parents may be less clear about how they can affect a child's feelings about himself in other ways. With an eye toward helping parents with this dilemma, I've outlined some ideas below that you may want to consider as you think about developing a healthy sense of self-esteem in your children.

An individual's self-esteem is the result of evaluations by one's self and others. For young children, the greatest influences on self-esteem—high and low—are others' evaluations, especially those of people closest to the child. The basis for self-esteem in childhood is the feeling of being loved and accepted, particularly by someone the child can look up to. This is one reason that parental support means so much to children and has such an extraordinary effect on their self-esteem.

Remember that it is not desirable to have excessive self-esteem. Indeed, an excessively high degree of self-esteem, confidence, or assurance might cause a person to be insensitive to others' reactions and feelings about him. Though it

Self-esteem is not acquired all at once early in life to last forever and be present in all situations.

is difficult to know precisely where the level is, the <u>optimum</u> level of self-esteem seems to be that which allows for the normal <u>fluctuations</u> in feelings of confidence, pride, and competence. The actual complexities of life are sufficient that all children (and adults) encounter situations in which it is realistic to have little confidence, hurt pride, or insufficient competence. Children can be helped by adults to accept the fact that such difficult situations are inevitable. They are also temporary, and in the scheme of things, they are only a small portion of the range of experiences they'll have in life.

Self-esteem varies from one interpersonal situation to another. Children do not have to be accepted or loved by everyone they encounter. Parents can help a child cope with occasions of rejection or indifference by reassuring her that Mom's and Dad's own acceptance of the youngster has not been shaken.

Self-esteem is not acquired all at once early in life to last forever and be present in all situations. A child may feel confident and accepted at home but the opposite in the neighborhood or preschool. Adults can generally avoid those situations in which their self-esteem is likely to take a beating, but children are limited to situations adults provide for them. They have few skills or resources for avoiding situations in which their self-assurance will be threatened. Parents should be aware that in some instances inappropriate behavior on the part of their child may be a signal that the child perceives the particular circumstance as threatening to his self-confidence.

Self-esteem is measured against certain criteria, typically acquired within the family. The criteria against which we are evaluated vary among families, ethnic groups, and neighborhoods. They also vary for boys and girls—more so in some communities than in others. In some families or groups esteem is based on physical beauty, in others on intelligence, athleticism, or toughness. Your child will need help in meeting your standards on those criteria. Whatever criteria for being an acceptable person make sense in your family, support your child's effort to meet them, but reassure her that, no matter what, she is loved and always belongs to the family.

Word count: 635

COPYRIGHT NOTICE

WHY I LIE

by Jacquelyn Mitchard
from *Parenting*

Some of the difficult words in the article are listed below in the order in which they appear. In the text, these words are underlined. As you preview, look at the context in which the words are used.

blanch	**repudiated**	**dissuade**
hypocrisy	**litmus test**	**scenario**
sangfroid	**debauched**	**purge**
humiliated	**harrowing**	**egregious**
paragons		

When children ask about their parents' past encounters with sex, drugs, and alcohol, honesty isn't always the best policy.

My friends and I play truth-or-dare games all the time. We ask one another, Would you ever leave your sleeping baby alone in the house for 20 minutes while you ran to the supermarket? Would you fake an excuse for school so your child could go to the circus? Would you give your three-year-old a pacifier?

But none of those is the biggie, the essay question that counts for a third of our grade: What would you tell your children, we ask one another, about the mistakes of your past—the sex, drugs, alcohol, and other awful things that still make you wince? Would you tell them the truth? Would you tell something that resembles the truth? Would you . . . lie?

When I say firmly, without hesitation, that I would lie, some of my friends blanch. Ours, after all, is the generation that founded its coming of age on a revolt against hypocrisy—and isn't that, after all, what I'm proposing: spin-doctoring my past with the sangfroid of a career politician?

How can you? they say; it's so unlike you.

True, lying to my children would be out of character for me. My kids have seen me drive back across town to pay for the toaster a salesclerk forgot to ring up. And they know I'd have done it even if they weren't in the car.

So I thought long and hard before I

could justify certain exceptions to the rule. My decision came gradually, only after I realized that there are several things in life even more important to me than my ideals: the health and safety of my children, and the love and protectiveness I feel for them.

My friend Steve, who has three young sons, could not disagree with me more. He thinks that withholding the truth is just as bad as telling a lie, and that you never do a child a favor by lying. "I think my oldest son respects me because I'm honest. I don't want him to think I'm perfect, because otherwise how is he ever going to learn that people can make mistakes and survive?"

Accordingly, Steve, in a discussion about bike helmets, has told his nine-year-old son, Chris, that he used to ride a motorcycle without a helmet—and what a stupid thing that was to do. When the subject arises years down the road, he'll also tell his son about the night he spent in jail after he went out drinking with friends and how, humiliated and sick, he had to face his mother's disappointment. "Honesty can be hard," he says, "but hypocrisy can kill you."

Much as I respect Steve, I don't entirely agree. Lucky people learn from their own mistakes, but they usually don't learn from other people's, even if those people are the most important figures in their lives.

What children come away with, after the hair-raising detours so many of them seem to take during their teens and twenties, is their parents' basic values and behavior. As compelling as peer pressure is, of the young people questioned in a 1991 Roper youth poll, the largest number cited their parents as their most influential role models.

I don't, however, think that parents should present themselves as paragons. And my husband and I don't. We apologize to our children when we've lost our tempers. We admit that we sassed our parents, broke the rules, slapped our

> ***...there are several things in life even more important to me than my ideals: the health and safety of my children....***

younger brothers. Would I try to keep it from my children that alcoholism ran like bitter sap through previous generations of our family tree? No. They have a right, and a need, to know that.

So what, exactly, would I fudge? Those stupid, rash mistakes that could have ruined a life or ended it. Unlike some of my peers, I haven't completely repudiated those salad days when indulging in casual sex and recreational drugs was a kind of litmus test to prove how antiestablishment we were. I don't think of those practices now as wholly evil or debauched. But neither were they, as people thought then, harmless. Twenty years of history bear witness to the fact that drugs can lay waste to families and whole neighborhoods, and that casual sex can have a lethal undertow.

Not long ago, a young college student in our community, one of those smart, funny young men who seem pointed like an arrow at success, fell to his death from the window of his seventh-story dorm room. His friends said it was only the second time he'd tried LSD. That tragedy strengthened my resolve. I silently vowed to throw all the furniture I could against the door of disaster—with education, role modeling, and long talks—to keep my children safe from such risks. Nor will I allow my own youthful mistakes to provide any possible justification for similar acts on their parts, for I suspect that if I did tell all, my sins might provide more of a rationale than a lesson.

On the day our 14-year-old was discovered to have a "friend's" cigarettes in her pocket, she didn't remember all the years I've spent as a nonsmoker; she reached back to the time before I quit: "*You* smoked! What's the big deal?" That she was just out of grade school and that I'd been in college when I took my first drag didn't matter to her; only that information about me was there, and it hung in the air between us.

After I told my friend Grace about this, she told me an even more harrowing story. When Grace (I'm changing her name here, as well as those of other parents, and you'll soon see why) was all of 15, she had a full-blown love affair with her 24-year-old gym teacher. Chances are, Graces children aren't going to ask her if she ever slept with a teacher while was in high school; they may, however, ask about their mom's youthful sexuality in general. What will Grace tell them? Not the truth, that's for sure. Such a revelation would

have more weight than it deserves, Grace believes, adding, "What possible lesson could they draw from what I did?"

My friend Sharon's plan is to reveal the truth by degrees. Sharon, now a pillar of the community and the mother of two children, didn't exactly have a wild youth, but she had her moments. If her children ask her if she has ever tried marijuana, she'll probably answer, "I did, but not very often or for very long."

If they ask about any other drugs, though, she'll answer firmly no—whether or not that is true. "We know now that even one experiment with cocaine can be a fatal one," she says. It isn't that Sharon doesn't want her children to be adventurous. Although her heart would be in her mouth, she wouldn't try to dissuade them from skydiving. But skydiving lessons come with a parachute; drugs don't.

Another mother I know plans to treat the drug issue differently. Janet's adolescent drug involvement was serious and long-term, and she intends to lay out that whole gruesome scenario for her children. "Drugs show up on the playground now," she says. "My kids will know the score."

But what effect will that information have on these children who have never known their mother to take more than a glass of wine? Will they admire her courage and the confiding atmosphere of mutual trust that she intends to foster? Or will they figure that since their mother survived some steep dives intact, so might they? Doesn't keeping your mouth shut and forgiving yourself for your own past take a kind of courage, too? Can't the urge to purge fall under the same heading as confessing an infidelity to your mate? It may feel like the right thing to do, but is it really? Can't the pain that the truth brings overwhelm the benefit of divulging it?

"Honesty isn't telling all," a child psychologist friend once told me. "We should show our children as much about our lives as they need to encourage their own growth." I agree. So when my children ask me, for instance, if I've ever driven drunk or ever gotten into a car with someone who was drunk, the answer will be no, or a variation such as, "That would have been an incredibly dumb thing to do." My answer will not comprise the whole truth and nothing but the truth, but it will be the answer that is most in line with what I want for my kids.

Now, I know that this strategy is full of land mines. What if an old friend of mine spilled the nasty beans about me one night? Would my children ever trust me again? Would they think I was a fraud?

It's not an inconsiderable risk. At least, though, they'd know that I had enough decency to be ashamed of my mistakes. What I'd tell them, in that painful situation, would probably go something like this: "I couldn't see a good reason for you to know this. We're a family, but we're also each individuals. Things may happen in your life that you won't confide to your own children, or even to me. There may be times when you'll just have to go on trust, as I trust you. But I want you to know that since I've been your parent, there's never been anything I've done that I wouldn't tell you about."

Bear in mind that I'm not trying to avoid owning up to a stretch in the pen for cocaine smuggling. No, my sins aren't

a source of horror to me; they're just better left unspoken.

I would also agree with the poet Emily Dickinson, who wrote, "The truth must dazzle gradually. . . ." Sharing the past, at the right time, on a need-to-know basis, should be every parent's right. Abortion is a good example. If I'd had an abortion, I might share that information with my 18-year-old daughter, provided she had a need to know. But face it, young children think of abortion only as eliminating the possibility of one of their own, and it could lead them to suspect that you're not all that crazy about them, either. In other words, age-appropriateness counts.

So how can I teach these children of mine to know the freedom of a truthful heart if I edit the most <u>egregious</u> mistakes out of the family history? I'm going to act honestly and speak honestly. I'm going to let them see me face up to my current failings as truly as I can. I'm not going to tell them that Dad and I were just talking things over when we were really having a fight. I'm not going to tell them that we can't afford a Nintendo when in fact we don't want to buy one because we think it's the Great Satan of Brain Death. I'm not going to tell them that I wish I could stay home when I'm really looking forward to going out. I'm not going to tell then that I threw the brownies out because they had gone stale when Dad and I ate them all.

And as for the past, I'm going to tell them as much as I—an adult who has their lives in my hands for only a short time— think can help them make choices with a critical mind and compassionate spirit, and not a sentence more. Will that choice protect them any more than the unvarnished truth? I can't know for sure, but this path feels farther from the cliff than the other one.

A family isn't, after all, a democracy, where everyone gets the facts and then votes. My husband and I are the only ones piloting this ship through rough passages. We have not only our consciences to guide us but also our responsibilities. When I'm tempted to tell all, I have only to look at the faces of my children to know that my love for them, so deep that it hurts, is more powerful than any ideal—even an important one.

Word Count: 2026

THE SEXES

The articles in this section, listed below, discuss intriguing topics relating to men and women getting along.

- **STAYING MARRIED**

- **WHY ISN'T A NICE PERSON LIKE YOU MARRIED?**

- **THE MYTH OF ROMANTIC LOVE**

- **MUST BOYS ALWAYS BE BOYS?**

- **SUPERWOMEN**

- **MARRIAGES MADE TO LAST**

STAYING MARRIED

by John K. Rosemond
from *Hemispheres*

Some of the difficult words in the article are listed below in the order in which they appear. In the text, these words are underlined. As you preview, look at the context in which the words are used.

proverbial	labyrinthine	unscathed
anomaly	perilous	insufferable
fidelity	visceral	autonomy
tomes		

Why are so many of today's marriages failing? Because the people in them just aren't stubborn enough. The key to successfully living together requires mutual respect, listening to one another, and sometimes saying, "I don't."

My wife, Willie, and I celebrated our 25th anniversary in July. Given that one out of every two marriages in our generation has already gone down the proverbial tube, having made it to our silver anniversary makes us somewhat of an anomaly. "What's your secret?" people will occasionally ask, as if the ongoing process of learning to live together boils down to a single kernel of wisdom that many seek but only the chosen few find. Willie and I did, however, pause to reflect upon our success as we passed this latest milestone in excellent repair. In addition to fidelity, learning to listen with respect, and giving one another "space" (pardon my lapse into trendiness), we came up with some counsel you aren't likely to find in any of the how-to books on marriage that have proliferated in this age of easy divorce:

Avoid How-to Books on Staying Married

The problem with these well-meaning tomes is the problem with self-improvement books in general: They cause the reader to think too much. The more one analyzes a marriage, the more labyrinthine the relationship is likely to seem. Finding one's way through the maze of "issues" that these books identify as musts for "working through" is, we discovered, decidedly perilous. Which is not, however, to say that marriage is really a simple thing, or that the best approach to conflict is to stick one's head in the sand and wait for it to go away. It isn't, and it won't. When it comes to conflict, Willie and I have come to rely on the <u>visceral</u> approach, as in, "I wish you'd stop doing that," or "Like it or not, this is the way I feel about what you did." The truth may, at times, hurt. But doing polite little intellectual dances around the truth often does a lot more damage in the long run.

Accept the Big Reality

Namely, that staying married is the single most difficult challenge you will ever undertake. Why? Because both you and your spouse are imperfect beings,

> *...staying married is the single most difficult challenge you will ever undertake.*

each no less so than the other. When two imperfect beings join together in an imperfect union, and their respective imperfections start to collide, the imperfections begin to multiply. Here's a fact: You are never so imperfect as you are a year after you tie the knot. If you don't believe me, just ask your mate. I have to laugh whenever I hear someone accuse their spouse of being "difficult to live with." The fact is, we're all, each and every one of us,

difficult to live with! Which is why, when my children were making college plans, we strongly advised that they not room with friends; not if they wanted to stay friends, that is. Now, on top of the relatively simple act of rooming together, add the complications of emotional commitment, children, shared financial responsibilities, different likes and dislikes, sexual drives that don't always mesh, and you begin to get the picture. Accept your equal part in all this and you will be able to retain your sense of humor, which is an outstanding feature of every truly successful marriage.

Compromise as Little as Possible

Yes, you read me right. Compromise is fine in certain situations, and may be the only way to emerge <u>unscathed</u> from certain conflicts, but compromise is often the weakest of three alternatives: You have your stubborn way of doing something; your spouse has his or her stubborn ideas on the same subject; then there's the compromise, which is a point approximately midway in between. As such, compromise is often more a means of resolving conflict than it is a means of resolving the problem at hand. Furthermore, by resolving the conflict rather than resolving the problem, you often only forestall more—and more serious—problems later.

Willie and I eventually realized, for example, that compromises concerning the manner in which the children were raised or the manner in which we ran our business resulted, more often than not, in further, and more serious, problems down the road. So we agreed that when we had differences concerning the children, we would both express our opinions, but the final call, in every case, was Willie's. On the other hand, when we disagreed concerning a business matter, the final call was mine. Knowing who was going to make the final decision forced us to frame our arguments persuasively, rather than emotionally. We were no longer trying to "out-gun" one another in discussions concerning the children or the business; therefore, these discussions didn't get heated. We also discovered that the more calm we were, the more persuasive we were. Lo and behold, I found myself agreeing with Willie concerning business matters, and she found herself agreeing with me concerning the children. Not always, mind you, but sometimes.

Accept That Neither of You Is Ever Likely to Change

Pretty pessimistic, eh? Perhaps, but I'm convinced that's the way it is. A few years back, I got together with several college chums I hadn't seen in over 15 years. After a couple of days of their company, I came to the conclusion that they hadn't changed a bit. They were more focused, their political views had swung to the right, their hairlines had receded, their tastes were more sophisticated, they acted generally more "mature," but their personalities were unchanged. Intrigued, I asked them if they felt I'd changed since they last knew me. The immediate, unanimous reply: "No." Funny. I thought I had. And they thought they had, too.

Thinking, as most of us do, that we've changed over the years leads us to believe

we can bring about change in someone else—our spouses, in particular. And then, when the change doesn't happen, we get frustrated, angry.

Understand that you are different people, with different backgrounds, with different likes and dislikes and different opinions. It is impossible to be married without conflict. To stay married, you must accept your differences and apply no value judgments to them, as in, "That's irrational." You must not only roll with your differences and the friction they create, but learn to celebrate them! That's what continuing to grow is all about.

Don't Pay too Much Attention to the Children

Children need attention, sure, but not a lot. The more attention they get, the more they want, and the more they want, the more <u>insufferable</u> they can become.

Despite what you may have heard, the relationship that requires the most quality time is not that of parent and child, but that of husband and wife. Over time, and after trying to always be One Big Happy Family, Willie and I came to realize that, for the most part, adults should interact with other adults, and children should interact with other children. By keeping the focus on the marriage, we allowed the children greater <u>autonomy</u>. In so doing, we promoted their emancipation. By being husband and wife first, Mom and Dad second, Willie and I also averted the debilitating effects of "empty nest syndrome." For us, the empty nest is cause for celebration, and our young-adult children wholeheartedly agree.

Be Stubborn

Huh? That's right, be stubborn, as in "I'm going to do my part to make this marriage work, no matter what!" Why are so many of today's marriages failing, or doomed to fail? In large part because the people in those marriages just aren't stubborn enough. Many of them have never had to work hard for anything, never had to persevere, never been forced to hang in there when the going got rougher than rough, never had to make great personal sacrifice. As a result, when it comes time in their marriages to do any or all of the above, they can't cut the mustard.

A young person, about to be married, recently expressed this attitude to me: "We've been going together for five years, so I guess it's time to see whether or not we can hack it being married."

If there's one thing Willie and I have discovered in 25 years of ups and downs, it's that you don't stay married because your marriage, in some magical way, manages to work; rather you stay married because you become determined to make it work. That means refusing to turn tail when nothing seems to be going right (and

hasn't been for quite some time), never allowing "boredom" through your front door, and remembering always that your marriage is far more important than you are, or ever will be.

So, on our 25th anniversary, when our friends and children were proposing the typical toasts, Willie and I raised our glasses "to hard-headed stubbornness, the essence of our commitment." That just about said it all.

Word count: 1456

WHY ISN'T A NICE PERSON LIKE YOU MARRIED?

by Elsie Bliss

> Some of the difficult words in the article are listed below in the order in which they appear. In the text, these words are underlined. As you preview, look at the context in which the words are used.
>
> **inordinately**   **c'est moi**   **twinge**
> **candidly**   **angst**

What are the advantages of being married? What are the advantages of being single? Some people react to single people as if something is wrong with them. This author presents a slightly different view—she prefers single life!

I am asked THE QUESTION by friends at every wedding reception. Also at every party and family gathering by well-meaning relatives and sometimes strangers. If it were not for this question and my creative response, some of the people I meet wouldn't find anything to say to me. But the time it hurts most is that moment when an eligible man I've just met wonders aloud, "Gee, it's a wonder you aren't married."

Am I supposed to admit that I am very insecure yet demanding? That no one I have ever met who was available was sufficiently desirable to justify giving up my precious independence? That no matter how I searched (while appearing not to be searching) there has not been anyone who met my rather rigid list of criteria? Am I expected to actually unload this emotional baggage on some poor schnook who might himself prove to be truly desirable? Of course not. Because then I would frighten him off.

Speaking for many nice, attractive, loving and desirable single people, I'd like to climb up on my soapbox and explain a few things. What I say may not hold true for all single people, but for some who have stayed single for an <u>inordinately</u> long time...

Being single is quite respectable. It is a valid way of life. It is not a tragedy or a handicap. It is being the boss; the captain of your ship. I quite like it, even though I readily admit that I frequently miss what married people have when their marriage is going well, just as they miss the freedom I have to decide my own goals and priorities.

I am sorry to say that statistics are against their marriages going well, unfortunately. Marriage in the 20th century is in trouble. Single is not in trouble, despite its bad press and your Aunt Sophie's opinion. Single has a lot going for it.

If you took a poll of your friends and their feelings about marriage, and if they responded <u>candidly</u>, you'd find that (as some brilliant mind once noted) marriage is like a besieged fortress; those who are inside want to get out and those who are outside want to get in. Perhaps the question should be put to married people, "Why is a nice person like you married?"

Some day I may find a partner who will allow me to be me and who will even respect and admire my need to be myself. He won't criticize my liking health foods or tell me I'm uptight because I won't go to a nude beach. He'll think I am fine, quirks and all, even though I love sitcoms and hate game shows and violent movies. If I am lucky, he will have the same desire for himself, and I'll respect and love him for it. Our two selves may join and become a couple of happy individuals. Note, I did not say we would become ONE, but a couple of individuals. Where did that myth originate that you become part of another? Better half, indeed.

Until that happens, no matter how long it takes (maybe never), I will not be categorized as a liberated woman or a Jewish Mother or anything else. I am all of these and none of them. I am the product of years of development and growth including experiences of joy and sorrow. I am like fine chocolate—bitter-sweet. I was liberated long before it was fashion-

Being single is quite respectable.... It is not a tragedy or a handicap.

able and I was a Jewish Mother type as a ten year old child. You don't have to be Jewish or a mother or even a female to be a J.M. If the definition is a protective, assertive, overly sensitive, deeply involved, demonstrative person, then hallelujah! <u>C'est moi</u>!

Probably what causes the greatest <u>angst</u> among single people is someone looking at us with a mixture of wonder and pity and saying, "You are so attractive, it's a shame you aren't married."

Would I gaze at anyone and say, "You are such an attractive person; it's a shame you are overweight"? Or, "How come a couple like you who argue so much are not divorced?" Or, "You seem so nice; why can't you find a good job?"

Of course no civilized person would ask these things. But there are those who consider being single a national dilemma and one that permits constant probing into the single person's psyche to learn the causes.

As with most things, being single is a trade-off. It is a mixed blessing of being private with time of your own to use as you see fit plus the occasional <u>twinge</u> of being left out as you observe hand-holding couples strolling down life's road together.

To some single people, the fear of failure is a great deterrent to marriage, especially if they have feelings of insecurity born of being the children of perfectionist parents. This can color all decision-making for them.

If you are single, and none of the above applies to you, then you will have no trouble replying easily when you hear that ageless question, "Why isn't a nice person like you married?" You'll smile sweetly at Aunt Minnie and say, "Gee, I've been too busy to notice it, but gosh, you're right, I'm not married; I didn't realize. I'll give it some thought and get back to you."

Word count: 894

THE MYTH OF ROMANTIC LOVE

by M. Scott Peck, M.D.

from *The Road Less Traveled*

Some of the difficult words in the article are listed below in the order in which they appear. In the text, these words are underlined. As you preview, look at the context in which the words are used.

illusion	**subjugates**	**rampant**
embody	**psychosomatic**	**colleagues**
ghastly		

You hear about people who marry their high school sweetheart and how fifty years later they are still married. You also hear about the high divorce rate and wonder why things go wrong with so many people who thought they were in love. See if you agree with this author that it is dangerous to believe in the idea of "living happily ever after."

To serve as effectively as it does to trap us into marriage, the experience of falling in love probably must have as one of its characteristics the illusion that the experience will last forever. This illusion is fostered in our culture by the commonly held myth of romantic love, which has its origins in our favorite childhood fairy tales, wherein the prince and the princess, once united, live happily forever after. The myth of romantic love tells us, in effect, that for every young man in the world there is a young woman and only one woman for a man and this has been predetermined "in the stars." When we meet the person for whom we are intended, recognition comes through the fact that we fall in love. We have met the person for whom all the heavens intended us, and since the match is perfect, we will then be able to satisfy all of each other's needs forever and ever, and therefore live happily forever after in perfect union and harmony. Should it come to pass, however, that we do not satisfy or meet all of each other's needs and friction arises and we fall out of love, then it is clear that a dreadful mistake was made: We misread the stars; we did not hook up with our one and only perfect match; what we thought was love was not real or "true" love; and nothing can be done about the situation except to live unhappily ever after or get divorced.

While I generally find that great myths are great precisely because they represent and <u>embody</u> great universal truths, the myth of romantic love is a dreadful lie. Perhaps it is a necessary lie in that it ensures the survival of the species by its encouragement and seeming validation of the falling-in-love experience that traps

> **But as a psychiatrist I weep in my heart almost daily for the ghastly confusion and suffering that this myth fosters.**

us into marriage. But as a psychiatrist I weep in my heart almost daily for the <u>ghastly</u> confusion and suffering that this myth fosters. Millions of people waste vast amounts of energy desperately and futilely attempting to make the reality of their lives conform to the unreality of the myth. Mrs. A. <u>subjugates</u> herself absurdly to her husband out of a feeling of guilt. "I didn't really love my husband when we married," she says, "I pretended I did. I guess I tricked him into it, so I have no right to complain about him, and I owe it to him to do whatever he wants." Mr. B. laments: "I regret I didn't marry Miss C. I think we could have had a good marriage. But I didn't fall head over heels in love with her, so I assumed she couldn't

be the right person for me." Mrs. D., married for two years, becomes severely depressed without apparent cause, and enters therapy stating: "I don't know what's wrong. I've got everything I need, including a perfect marriage." Only months later can she accept the fact that she has fallen out of love with her husband but that this does not mean that she made a horrible mistake. Mr. E., also married two years, begins to suffer intense headaches in the evenings and can't believe they are <u>psychosomatic</u>. "My home life is fine. I love my wife as much as the day I married her. She's everything I ever wanted," he says. But his headaches don't leave him until a year later, when he is able to admit, "She bugs the hell out of me the way she is always wanting, wanting things without regard to my salary," and then is able to confront her with her extravagance. Mr. and Mrs. F. acknowledge to each other that they have fallen out of love and then proceed to make each other miserable by mutual <u>rampant</u> infidelity as they each search for the one "true love," not realizing that their very acknowledgment could mark the beginning of the work of their marriage instead of its end.

Even when couples have acknowledged that the honeymoon is over, that they are no longer romantically in love with each other and are able still to be committed to their relationship, they still cling to the myth and attempt to conform their lives to it. "Even though we have fallen out of love, if we act by sheer will power as if we still were in love, then maybe romantic love will return to our lives," their thinking goes. These couples prize togetherness. When they enter couples group therapy (which is the setting in which my wife and I and our close <u>colleagues</u> conduct most serious marriage counseling), they sit together, speak for each other, defend each other's faults and seek to present to the rest of the group a united front, believing this unit to be a sign of the relative health of their marriage and a prerequisite for its improvement.

Sooner or later, and usually sooner, we must tell most couples that they are too much married, too closely coupled, and that they need to establish some psychological distance from each other before they can even begin to work constructively on their problems. Sometimes it is actually necessary to physically separate them, directing them to sit apart from each other in the group circle. It is always necessary to ask them to refrain from speak-

ing for each other or defending each other against the group. Over and over again we must say, "Let Mary speak for herself, John," and "John can defend himself, Mary; he's strong enough." Ultimately, if they stay in therapy, all couples learn that a true acceptance of their own and each other's individuality and separateness is the only foundation upon which a mature marriage can be based and real love can grow.

Word count: 961

MUST BOYS ALWAYS BE BOYS?

from *Newsweek*

Some of the difficult words in the article are listed below in the order in which they appear. In the text, these words are underlined. As you preview, look at the context in which the words are used.

pubescent	**invoked**	**gauntlet**
assert	**statute**	**plaintiffs**
anecdotal	**analogy**	

In the wake of the Clarence Thomas hearings, girls are suing to fight sexual harassment at school.

It's hard to be a little girl, going to school every morning with boys who believe in their wormy little hearts that *girls stink*. It was particularly hard for 7-year-old Cheltzie Hentz, who had to ride to her school in Eden Prairie, Minn., on a bus with boys who called her "bitch" and a driver who seemed to think it was funny. "These boys were making fun of the little girls because they don't have penises!" recalls her horrified mother, Sue Mutziger. Over five months Mutziger sent 22 pages of complaints to school officials, who lectured the boys and briefly suspended several troublemakers from riding the bus. With a new driver this year, the teasing stopped—but Mutziger still thought the schools weren't doing enough to protect her daughter. So she took stronger action:

she filed a complaint with the state Department of Human Rights.

In the fight against sexual harassment, schools are the last frontier. The Clarence Thomas hearings raised awareness of harassment on the job, but "there are things that go on in the hallways, the parking lots, at band practice, that are as bad if not worse," says Pat Callbeck Harper, a "gender-equity specialist" for the Montana schools. Experts also believe that the boy who throws spitballs at girls in his class will grow up to be the man who tries to drop peanuts down their dresses at bars. "There are still too many people who say 'boys will be boys,'" warns Leslie Wolfe of the Center for Women Policy Studies in Washington. "If no one teaches boys that harassment is wrong, why should they stop harassing women as adults?" And by characterizing as "harassment" the activities of second graders, the women's movement has achieved a major political breakthrough: a definition of oppression so broad that no man alive can be sure he's innocent.

Teasing is a problem that dates back at least to the first inkwell and pigtail, and underline{pubescent} girls have long suffered truly degrading abuse from adolescent boys.

> ***Teasing is a problem that dates back at least to the first inkwell and pigtail, and pubescent girls have long suffered truly degrading abuse from adolescent boys.***

Authorities underline{assert} the problem is worsening, although they can't be sure, since the only study was done at a single high school in 1986. There, half the girls reported harassment of various kinds, including remarks, touching, gestures and staring. Most other evidence is anecdotal, such as the long-standing tradition of "Friday flip-up day" at Montana elementary schools, a competition among boys to see how many girls' skirts they can lift. But now prominent scholars such

as Nan Stein of Wellesley College Center for Research on Women are studying it— and finding it, in Stein's words, "an everyday phenomenon."

What has changed is that girls and their parents are less disposed to accept harassment as a normal part of growing up. They have discovered a powerful weapon in the ban on sex discrimination in Title IX of the Education Act of 1972. This provision has usually been underline{invoked} over issues such as equality in sports programs, but last February the Supreme Court ruled that under the underline{statute} students can sue for harassment—and collect damages. That case involved a high-school student who claimed her teacher forced sex on her. But by underline{analogy} to the workplace—where the court has held companies liable if their employees create a "hostile environment" for co-workers—the principle is likely to be extended to cases where boys make life miserable for their classmates, as only they know how.

Running the underline{Gauntlet}

This is already happening in some states, notably in Minnesota, which has recently begun to require schools to have policies prohibiting student-on-student harassment. In Chaska, Minn., Jill Olson was appalled that boys were circulating a list of the 25 most desirable—they used a very different word—girls in her high school, and that she was one of them. (She was even more appalled to learn that some of the other girls on the list were flattered.) Her complaint was investigated by the Minnesota Department of Human Rights and referred to the state attorney general. In Petaluma, Calif., eighth grader Tawnya

Brawdy had to run a gauntlet of boys gathered outside her school who would begin mooing as she approached. "It went on before school, during classes, in between classes and during lunch," says Tawnya, adding that her teacher told her she'd just have to put up with it. Boys continued to moo at her all through high school. The U.S. Department of Education found, in a 211-page report, that the schools had failed to protect her. Her mother, Louise, now heads a group called Parents for Title 9.

In what other school boards might consider a warning, Brawdy sued her district over "emotional distress" and collected $20,000 in an out-of-court settlement. Most judgments in these cases have been small, but the potential number of <u>plaintiffs</u> is huge. So it's likely that what has usually been treated as a routine nuisance will increasingly become a serious disciplinary matter. And, while there may not be a man today who can honestly say he never spent most of a math period staring at the prettiest girl in his class instead of a blackboard . . . someday there might be.

Word Count: 876

SUPERWOMEN

by Edward Dolnick
from *Health*

Some of the difficult words in the article are listed below in the order in which they appear. In the text, these words are underlined. As you preview, look at the context in which the words are used..

swaddled   lamented   innate
trundling   resilient   panache
epidemiologist   acute   camaraderie
satirizing   conscientious

Women have often been called the "weaker" sex. According to Edward Dolnick, this description is highly inaccurate.

Look at a school photo of a fifth-grade class, the boys in their coolest T-shirts, the girls just starting to grow gangly. Look at the nursery in a big-city hospital, at row upon row of swaddled babies. Look at the teenagers working at McDonald's or at the 60-year-olds trundling off the bus behind their tour guide at the Washington Monument.

Then look again in a few years. In every case, if you tried to put together a reunion, you'd find that more males than females had died. If you could take an immense group snapshot of everyone in the United States today, females would outnumber males by 6 million. In this country, women outlive men by about

seven years, and the figure is close to that in all industrialized nations.

Throughout the modern world, cultures are different, diets are different, ways of life and causes of death are different, but one thing is the same: Women outlive men.

It starts even before birth. At conception male fetuses actually outnumber females by about 115 to 100; at birth, the ratio has already fallen to about 105 boys to every 100 girls. By about age 30, there are only enough men left to match the number of women. And from there on, women start building a lead that just grows and grows. Beyond age 80, there are twice as many women as men.

"What's dramatic," says Deborah Wingard, an <u>epidemiologist</u> at the University of California at San Diego, "is that if you look at the top 10 or 12 causes of death, EVERY SINGLE ONE kills more men." She runs a finger down this melancholy Top 10 and rattles off one affliction after another—heart disease and lung cancer and homicide and cirrhosis of the liver and pneumonia. Each kills men at roughly twice the rate it does women.

"Diabetes," Wingard resumes after catching her breath , "is the only one that even comes close to being"—she pauses, in search of a non-judgmental word—"to being equitable."

Women's superiority extends far beyond merely living longer. Women are better than men at distinguishing colors. They have a sharper sense of taste and a better sense of smell. Would any child, confronted with a dubious-looking glass of milk, be so foolish as to give it to his father, rather than his mother, to sample?

The differences between men's and women's sexual capacities are much too familiar to need repeating here. Mark Twain once devoted a bitter essay to <u>satirizing</u> the workmanship of a creator who had come up with two such mismatched creatures. "After 50, a man's performance is of poor quality, the intervals between are wide, and its satisfactions of no great value to either party," Twain <u>lamented</u> in his old age. "Whereas his great-grandmother is as good as new."

In outdoor athletics, women aren't a match for men. But one trend is worth noting: The more a competition requires stamina, the better women fare. The first woman to win a mixed-sex national championship did so in a 24-hour endurance race. Ann Trason ran 143 miles' worth of circles around a track, four miles more than the (male) runner-up. Helen Klein, a 68-year-old who considers a 50-mile race routine, holds all the "ultramarathon" records in her age group. Women win so many long-distance dogsled races that one musher has designed a "Save the Males" T-shirt.

Women's superiority extends far beyond merely living longer.

In real-life ordeals, too, women seem at least as durable as men. One man trapped in the Warsaw Ghetto by the Nazis kept a journal in which he recorded the growing misery of his fellow Jews.

"At 14 Ostrowska Street is a house where there are only women and children," he wrote in the cold and hungry winter of 1942. "All the menfolk have died. In general, men have a markedly higher mortality— the reason being that men have less endurance, work harder, and so forth." Six miserable months later, the diarist continued to marvel at "the courage and endurance of our women" who were now "coming forward to replace the men, who fall out exhausted."

In bad times, women may also be psychologically more <u>resilient</u> than men. A study of areas of London heavily bombed during World War II, for example, found that 70 percent more men than women became psychiatric casualties. The study's (male) author summarized its findings: "It may be true that women are more emotional than men in romance, but they are less so in air raids."

Women have more <u>acute</u> hearing than men, and keep their hearing longer. Women have colder hands and feet than men, but complain and suffer less when exposed to bitter cold.

Are you beginning to detect a pattern?

Men out-stutter women 4 to 1. Men go bald, and sprout hair from their ears to make up for it. They're more likely to be color-blind, 16 to 1, and are especially prey to ulcers and hernias and back problems. Faced with such a list of defects, any <u>conscientious</u> manufacturer would have issued a product recall.

Why are men so puny? A century ago, the question would have made no sense. In 19th-century America, men outnumbered and outlived women. This situation presented no challenge to conventional wisdom. Women were, authorities from the Bible to Shakespeare agreed, "the weaker vessel."

God was in his heaven, all was right with the world. But in the 20th century, the trend reversed itself. Women began living longer than men, primarily because pregnancy and childbirth had become less dangerous. The gap grew steadily through the decades. In 1950, for the first time ever in the United States, females outnumbered males.

That made for some wrinkled brows. If men were so strong, why were they all dying? Part of the damage turned out to be self-inflicted.

Overall, statisticians figure that one-third of the longevity gap can be attributed to the ways men act. Men smoke more than women, drink more and take more life-threatening chances.

Men are murdered (usually by other men) three times as often as women are. Overall, they commit suicide at a rate two or three times higher than that of women. This fact holds for every age group, without exception, whether you compare teenagers or the middle-aged or the elderly. If men don't have guns or knives, they make do with cars. Men have twice as many fatal accidents per mile driven as women do. Men are more likely to drive through an intersection when the light is yellow or red, less likely to signal a turn, more likely to drive after drinking. Men drivers!

But behavior doesn't explain away the longevity gap. Women seem to have an <u>innate</u> health advantage. Even among people who have never smoked regularly, for example, the death rates from heart disease, lung cancer and emphysema are between two and four times higher for men than women.

As the '50s drew to an end, conventional wisdom finally came up with an explanation. Men's problem wasn't biology so much as a newly discovered killer called stress. Heart disease was claiming more and more male victims, and the reason, according to the new way of thinking, was that stress lurked in office buildings and corporate boardrooms, the very places men spent their days.

Breadwinning in earlier eras may have had more <u>panache</u>—slaying a lion with a spear called for a certain flair—but earning a living in the modern workplace was portrayed as just as dangerous. A popular book called "Stress and Your Heart," published in 1961, summed it all up: "It seems that being the breadwinner—whether man or woman—is a difficult job. Tension is inevitable. The job of homemaker, on the other hand, gives the woman some time—if she desires it—to relax and let some things go."

Let women be so foolish as to venture out of the home and into the line of fire, the good doctors thundered, and they would begin dying at the same rate as men. But a funny thing happened on the way to the funeral. Between 1950 and 1985, the percentage of employed women in the United States nearly doubled. Those working women, study after study has found, are as healthy as women at home. And where differences between the two groups have been reported, the advantage has gone to the working women.

The doomsayers had predicted that employed women would collapse under the stress of "role overload," as they tried to juggle work, children and homemaking. The extra stress is there, surveys confirm, but it hasn't brought ill health along with it. The reason, it seems, is that paid work provides women with feelings of self-esteem, responsibility, and camaraderie that outweigh its drawbacks. Work is no picnic—that's why they call it work—but it appears to beat staying home.

Word count: 1475

COPYRIGHT NOTICE

MARRIAGES MADE TO LAST

by Jeanette and Robert Lauer
from *Psychology Today*

Some of the difficult words in the article are listed below in the order in which they appear. In the text, these words are underlined. As you preview, look at the context in which the words are used.

trite   **incongruous**   **egalitarian**
inexorably   **catharsis**

What is the secret to a lasting marriage? What keeps married partners together? The authors of this article asked these questions of several couples who have had a long-lasting marriage. The answers may surprise you.

Americans are keenly aware of the high marital breakup in this country. More than a million couples a year now end their expectations of bliss in divorce; the average duration of a marriage in the United States is 9.4 years. The traditional nuclear family of husband, wife, and children is less and less common. Indeed, it seems at times that no one out there is happily married. But in the midst of such facts and figures, another group tends to be overlooked: those couples who somehow manage to stay together, who allow nothing less than death itself to break them up.

Social scientists have long been concerned about the causes of marital disruption. There are numerous works that tell us why people break up.

But as J.H. Wallis wrote in his 1970 book, *Marriage Observed*, "we have still not quite come to grips with what it is that makes marriages last, and enables them to survive." His conclusion remains valid. The books that tell couples how to construct a lasting and meaningful marriage tend to be based either upon the clinical experiences of those who have counseled troubled and dissolving marriages, or upon the speculations of those who believe that they have found the formula for success.

We recently completed a survey of couples with enduring marriages to explore how marriages survive and satisfy in this turbulent world. Through colleagues and students, we located and questioned 351 couples married for 15 years or more.

Of the 351 couples, 300 said they were happily married, 19 said they were unhappily married (but were staying together for a variety of reasons, including "the sake of the children"); and among the remaining 32 couples only one partner said he or she was unhappy in the marriage.

Each husband and wife responded individually to our questionnaire, which included 39 statements and questions about marriage—ranging from agreement about sex, money and goals in life to attitudes toward spouses and marriage in general. We asked couples to select from their answers the ones that best explained why their marriages had lasted. Men and women showed remarkable agreement on the keys to an enduring relationship (see list at end of article).

The most frequently named reason for an enduring and happy marriage was having a generally positive attitude toward one's spouse: viewing one's partner as one's best friend and liking him or her "as a person."

As one wife summed it up, "I feel that liking a person in marriage is as important as loving that person. Friends enjoy each other's company. We spend an unusually large amount of time together. We work at the same institution, offices just a few feet apart. But we still have things to do and say to each other

on a positive note after being together through the day."

It may seem almost <u>trite</u> to say that "my spouse is my best friend," but the couples in our survey underscored the importance of feeling that way. Moreover, they told us some specific things that they liked about their mates—why, as one woman said, "I would want to have him as a friend even if I weren't married to him." For one thing, many happily married people said that their mates become more interesting in time. A man married for 30 years said that it was almost like being married to a series of different women: "I have watched her grow and shared with her both the pain and the exhilaration of her journey. I find her more fascinating now than when we were first married."

A common theme among couples in our study was that the things they really liked in each other were qualities of caring, giving, integrity and a sense of humor. In essence, they said, "I am married to someone who cares about me, who is concerned for my well-being, who gives as much or more than he or she gets, who is open and trustworthy and who is not mired down in a somber, bleak outlook on life." The redemption of difficult people through selfless devotion may make good fiction, but the happily married people in our sample expressed no such sense of mission. Rather, they said, they are grateful to have married someone who is basically appealing and likable.

Are lovers blind to other's faults? No, according to our findings. They are aware of the flaws in their mates and acknowledge the rough times, but they believe that the likable qualities are more important than the deficiencies and the difficulties. "She isn't perfect," said a husband of 24 years. "But I don't worry about her weak points, which are very few. Her strong points overcome them too much."

A second key to a lasting marriage was a belief in marriage as a long-term commitment and a sacred institution. Many of our respondents thought that the present generation takes the vow "till death us do part" too lightly and is unwilling to work through difficult times. Successful couples viewed marriage as a task that sometimes demands that you grit your teeth and plunge ahead in spite of the difficulties. "I'll tell you why we've stayed together," said a Texas woman married for 18 years. "I'm just too damned stubborn to give up."

Some of the people in the survey indicated that they would stay together no matter what. Divorce was simply not an option. Others viewed commitment somewhat differently. They saw it not as a chain that <u>inexorably</u> binds people together despite intense misery but rather as a determination to work through difficult times. "You can't run home to mother when the first sign of trouble appears," said a woman married for 35 years.

"Commitment means a willingness to be unhappy for a while," said a man married for more than 20 years. "I wouldn't go on for years and years being wretched in my marriage. But you can't avoid troubled times. You're not going to be happy with each other all the time. That's when commitment is really important."

In addition to sharing attitudes toward the spouse and toward marriage, our respondents indicated that agreement about aims and goals in life, the desire to make the marriage succeed, and laughing together were all important.

It may seem almost trite to say that "my spouse is my best friend," but the couples in our survey underscored the importance of feeling that way.

tant. One surprising result was that agreement about sex was far down the list of reasons for a happy marriage. Fewer than 10 percent of the spouses thought that good sexual relations kept their marriage together. Is sex relatively unimportant to a happy marriage? Yes and no.

Although not many happily married respondents listed it as a major reason for their happiness, most were still generally satisfied with their sex lives. Seventy percent said that they always or almost always agreed about sex. And indeed for many, "satisfied" seems too mild a term. A woman married for 19 years said: "Our sexual desire is strong, and we are very much in love." One man said that sex with his wife was like "a revival of youth." Another noted that for various reasons he and his wife did not have sex as frequently as they would like to, but when they do "it is a beautiful act of giving and sharing as deeply emotional as it is physical."

While some reported a diminishing sex life, others described a relatively stable pattern and a number indicated improvement over time. "Thank God, the passion hasn't died," a wife said. "In fact, it has gotten more intense. The only thing that has died is the element of doubt or uncertainly that one experiences while dating or in the beginning of a marriage."

On the other hand, some couples said they were satisfied despite a less-than-ideal sex life. A number of people told us that they were happy with their marriage even though they did not have sex as frequently as they would like. Generally men complained of this more than women, although a number of wives desired sex more than did their husbands. There were various reasons for having less sex than desired, generally involving one partner's exhaustion from work or family circumstances ("We are very busy and very involved," reported a husband, "and have a teenager who stays up late. So we don't make love as often as we would like to").

Does this dissatisfaction with sex life lead to affairs? We did not ask about infidelity directly, but the high value that most of our subjects placed on friendship and commitment strikes us

as <u>incongruous</u> with infidelity. And in fact only two of those we questioned volunteered that they had had brief affairs. One husband's view might explain the faithfulness of the group: "I get tempted when we don't have sex. But I don't think I could ever have an affair. I would feel like a traitor."

Such treason, in fact, may be the one taboo in enduring relationships. A wife of 27 years said that although she could work out almost any problem with her husband given enough time, infidelity "would probably not be something I could forget and forgive." The couples in our sample appear to take their commitment to each other seriously.

Those with a less-than-ideal sex life talked about adjusting to it rather than seeking relief in an affair. A woman married 25 years rated her marriage as extremely happy even though she and her husband had had no sexual relations for the past 10 years. "I was married once before and the marriage was almost totally sex and little else," she said. "So I suppose a kind of trade-off exists here—I like absolutely everything else about my current marriage."

Many others agreed that they would rather be married to their spouse and have a less-than-ideal sex life than be married to someone else and have a better sex life. As one wife put it, "I feel marriages can survive and flourish without today's emphasis on sex. I had a much stronger sex drive than my husband and it was a point of weakness in our marriage. However, it was not as important as friendship, understanding and respect. That we had lots of, and still do."

We found some beliefs and practices among our couples that contradict what some therapists believe is important to a marriage. One involves conflict. Some marriage counselors stress the importance of expressing feelings with abandon—spouses should freely vent their anger with each other, letting out all the stops short of physical violence. According to them, aggression is a <u>catharsis</u> that gets rid of hostility and restores harmony in the marital relationship. But some social scientists argue that intense expressions of anger, resentment, and dislike tend to corrode the relationship and increase the likelihood of future aggression.

Happily married couples in our survey came down squarely on the side of those who emphasize the damaging effects of intensely expressed anger. A salesman with a 36-year marriage advised, "Discuss your problems in a normal voice. If a voice is raised, stop. Return after a short period of time. Start again. After a period of time both parties will be able to deal with their problems and not say things that they will be sorry about later."

Only one couple said that they typically yelled at each other. The rest emphasized the importance of restraint. They felt that a certain calmness is necessary in dealing constructively with conflict.

Another commonly held belief that contradicts conventional wisdom concerns equality in marriage. Most social scientists note the value of an <u>egalitarian</u> relationship. But according to the couples in our sample, the attitude that marriage is a 50-50 proposition can be damaging. One husband said that a successful marriage demands that you "give 60 percent of the time. You have to be willing to put in more than you take out." A wife happily married for 44 years said she would advise all young couples "to be willing to give 70 percent and expect 30 percent."

In the long run, the giving and taking should balance out. If either partner enters a marriage determined that all transactions must be equal, the marriage will suffer. As one husband put it, "Sometimes I give far more than I receive, and sometimes I receive far more than I give. But my wife does the same. If we weren't willing to do that, we would have broken up long ago."

Finally, some marriage experts have strongly advocated that spouses maintain separate as well as shared interests. It is important, they argue, to avoid the merging of identities. But those in our survey with enduring, happy marriages disagree. They try to spend as much time together and share as many activities as possible. "Jen is just the best friend I have," said a husband who rated his marriage as extremely happy. "I would rather spend time with her, talk to her, be with her, than with anyone else."

"We try to share everything," said another. "We even work together now. In spite of that, we often feel that we have too little time together."

We did not detect any loss of individuality in these people. In fact, they disagreed to some extent on many of the questions. Their intense intimacy—their preference for shared rather than separate activities— seems to reflect a richness and fulfillment in the relationship rather than a loss of identity. "On occasion, she has something else to do and I enjoy the time alone. But it strikes me that I can enjoy it because I know that soon she will be home, and we will be together again."

Our results seem to underscore Leo Tolstoy's observation that "Happy families are all alike." Those who have long-term, happy marriages share a number of attitudes and behavioral patterns that combine to create an enduring relationship. For them, "till death us do part" is not a binding clause but a gratifying reality.

What keeps a marriage going?

Here are the top reasons respondents gave, listed in order of frequency.

MEN

My spouse is my best friend.
I like my spouse as a person.
Marriage is a long-term
   commitment.
Marriage is sacred.
We agree on aims and goals.
My spouse has grown more
   interesting.
I want the relationship to succeed.
An enduring marriage is important
   to social stability.
We laugh together.
I am proud of my spouse's
   achievements.
We agree on a philosophy of life.
We agree about our sex life.
We agree on how and how often
   to show affection.
I confide in my spouse.
We share outside hobbies and
   interests.

WOMEN

My spouse is my best friend.
I like my spouse as a person.
Marriage is a long-term
   commitment.
Marriage is sacred.
We agree on aims and goals.
My spouse has grown more
   interesting.
I want the relationship to succeed.
We laugh together.
We agree on a philosophy of life.
We agree on how and how often
   to show affection.
An enduring marriage is important
   to social stability.
We have a stimulating exchange
   of ideas.
We agree about our sex life.
I am proud of my spouse's
   achievements.

Word count: 2496

CULTURAL VIEWPOINTS

The articles in this section, listed below, present ideas about the dynamic and unique multicultural American society.

I WANT MY SON TO BE PROUD

by Casey Kasem
from *Parade*

Some of the difficult words in the article are listed below in the order in which they appear. In the text, these words are underlined. As you preview, look at the context in which the words are used.

heritage	**sequel**	**pioneered**
ethnic	**bigotry**	**alleviated**
invariably	**hindrance**	**defamation**
Semite		

Bias in American society affects those who feel it as well as those to whom it is directed. Arab-Americans are one of many groups who regularly face subtle racism as well as obvious cases of it.

When he was 12, my son, Mike, walked into our living room and said to me, "Dad, I hate Arabs."

I was shocked. My parents' background is Lebanese. I thought I'd taught Mike to be proud of his Arab heritage. Of course, like most kids born here, he thought of himself as American, period.

I asked why he hated Arabs. Mike said it was because of what he saw in films and on TV.

As a student at Detroit's Wayne State University, I'd learned how media stereotypes can create public attitudes. But that lesson only hit me emotionally when I saw how it had affected my son's self-image. I became more aware of how traditional Arab stereotypes get full play: from Rudolph Valentino's 1921 portrayal of *The Sheik* (with its memorable line, "When an Arab sees a woman he wants, he takes her"); to bad Arabs with big swords pursuing everyone across the desert, from The Three Stooges and Hope & Crosby to Beatty & Hoffman; all the way to recent films, where Arabs appear only as terrorists. At the same time, the *positive* contributions of Arabs throughout history—and of the Arab-American community—are skipped over as if they didn't exist.

That imbalance creates racism.

Americans with Arab heritage who have contributed to our nation include innovators in science and medicine like Dr. Michael DeBakey, the pioneer heart surgeon, and Prof. Elias Corey, winner of the 1990 Nobel Prize for chemistry; entertainers like Paula Abdul and Paul Anka; political figures like John Sununu, President Bush's former chief of staff, George Mitchell, former Senate Majority Leader, and Donna Shalala, President Clinton's Secretary of Health and Human Services; and sports figures like Doug Flutie, the 1984 Heisman Trophy-winner who is now a quarterback for the Calgary Stampeders, and Rony Seikaly, the pro basketball star.

Recently, I asked prominent Americans of Arab descent how they had dealt with racism. The answers ranged from confronting it head-on to staying silent. But, in every case, they rose above it.

James Abourezk, a former Senator who heads the American Arab Anti-Discrimination Committee (ADC), confronted the racism. Abourezk, whose parents were Lebanese, was called a "damn Jew" by some people in his hometown of Wood, S.D., who knew nothing about Arabs or Lebanese.

Arab-bashing ballooned in the '70s. After the Abscam scandal, where FBI agents posed as oil sheiks to "sting" law-breaking members of Congress, outraged Arab-Americans asked for Abourezk's help. Turning down another term as Senator, he founded the ADC in 1980. The organization, which calls attention to instances of bias, today has 30,000 members in more than 70 cities. Abourezk, who once was nicknamed the "Syrian Sioux," also defends the rights of Native Americans.

"You look at the popular media," he says, "and you don't find any Arab or Arab-American portrayed in a positive light. The last one was Danny Thomas in his TV shows [in the '5Os and '60s], and then they were called Lebanese. I think the only movie where I've seen a positive Arab was Kevin Costner's *Robin Hood*. But 99.95 percent of all portrayals of Arabs are vicious. *That's* why Arab-Americans are invisible.

"We've found in ADC that some Arab-Americans have changed their names to make them sound more Anglo, because they just don't want to get in trouble," he adds. For example, F. Murray Abraham—the American-born, Oscar-winning actor (*Amadeus*)—uses an initial because, as he told one reporter, his Syrian name, Fahrid, "would typecast me as a sour Arab out to kill everyone."

Joseph Jacobs grew up in Brooklyn, where the goal was to blend in as Americans. He worried less about taunts like "camel jockey" and more about whether his mother spoke Arabic in front of his friends. Today, he says he feels lucky to have his heritage: "The ethics, pride and sense of honor I learned in my <u>ethnic</u> community were important contributors to my business career."

Businessmen and intellectuals were Jacobs' role models. He recalls that many uneducated immigrants like his dad made great successes of themselves: "'What business are you in?' was a question I <u>invariably</u> heard asked when a Lebanese came to visit us."

Jacobs became a professor of chemical engineering, but his mother insisted he'd never be a success until he went into business for himself. So, in 1947, he started a one-man consulting firm. Today, Jacobs Engineering Group, based inPasadena, is one of America's largest professional service firms—a billion-dollar international corporation.

Any racism he experienced as a youth, Jacobs says, gave him "additional incentive to *accomplish* something and get the respect of your peers." He adds, "Being accepted and respected in the American culture was a powerful motivator for me."

Candice Lightner's Lebanese-American mother was taught to "mainstream" and wouldn't teach her daughter to speak Arabic. But there was still Arabic culture at home. Lightner first experienced the pain of discrimination at 13, when a school friend's parents refused to let her visit Lightner because she was Lebanese. "I remember telling my parents and being very hurt," she says.

In 1980, after losing her daughter in a car accident caused by a drunk driver, Lightner founded MADD (Mothers Against Drunk Driving), lobbying across the nation for tougher laws. Today—2000 new laws later—"drunk driving is no longer socially acceptable," she says.

"The press would never *print* that I was an Arab-American," she asserts. "So, when I started doing live media, I'd bring it up." When Lightner protested the 1982 Israeli invasion of Lebanon, her boyfriend called her "anti-Semitic." Their relationship ended. Her non-Arab father knew better. "Honey, you *are* a Semite," he said. "That's the way I was raised," says Lightner. "We [Arabs and Jews] are all Semites."

Prejudice may have held back Fawaz "Tony" Ismail's dream of a pro football career. As a high school student in Texas, the Palestinian-American got good grades and excelled in soccer, track and weightlifting. But, for three seasons, a new coaching staff didn't start him in a football game. "I felt I was being discriminated against because my name was different," he says.

> *"You look at the popular media,"* he says, *"and you don't find any Arab or Arab-American portrayed in a positive light.... That's why Arab-Americans are invisible."*

In 1985, Ismail joined his father, selling flags on the road. Today, his Virginia-based Alamo Flag Co. is the largest retailer of flags and flag-related items in the U.S. Ismail has sold Swedish flags in Minnesota, Italian and Irish flags in New York, and flags to citizens whose ancestries reach around the globe. [In September of 1993], he supplied the Palestinian flags and lapel pins for the historic signing of the Israeli-Palestinian peace accord at the White House.

Kathy Najimy grew up in San Diego proud of *her* heritage. The actress says she thought being Lebanese "was the coolest thing to be."

One of her feminist role models was Marlo Thomas, Danny's daughter and star of *That Girl* on TV (1966-71). "She was the first actress in [television] history whose character was single, *independent*, had a job and didn't live with her parents!" says Najimy.

As an aspiring actress who wasn't built like a "Barbie doll," Najimy succeeded through comedy. She wrote and co-starred in a feminist cabaret hit, *The Kathy & Mo Show*. She played a bubbly nun in the popular film *Sister Act* and its recent sequel.

While she didn't suffer racism as a child, Najimy ran into bigotry in the late 1970s, when anti-Iranian sentiment swept the country. Technically, Iranians aren't Arabs, but it made no difference. Angered by the intellectual stupidity expressed in anti-Iranian bumper stickers, Najimy went around ripping them off cars.

People "need to have . . . someone they can feel *better* than—or hate," Najimy says. It's "sad," she adds, "because it comes from wanting to belong, to feel like part of a group."

The actress believes that all ethnic groups benefit from knowing their own heritage: "Identifying yourself as something strong and positive helps you to overcome the things that you're going to meet along the way as a woman."

Farouk El-Baz identified himself as a conservative Muslim raised in Cairo when he came to the United States in 1960 to earn a Ph.D. in geology. He soon learned that the beliefs of Egyptians about Americans were as incorrect as those of Americans about Arabs. "Americans did not really know about the Arab world—except for what was presented in the media, especially the movies," he recalls.

His accent was no hindrance when he joined America's space program in 1967. "In social settings, it even served as an icebreaker," he says. El-Baz worked on Apollo missions 8 through 17, helping to select landing sites, training astronauts in visual observations and photography, and naming features on the moon. He pioneered the use of space photography to locate groundwater and petroleum in the Earth's deserts. Today he directs Boston University's Center for Remote Sensing.

In 1971, El-Baz was interviewed for a TV special. Rick Berman, the sound man, was so impressed that in 1989, as executive producer of TV's *Star Trek: The Next Generation*, he named a shuttle craft El-Baz in the scientist's honor.

Arab-Americans are more visible today than when he was starting out, El-Baz says, but they still experience racism. "Racism originates from fear of the unknown or lack of knowledge," he says, adding that this is "usually alleviated by the spread of information on the Arab culture and its diversity."

Information is Helen Thomas' life. She fell in love with journalism in high school and has pursued it ever since.

A 50-year veteran with UPI, Thomas has covered eight Presidents and was the first woman admitted to Washington's

Gridiron Club for journalists (1975)—as well as its first woman president (1992). She alternates with the AP reporter in opening Presidential news conferences and closes them with the words, "Thank you, Mr. President."

Thomas, whose parents were Lebanese, was raised in an ethnically mixed neighborhood in Detroit and doesn't recall feeling set apart from others. Her parents were determined to be American, says Thomas. They taught her "a sense of justice, love of freedom, democracy... really cherishing and appreciating what this country had given them and their children."

Thomas rejects labels and hyphens. "I think everybody who was born here or becomes a naturalized citizen is an American, period," she says. "You shouldn't have to have a hyphen between your nationality and your ethnic background or your religion or anything else." To improve race relations today, Thomas says she would teach tolerance in the schools, from kindergarten on.

In the years since my son said he hated Arabs, I've confronted Arab <u>defamation</u>

in our society by highlighting positive contributions made by Arab-Americans. "Ask not what your country can do for you; ask what you can do for your country." Those sentiments, spoken by President Kennedy, were expressed earlier by, among others, an Arab-American philosopher and poet—Kahlil Gibran, author of *The Prophet*. He was proud of his Arab heritage *and* a champion of U.S. citizenship. Arab-Americans have reflected that sentiment ever since they first arrived, more than 100 years ago.

Word Count: 1880

[Written with the help of Jay Goldsworthy]

LOS ANGELES 2010: A LATINO SUBCONTINENT

from *Newsweek*

Some of the difficult words in the article are listed below in the order in which they appear. In the text, these words are underlined. As you preview, look at the context in which the words are used.

silhouette	invigorated	disintegration
denounced	decry	prosperity
vestige	cites	barrio
phenomenon	Hobbesian squalor	exudes
defies	criminality	entrepreneurial
demographically	cohesion	infrastructure
megalopolis	vibrancy	disparate

Hundreds of Latinos are pouring into Southern California almost daily. This author believes that these Latino immigrants will strengthen *not* weaken *the economy and social values.*

A few miles south of San Diego, along the stretch of Interstate 5 approaching the Mexican border, there's a road sign to California's future. CAUTION! it warns, and shows a silhouette of two running adults, a child scurrying along behind. Like deer or cattle elsewhere in the country, people here are a motorist's hazard. Most are illegal immigrants from Mexico, heading for jobs to the north. Because Highway 5 lies between them and their dreams, they dash across six lanes of traffic as if it were a short wade across the Rio Grande.

Farther to the south stands the Fence, a 13-mile barrier of floodlighted steel and concrete. When it went up, two years ago, the Fence was denounced worldwide as a vestige of the old world order. The Berlin wall was gone. Why need America build its own? But those who lived along the border, north or south, knew different. "It isn't meant to stop anyone," said a border guard recently, gesturing toward one short stretch of barrier and the hundred or so youths perched along its top. His job, as he described it, was merely "crowd control."

This mass migration, now so routine as to be signaled by road signs, is a phenomenon that defies change or control. Already it has transformed southern California. One in four Californians is Latino; nearly 4 million Latinos live in Los Angeles County alone. Counting illegals, they make up almost half the population. Two million more live in the neighboring counties of Orange, San Diego, Riverside and San Bernardino. These figures will quickly grow. By the year 2010, southern California will have become a Latino subcontinent—demographically, culturally and economically distinct from the rest of America.

The question is not whether this *reconquista*—"reconquest"—will take place, but how and with what consequences. Pessimists evoke visions of the 1982 film "Blade Runner": Los Angeles as an American Third World, a sprawling megalopolis of 20 million, horribly polluted and only slightly more prosperous than Tijuana. But others see a different picture: an L.A. that's an even more thriving world city than it is today, invigorated by its diversity.

Sociologists such as David Hayes-Bautista, director of UCLA's Center for the Study of Latino Health, decry the negative stereotypes that decades of illegal immigration have attached to Mexican-Americans. He cites letters to the editor of the Los Angeles Times that are full of references to the immigrant "invasion" and often express the fear that im-

poverished Mexicans will overrun the welfare rolls, swamp social services and create sprawling barrios of almost Hobbesian squalor—high in criminality, low in health, education and family cohesion. "These are myths," says Hayes-Bautista, "and they are wrong."

'Social Values'

For evidence, he offers the results of a sweeping survey of southern California's Latino population released earlier this year by UCLA. "Yes, these immigrants are poor," he says. "Yes, they are under educated." But according to Hayes-Bautista's study of Los Angeles County's various ethnic groups, Latinos are least likely to

"Latinos have thrived," says Kotkin, "because they've kept their capital and community intact."

claim public assistance. (More than a third of L.A.'s African-Americans, and 12 percent of whites, are on welfare, compared with 6 percent of Latinos.) They exhibit an extraordinary work ethic. (In 94 percent of Latino households, at least one family member—and usually everyone over 18 years of age—works full time, with most in blue-collar jobs. Those who hold a job seldom lose or leave it.) Latino families are twice as likely as Anglo and black ones to comprise a classic married couple with children. (Divorce rates are among the lowest of all ethnic groups'.) As for health, Latinos live an average of four years longer than whites and 11 years longer than blacks. They have the lowest rates of infant mortality, and the lowest incidence of strokes, heart attacks and cancer, as well as alcohol and drug abuse. "When we look at the data," Hayes-Bautista concludes, "we get a very different picture of Latino immigration. Rather than being viewed as a threat, it should be seen as strengthening our economy and social values."

Bill Clinton might have seen that for himself had he strayed several blocks east during a September campaign rally in Watts. He was appearing at an African-American community center rebuilt with government funds after the riots of '68. The immediate vicinity was upscale and modern; the surrounding neighborhoods were downtrodden and, commercially, nearly dead. That abruptly changes as you cross into adjoining Lynwood, a largely Mexican community that, official statistics say, is even poorer than Watts. There, emptiness suddenly gives way to vibrancy. Instead of one or two shops to a city block, there are three or four or 10. People crowd the streets. There are mom-and-pop *carnicerías*, Mexican *mercados*, branches of Mexico City banks, shops of every description— even motels, lighted with neon flamingos and bursting with immigrants just arrived from the south.

Why does Watts decline as its neighbor rises? The reasons range from destructive welfare policies to the disintegration of traditional families to black flight to the suburbs. Equally important, though, is what L.A. sociologist Joel Kotkin calls "the Latin community of culture and language." Latinos shop at Latino stores, consult Latino doctors, hire Latinos, read L.A.'s 37 Spanish-language newspapers and listen to its 17 Spanish radio and TV stations. "Latinos have thrived," says Kotkin, "because they've kept their capital and community intact."

The measure of prosperity can be glimpsed still farther to the east, in Santa Fe Springs, heart of the overwhelmingly Latino third of the city known as East L.A. Once a working-class barrio like Lynwood, Santa Fe Springs now exudes middle-class affluence. New cars stand outside tidy bungalows; glass-and-steel offices and business parks dot the landscape. "Welcome to the new America," says Victor Valle, a professor at California Polytechnic. Places like Santa Fe Springs, he argues, will lead southern California's demographic transformation, and not merely by weight of numbers. As traditional industries decline—defense, chemicals, heavy manufacturing—a host of small and medium-size firms are growing up to take their place. Many are Latino-owned; others are relocating to East Los Angeles in search of reliable low-cost labor. "Latinos are California's emerging entrepreneurial class," says Valle. "We are engines for growth in the 21st century."

Not everyone thinks the future will be quite so bright. Time is one problem. For most immigrants, the leap from poverty to affluence can be measured in generations rather than decades. And the facts are clear: southern California's new immigrants, however hardworking, are almost uniformly poor and undereducated. The prospect is thus a rapidly rising population coupled with sharp declines in average regional income—with obvious implications for taxes, schools and social infrastructure.

Political Power

Nor do southern California's ethnic groups easily coexist. As Latinos continue to move into traditionally African-American neighborhoods, racial tensions will rise. David Ayón, at the University of Southern California's California-Mexico Project, anticipates years of what he calls "low-intensity conflict," characterized by gang warfare, fire-bombings and, perhaps, riots similar to those of last spring. Moreover, Latinos will eventually demand—and get—political power in proportion to their numbers. Not only will they likely displace blacks, says Ayón; they will challenge Anglos and traditional elites for representation on everything from school boards and labor unions to the highest municipal offices.

That presumes another accommodation, for the Latino reconquista is less a political or economic phenomenon than a cultural one. Carlos Fuentes, the Mexican author and social historian, writes of the region's transformation in his recent book "The Buried Mirror." Mexico City and Los Angeles are the southern and northern poles of a cultural evolution, a meeting and melding of disparate civilizations. Southern California, he suggests, already beats with a "hispanic pulse," evident in the arts, popular music, language and cuisine, and the ebb and flow of L.A. life. "We should rejoice in this culture we are creating together," says Fuentes, and no doubt he is right. Besides, the multitudes flocking across Highway 5 leave very little choice.

Debunking Immigration Myths

A recent study predicts that Latinos could have a stabilizing effect on Southern California.

	Latino	Black	White
Population in LA. County	38%	11%	41%
Traditional households (two parents with children)	43%	14%	16%
Low birth-weight babies	5.3%	13%	5.5%
On welfare	6.0%	35%	12%
Males in labor force	80.6%	66.7%	76.2%
Life expectancy (in years)	79.4	68.7	75.1

Word Count: 1379

She Leads a Nation

by Hank Whittemore

from *Parade*

Some of the difficult words in the article are listed below in the order in which they appear. In the text, these words are underlined. As you preview, look at the context in which the words are used.

tenacity	exodus	procure
adversity	trudged	introspective
uncannily	articulate	

Wilma Mankiller is the first woman to become chief of the Cherokee Indian Nation. Read to see the obstacles she has overcome and some of the reasons she is considered such a good leader

"My life may be unusual, but not to the Indian world," says Chief Wilma Mankiller, 45, whose name goes back to that of a Cherokee warrior. "My ability to survive personal crises is really a mark of the character of my people. Individually and collectively, we react with a tenacity that allows us again and again to bounce back from adversity."

The first woman to become principal chief of the Cherokee Nation of Oklahoma, she speaks softly but with an undercurrent of urgency and commitment. From the Cherokee capital of Tahlequah in northeast Oklahoma's "green country," where she was born, Wilma Mankiller guides the second-largest Indian nation in the U.S. (only the Navajo Nation is larger), with a population of more than 120,000, an annual budget of $54 million and more than 800 employees spread across 7000 square miles. "It's like running a big corporation and a little country at the same time," she says with a laugh.

Today, wearing an orange blouse and purple skirt in her office at the tribal headquarters, the chief gives no sign of having had a bout with myasthenia gravis after a car accident in 1979, and while her face is puffy from medication following a kidney transplant last year, she radiates health and energy.

Chief Mankiller's rapid rise to Cherokee power—and her accomplishments in economic development, health care and tribal self-governance—already are legendary in the Native American community. She has helped develop new projects from waterlines to nutrition programs, from rural health clinics to a $9 million vocational training center.

Mankiller freely admits, meanwhile, that her people face a continuing crisis in housing, that too many Cherokee youngsters still drop out of high school, that unemployment remains about 15 percent and that decades of low self-esteem cannot be reversed overnight.

"Although we've been affected by a lot of historical factors," she insists, "nobody's going to pull us out but ourselves." In 1975, nearly all Cherokee income came from the federal government, but today more than 50 percent of the tribe's revenues are from its own enterprises, such as an electronics plant.

While leading her tribe to greater self-reliance, Mankiller draws inner strength from the values passed down to her through generations. In many ways, her own life reflects the historic struggle of the Cherokee Nation itself.

One of 11 children, Mankiller spent her earliest years on "allotted" Oklahoma land amid woodsy hills without electricity or running water.

Her full-blooded Cherokee father, who married a Dutch-Irish woman, was directly related to the tribal members who had been forcibly removed from their original homeland in the southeastern Appalachian states. That exodus in the winter of 1838-39 turned to tragedy as some of 18,000 Cherokees, suffering from hunger and disease, trudged westward and

left about 4000 dead on "the trail where they cried," later called the Trail of Tears.

"We knew about it from family stories," Mankiller says, recalling how one of her aunts had a cooking utensil from ancestors on the trail. "Later we learned how our people had left behind their homes and farms, their political and social systems, everything they had known, and how the survivors had come here in disarray—but how, despite all that, they had begun almost immediately to rebuild."

When Mankiller was 12, in 1957, her family was again relocated—in this case, by a federal program designed to "urbanize" rural Indians. Sent from the Oklahoma countryside to a poverty-stricken,

In many ways, her own life uncannily reflects the historic struggle of the Cherokee Nation itself.

high-crime neighborhood in San Francisco, they were jammed into "a very rugged" housing project. Like their ancestors, they were forced to start over.

"My father refused to believe that he had to leave behind his tribal culture to make it in the larger society," Mankiller recalls, "so he retained a strong sense of identity. Our family arguments were never personal but about some social or political idea. That stimulating atmosphere, of reading and debating, set the framework for me."

During the 1960s, Wilma Mankiller got married and had two children. She also studied sociology at San Francisco State University. In 1969, when members of the American Indian Movement took over the former prison at Alcatraz to protest the U.S. government's treatment of Native Americans, she experienced an awakening that, she says, ultimately changed the course of her life.

"I'd never heard anyone actually tell the world that we needed somebody to pay attention to our treaty rights," she explains. "That our people had given up an entire continent, and many lives, in return for basic services like health care and education, but nobody was honoring those agreements. For the first time, people were saying things I felt but hadn't known how to <u>articulate</u>. It was very liberating."

So, in the 1970s, Wilma Mankiller began doing volunteer work among Native Americans in the Bay Area. Learning about tribal governance and its history compelled her to take a fresh look at the Cherokee experience; and what she saw, in terms of broken promises and despair, made her deeply angry.

After the Trail of Tears in 1839, rebuilding by the tribe in Oklahoma proceeded with the creation of a government, courts, newspapers and schools. But this "golden era" ended with the Civil War, followed by the western land rush by settlers who devoured Cherokee holdings. In 1907, Washington gave all remaining Indian territory to the state of Oklahoma and abolished the Cherokees' right to self-government. "We fell into a long decline," Mankiller says, "until, by the 1960s, we had come to feel there was something wrong with being an Indian."

Not until 1975 did U.S. legislation grant Cherokees self-determination. As rebuilding began yet again, Mankiller's own transformation was progressing as well. In 1977, after being divorced, she returned with her children to Oklahoma.

Working in community development, Mankiller saw that the tribe's need for adequate housing, employment, education and health care was staggering. She helped to <u>procure</u> grants and initiate services; but, she says, she was still angry and bitter over conditions—not yet the calm, <u>introspective</u> woman capable of leading the Cherokee Nation.

Then, in the fall of 1979, an oncoming car collided with her station wagon. She regained consciousness in the hospital, with her face crushed, ribs broken and legs shattered. Months of recovery included a series of operations and plastic surgery on her face. Then she developed myasthenia gravis, which sent her nerves out of control. Surgery on her thymus was followed by steroid therapy. Yet, in December 1980—just over a year after the accident—she went back to work.

In a profound way, however, Wilma Mankiller was a different person. "It was a life-changing experience," she says. To sustain herself through recovery, she explains, she drew upon precepts that the Cherokee elders had taught her:

■ *"Have a good mind.* No matter what situation you're in, find something good about it, rather than the negative things. And in dealing with other human beings, find the good in them as well.

■ *"We are all interdependent.* Do things for others—tribe, family, community—rather than just for yourself.

■ *"Look forward.* Turn what has been done into a better path. If you're a leader, think about the impact of your decisions on seven generations into the future."

The same woman who had been immobilized became a bundle of energy relentlessly focused on getting things done. After she helped obtain a grant enabling rural Cherokees to build their own 26-mile waterline, male leaders took notice. By 1983, she was being asked to run for election as deputy chief. Two years after that victory, when Chief Ross Swimmer was named head of the Bureau of Indian Affairs, Mankiller became the principal chief. Then, in the 1987 election, she ran for a full four-year term, becoming the first woman elected as Cherokee chief.

"Wilma is a breath of fresh air in Indian leadership," says Peterson Zah, 58, president of the Navajo Nation and a friend. "She is a visionary who is very aggressive about achieving the goals she has in mind for her people. She truly cares about others."

As chief, Mankiller works 14-hour days filled with meetings in Tahlequah and frequent twin-engine flights to the state capital in Oklahoma City; and she is often in Washington, D.C., lobbying Congress. Her second husband, Charlie Soap, a full-blood Cherokee, keeps up a similar pace developing community programs. "We can't wait until the end of the day," Mankiller says, "to tell each other what went on."

They had long talks before Wilma decided to run for a second full term in June. Her recent kidney transplant was successful (the donor was her oldest brother, Donald Mankiller), but she has yearned to do more "hands on" work in rural communities; and there have been enticing offers to teach.

"Committing to another four years was a big decision," she says. "Basically it came down to the fact that there are so many programs in place that have been started but aren't yet finished."

On June 15—with 83 percent of the vote—Wilma Mankiller was re-elected for four years, beginning August 14.

As she starts her second term, Mankiller sees clearly the depth of problems of her own people, but her vision also includes a national agenda for all Native Americans, whose emerging leadership has heartened her.

One afternoon recently, Mankiller joined other tribal chiefs in Oklahoma City in a meeting with the governor's staff about a plan to tax Indian-owned stores. During a long discussion, Chief Mankiller kept silent; but when she finally spoke up, it was in a way typical of her strong, yet quiet leadership. "I suggest you look at existing tribal contributions to the state," she said in a soft voice, "and decide not to impose any new taxes on us. This is an opportunity for the state to begin a new day, an era of peace and friendship, with the tribes. Deciding against a tax would send a clear signal to the Indian population with long-term, positive impact."

Although the decision was left hanging and has yet to be resolved, in a single stroke Mankiller had elevated the meeting's theme. Then she was off to board a small airplane back to Tahlequah.

Flying over the lush green countryside where her people have lived for a century and a half, she could see the Cherokee Nation spread beneath her.

"We can look back over the 500 years since Columbus stumbled onto this continent and see utter devastation among our people," she says. "But as we approach the 21st century, we are very hopeful. Despite everything, we survive in 1991 as a culturally distinct group. Our tribal institutions are strong. And I think we can be confident that, 500 years from now, someone like Wilma Mankiller will say that our languages and ceremonies from time immemorial still survive."

As her plane descended, some children paused briefly to glance upward before returning to their lives and to the "new day" that Wilma Mankiller was trying to create for them.

The chief was home.

Word count: 1819

COPYRIGHT NOTICE

Ly Tong's Long Trek to Freedom

by Anthony Paul
from *Reader's Digest*

Some of the difficult words in the article are listed below in the order in which they appear. In the text, these words are underlined. As you preview, look at the context in which the words are used.

queued	**cannibalizing**	**berth**
plumeting	**genocidal vengeance**	**causeway**
yoke	**consigned**	

Many U.S. Vietnam War Veterans and Vietnamese refugees have something in common—their experiences as prisoners-of-war in Vietnam. The following story describes one man's hardships as he makes many attempts to escape.

More than one million Vietnamese—primarily "boat people" who risked the South China Sea—are estimated to have fled their country since the end of the Vietnam war in April 1975. Hundreds of thousands have died in the attempt.

For five years, former South Vietnamese jet pilot Ly Tong was an inmate of various prisoner-of-war camps. During that time he often defied his captors and risked his life in abortive escapes. Eventually he managed to flee overland, and for 17 months he walked, rode, swam and crawled through five countries. His flight has become one of the great sagas of our time.

The way his friend died convinced 27-year-old Ly Tong that he had to escape. It was visitors' day in the summer of 1975, and Ly Tong was watching as married prisoners queued for a 15-minute talk with their families waiting outside the camp's barbed-wire fence. Excited by the sight of his wife and family, his friend broke line and stepped toward the fence. A North Vietnamese guard opened fire, and Ly Tong's friend died instantly, under the eyes of his horrified family.

A couple of months later, Ly Tong and a fellow prisoner escaped from a lightly guarded wood-chopping detail. On their second evening at large, a roadblock guard demanded to see identification. Ly Tong's companion panicked and blurted out the story of their escape.

I must go alone, Ly Tong told himself as they were taken back to camp. A bachelor with both parents deceased, he was responsible only for himself. *I will turn these circumstances into a strength.*

And strength he needed immediately. Hauled before a "people's court," he was ordered to kneel as the charges were read. Ly Tong refused and was sentenced to "conex" imprisonment.

Once simple jargon for a type of freight compartment, conex has become a most feared word in Vietnamese prison vocabulary. The metal boxes are now used as solitary-confinement cells. For six months, Ly Tong existed in an eight-foot-high by 4½-foot-wide conex. Interior daytime temperatures exceeded 100 degrees Fahrenheit. At night, <u>plummeting</u> temperatures stiffened Ly Tong's limbs. Stones thrown against the conex boomed like out-of-tune drums and denied him sleep. Air, food—handfuls of rice and salt—and Ly Tong's own wastes passed through the same few holes in a side of the box.

Though he was finally released from the conex, the Communists did not forgive Ly Tong's "bad attitude." After a year, he was transferred to one of Vietnam's worst camps.

As the story of his defiance became legion, his continued refusal to kneel to his captors strengthened their resolve to break him. Guards at Camp 52 knocked him down and jeered, "Not on your knees here. On your face. How do you feel now?"

"Honorable!" Ly Tong spat back. "Six men treat me like an animal. But who is the animal, who the man?"

He was ordered to construct a scaffold and to dig a grave. "When I gut you with this knife, how happy I'll feel," one guard taunted. Eventually tiring of their sport, the guards tied Ly Tong in a <u>yoke</u> and left him in it for two weeks.

As soon as he was released from the yoke, Ly Tong began planning his next escape. To toughen himself, he put aside what meager comforts camp life provided. In cold weather he would sleep without a blanket. On the hottest day, he worked without head-covering.

Ready to Try

On July 12, 1980, at Camp A30 in Phu Khanh Province, some 240 miles northeast of Ho Chi Minh City (Saigon), he made his move. After ten days of laboriously working a nail to loosen the bar on a toilet-hut window, he crawled out and inched his way across the prison yard. With small pilfered scissors, he broke through the strands of two barbed-wire fences, and then walked all night to Tuy Hoa, the nearest big city. There a friend gave him money, and he finally hailed a bus headed for Nha Trang.

"You're from A30 prison, aren't you?" asked the conductor, spotting Ly Tong's hunted look. "Then you've got trouble. There's a control post dead ahead. Get off and walk through with a crowd of local people. They seldom check all ID cards. I'll wait for you on the road beyond."

Once in Nha Trang, Ly Tong got in touch with an old girlfriend, who furnished him with clothes, cash and a train ticket to Ho Chi Minh City.

But he had not run more than 100 yards when he heard warning shots and had to surrender.

There Ly Tong joined the new Saigon's shadow world of Vietnamese in flight from communism's controls. Until September 1981 he lived by selling fake identity cards, so desperately needed by "shadows" like himself. A plan to escape in a boat fell through. Then a new idea formed: *I'm a pilot. Why not steal a plane?*

Ly Tong had once been based at Tan Son Nhut airport. But when he penetrated the base, he found no suitable aircraft. Cut off from U.S.-made spare parts, Vietnamese mechanics had kept only a handful of planes in the air by <u>cannibalizing</u> those on the ground.

Reluctantly, Ly Tong concluded that he must escape overland. With just 150 dong ($7.50 on the black market), he took a bus to the Kampuchean (Cambodian) border, where he crossed by foot on smugglers' tracks.

The country in which Ly Tong would spend the next five months had endured a bloody five-year civil war ending in 1975, followed by some three years of <u>genocidal vengeance</u> by Communist Pol Pot's victorious forces and invasion by Vietnam in 1978-79. Although the Vietnamese occupation army had pacified main population centers and most highways, guerrilla war still raged in much of the countryside.

"Catch Him!"

Roadblocks constantly halted travelers, but as long as Ly Tong was on foot or in a crowded bus, he was relatively safe. It was in a bus that he reached Phnom Penh, the national capital.

There he bought a train ticket to Batdambang, close to the Thailand border, but a Kampuchean station guard took a second look at him. Once again, Ly Tong was under arrest.

The police locked him in a small room. Outside the door a guard settled with a machine gun and a guitar. As the Kampuchean plucked out a tune, Ly Tong squeezed through the small, solitary window. But he had not run more than 100 yards when he heard warning shots and had to surrender.

This time he was handed to the Vietnamese police, who threw him into Phnom Penh's 7708 jail, a notorious prison camp. In a few weeks, he was told, he would be transported back to Vietnam.

By now, however, Ly Tong had confidence in his jail-breaking ability. Here the weakest spot was his dormitory window, a wooden frame with six iron bars. Before dawn one morning, with guards drowsing, he tested the bars. After three hours of tugging—and using the first-freed bar as a lever—the last bar came loose. Ly Tong crawled through.

For the next four months, he moved northwest across Kampuchea, following the mighty Mekong River. At one river village near Kampong Chhang, he worked for three months clearing fishing traps and earned about 1500 riels ($75 on the black market)—enough for a bicycle, food, and clothes. Then it was time to move north again.

The jungle and rice paddies surrounding Sisophon, the last major town on Ly Tong's route to Thailand, harbor one of Asia's nastiest guerrilla wars. To avoid danger, Ly Tong carted his bicycle into the jungle. Reaching a river, he asked some fishermen to help him cross, but they shook their heads.

Their unfriendliness bothered Ly Tong—and for good reason. Suddenly, an armed Kampuchean soldier on a motorbike barred his way. "So you're the man with the bike and the funny accent," he said. "Follow me!" As they passed a dense section of jungle, Ly Tong leaped from his bike and scrambled into the undergrowth. The soldier opened fire, missed, and then roared off in search of help.

The Phantom

Now in his path lay many creeks and large ponds. So often was he forced to strip for a swim that after a while he went naked, holding his clothes in a bag on his head. His strange appearance may have saved him. As he walked along a riverbank, he saw four young soldiers coming his way, speaking Vietnamese. Unable to avoid them, he crouched beside the water. When they spotted him, he leaped into the air with an unearthly yell: "WHOOOOO!" Though armed, the youths fled.

Ly Tong ran in the opposite direction—straight into a Vietnamese camp! All around him stood two-story huts housing sleeping soldiers. He could hear soldiers scouring the riverbank for a "phantom." By inching himself on his stomach through the darkness, he finally cleared the compound.

After walking for several more hours, he thought: *By now, Thailand must be very close, probably under my feet already.* With the sunrise came a feeling of elation until he spotted a camouflaged sniper on a platform high in a tree. *I haven't crossed the border.* And ahead lay great danger: mines.

From his mine-clearing labors as a prisoner, he remembered that the Hanoi army is taught to place small anti-personnel mines wherever a man might take cover: beside a tree trunk or boulder, under a bush. *Avoid cover,* he told himself. *And move only by night.*

For two days Ly Tong hadn't eaten. There was no water. Half-crazed by thirst, he lost track of time. Then, suddenly, he heard the sound of barking. For more than seven years of famine, Kampucheans had been eating their dogs. *Dogs mean a food surplus,* he reasoned. *This must be Thailand!*

And it was. Creeping to within earshot of a peasant's hut, he could hear a language that was neither Kampuchean nor Vietnamese. Following the sound of traffic to a highway, he waved down a passing motorcyclist and asked to be taken to the Red Cross.

Into Prison

But Ly Tong's troubles were not over. To deter an endless stream of refugees, and because Hanoi often "seeds" new waves of refugees with subversives, Thai police first jail and interrogate border-crossing Indochinese. For ten months, despite repeated protests and a hunger strike, Ly Tong was kept in prison in the Thai border town of Aranyaprathet. Finally, his story reached United States consular officials in Singapore, who confirmed Ly Tong's air force service.

Instead of passage to the United States, however, Ly Tong was <u>consigned</u> by a Thai colonel, whom he had offended during one of his protests, to a sprawling refugee settlement at Nong Samet, on the Kampuchean side of the border. It was time, yet again, to escape.

For months Ly Tong had been studying English and questioning refugee-relief workers about conditions in countries west and south of Aranyaprathet. Now he planned to escape across south Thailand and Malaysia to Singapore—perhaps 1,400 miles and three more borders.

On February 1, 1983, Ly Tong climbed over his camp's fence, picked his way through a minefield, swam five creeks, pushed through jungle and headed for Aranyaprathet, 15 miles to the southwest.

The next morning, however, at the first Thai roadside checkpoint, he ignored an order to halt, and the soldiers began shooting. He managed to race ahead of them to a field where he hid in a clump of tall grass. Some minutes later, he heard soldiers run up and then the sound of a cigarette lighter, as one of them tried to set fire to the grass.

For 15 years Ly Tong had not wept. Now, crying softly to himself, he began to pray. *With your help I have come so far. If I am no longer worthy, kill me now! Don't let me fall into enemy hands.* When the grass failed to catch fire, the soldiers finally walked away. *I believe in God,* Ly Tong told himself. *I cannot die anymore.*

The next day Ly Tong reached the house of a young woman he had met when she visited the Nong Samet settlement. Despite the risk to her own life, she had offered help, and now the pair set out for Bangkok by bus, passing themselves off as husband and wife. At the Bangkok railroad station, she handed him money for a train heading south.

Ly Tong left the train at Hat Yai, Thailand's southernmost large town, reasoning that it would be better to cross the border on foot than to face guards and immigration officials at the regular checkpoint. He followed the railroad tracks until night fell and he saw lights, trucks, uniforms. *The Malaysian border!*

Giving the immediate area wide <u>berth</u>, he detoured through the jungle and, doubling back to the highway, saw the sun rise on Kanger, the first town inside the border.

Ly Tong had no trouble catching a bus to Kuala Lumpur, and then another to his last border, Malaysia-Singapore. At about 8 p.m., the bus reached the checkpoint at the Malaysian end of the <u>causeway</u> to

Singapore, across the Jonore Strait. Ly Tong slipped away into the darkness and walked about two miles west along the seaside.

Winds whipped the channel. Tying his clothes in a bundle on his back, he entered the water. Singapore's lights beckoned, and at the halfway point of the nearly two-mile swim came a fresh surge of energy. Soon there was sand beneath his feet.

After a few hours' sleep in a seaside park, Ly Tong made his way to the United States embassy. "I'm a Vietnamese," he explained to an official, "and I've just swum the Strait from Malaysia."

"In last night's weather?" said the American. "Impossible."

It was February 10, 1983. Behind Ly Tong were almost 2,000 miles of land and water, five countries, four border crossings, a half-dozen escapes from custody.

"If you've got a moment," said Ly Tong, "Let me tell you my story...."

Reader's Digest Editor's Note: After six months in a refugee-processing center, Ly Tong flew to the United States. He is now living in Texas and has just finished a book about his escape. He hopes to qualify soon for a scholarship to study political science, "to prepare me for the day my country is free again."

Word count: 2374

BEYOND BLACK AND WHITE

by Tom Morganthau

Some of the difficult words in the article are listed below in the order in which they appear. In the text, these words are underlined. As you preview, look at the context in which the words are used.

divisive	spurious	legitimizing
mayhem	ceded	endemic
searing	demagogues	elusive
multiethnic	retrograde	societal norms
mosaic	fixated	ambivalent
subsumed	disentangle	bombard
depict	ethnicity	enigma
relic		

The riots in Los Angeles left many people wondering, "How can people of different races and cultures survive in the 21st century?" Read to learn this author's suggestions.

Out of the ashes, Los Angeles began the hard task of rebuilding its future. One of the century's deadliest riots left deep scars on the face of the city—and the soul of the nation. In all the debate that followed, one thing became clear: the country must find new ways of thinking and talking about the <u>divisive</u> questions of race, crime and leadership.

Most Americans see the terrible events in Los Angeles as an unwanted flashback to the 1960s—to the civil-rights movement, the riots of 1965 and 1968 and to what we then saw, accurately, as the inevitable crisis of race in America. Once again, young blacks are taking to the streets to express their outrage at perceived injustice and once again, whites are fearful that The Fire Next Time will consume *them*. Looting, arson and mindless <u>mayhem</u> fill our television screens with <u>searing</u> images: we can only wonder whether the nation will ever move beyond what the Kerner Commission described as two societies, separate and unequal, one black, the other white.

The short answer is, we already have—for better or worse. The most important facts about the riots of 1992 are that upwards of 30 million African-Americans did *not* take to the streets, and that those who did are clearly part of a relatively small urban underclass that is now as distinct from the black middle class as it is from the white middle class. The devastated hopes of L. A.'s Korean-immigrant community, meanwhile, are a powerful reminder that the nation is rapidly moving toward a <u>multiethnic</u> future in which Asians, Hispanics, Caribbean islanders and many other immigrant groups compose a diverse and changing social <u>mosaic</u> that cannot be described by the old vocabulary of race relations in America. The race crisis of the 1960s has been <u>subsumed</u> by the tensions and opportunities of the new melting pot: the terms "black" and "white" no longer <u>depict</u> the American social reality.

It follows that much of the sputtering national debate over race is outdated, too. It is arguable, for example, that the very concept of race itself is a <u>relic</u> of our bitter past—a throwback to the days of slavery and Jim Crow, and a scientifically <u>spurious</u> rationale for keeping African-Americans down. The truth is, there is no such thing as "black." Why, exactly, should the child of an interracial couple be identified only as "black"? Why not brown or tan—or white? Why do we persist in categorizing people as white, black, Asian and Hispanic? "Hispanic" is a meaningless term that lumps together a bewildering array of nationalities and ethnic groups. "White," obviously, plays to our national obsession with skin color and refers to people of European descent. But it does not define a race, and the now un-

fashionable term "Caucasian" (or, more accurately, "Caucasoid") in fact refers to a far-flung Indo-European ethnic group that includes millions of dark-skinned

...we are likely to become both more diverse, and more nearly like each other, as time goes by.

people. Like it or not, we Americans are a hyphenated, intermarrying and increasingly blended people—and we are likely to become both more diverse, and more nearly like each other, as time goes by.

Or take poverty and crime, two bitterly divisive subjects that many Americans believe to be race-related. Blacks have no monopoly on crime and poverty, and they never did. Why did we allow the debate on these issues to become intertwined with race? Liberals, too fearful of seeming to be racist, have <u>ceded</u> the crime issue to hard-liners and <u>demagogues</u>, a departure from courage and common sense that has allowed some politicians to turn legitimate fears about crime into <u>retrograde</u> anxieties about race.

The poverty debate, similarly, has in many respects become a coded discussion of race. Some liberals, <u>fixated</u> by the problem of historic discrimination, insist that poverty will not disappear until all barriers to opportunity are removed, a contention that is plainly undercut by the fact that about 40 percent of all African-American families can now be classified as middle class or upwardly mobile working class. Others think poverty is nothing more than the lack of money or jobs, a belief that is instantly refuted by the hard-won success of new immigrants like the Koreans. "I hear black people say Koreans and Vietnamese and other Asians have an easier time getting grants from the government," says Edward Lee, 34, a Korean-born shop owner in Atlanta. "I know nobody who gets this free money. . . When my family came here we had nothing. We worked our ass off to get where we are."

Like Lee, we have no real choice but to try to <u>disentangle</u> this infinitely sensitive, infinitely complicated subject—to separate, as best we can, the residual problems of race and <u>ethnicity</u> from the problems of crime, poverty and despair that so frustrate public policy and public discourse. That racism and race friction still exist is undeniable. But neither can any longer be taken as a <u>legitimizing</u> rationale for violence, crime or the <u>endemic</u> problems of the urban poor. Those problems—all of them—are the result partly of the increasing concentration of poverty in the nation's cities and partly of an accelerating breakdown in the value structure that made American the least class-ridden, and most optimistic society in the world. We all share the blame for this, as citizens, taxpayers and voters who supported and approved the spectacular lack of political leadership of the past two

decades. But sharing the blame does not tell us how to proceed.

Finding the right answers will require us to suspend belief in fashionable myths and to think without stereotypes. We tend to believe, for example, that the nation's cities now house a growing and increasingly violent underclass that is majority-black. We recite alarming statistics about black-on-black crime and the number of black children born out of wedlock. We accept the consensus verdict that low-income black Americans are reluctant to accept easily found (though admittedly low-paying) jobs. But hard facts about the urban underclass are maddeningly <u>elusive</u>. Estimates of its size vary from about 2 million to about 8 million persons; no one knows with precision how many of these people are African-American or whether the number of underclass blacks is rising or falling. What seems clear, if only because so many experts agree on it, is that black poverty and crime are somehow associated with a breakdown in <u>societal norms</u>. As a result, we now believe government must teach the values of work, thrift, marriage and personal responsibility to millions of resisting subjects.

We should look to ourselves first—for most Americans are deeply <u>ambivalent</u> about these homely virtues, and the poor receive a steady diet of mixed messages from society at large. We say, for example, that the rise in single-parent families is a key to hard-core poverty. But divorce and single-parenting are epidemic in American society, and no one wants to restrict the right of middle-class adults to break off failing marriages. We say inner-city kids should avoid the fast money that can be made by selling drugs, but we <u>bombard</u> them with advertising for clothes and shoes and high-priced trinkets. We crack down on street crime, while most of the crooks who looted the nation's savings-and-loan industry go unpunished. Solving the <u>enigma</u> of urban poverty is an issue that should be high on the national agenda, and the new gospel of family values and personal responsibility is clearly part of the solution. But reviving the power of the American dream would be much easier if we practiced what we preach.

Word Count: 1270

WHEN MISS AMERICA WAS ALWAYS WHITE

by Navita Cummings James

Some of the difficult words in the article are listed below in the order in which they appear. In the text, these words are underlined. As you preview, look at the context in which the words are used.

refuted	masonry	milieu
treachery	siblings	overt
roulette	profanity	covert
folly	stereotypes	metaphorical
lynchings	treacherous	definitive
castrating	dialectic	

What beliefs and stereotypes do you have about Black people? About White people? This author talks about the stories she heard as she was growing up that helped shape her beliefs.

Family Stories

The telling of family stories not only informs children about their past, but also passes on family values and helps prepare them to live in the world beyond the family. I was born in 1952 in Columbus, Ohio. One of the duties of my parents in the 1950s and 1960s was to help prepare my sister and me for a world that would attempt to put limitations on what we could achieve because of our race. Our family always <u>refuted</u> the dominant culture's message of what it meant to be "colored" or "Negro." Race was a frequent topic of discussion in our family, especially among the adults.

The most vivid race-related stories of my youth were about the <u>treachery</u> and violence of White men, how Whites could get away with any crime committed against Black[1] people. These stories led me to believe that Black life was not highly valued by White people and that, in the eyes of White society, Black women had no virtue worth respecting or protecting.

The single most upsetting story I can recall, related to me by an aunt, happened to a young Black girl in Georgia in the 1920s. Two young school girls were walking down a road and met a drunken White man carrying a gun. He pulled one of the girls aside, put the gun in her mouth, and began to play a form of Russian <u>roulette</u>. One of the chambers was loaded, and he blew the back of the girl's head off. I expected my aunt to say that the man was punished and sent to jail. But *nothing* happened to him. Instead, White people felt pity for the man because he was drunk and had to witness his own <u>folly</u>, rather than for the murdered child and her family. I remember my horror that such a man could get away with killing a little Black girl *like me*.

The story taught me that White men were violent and not to be trusted. Other stories I heard about <u>lynchings</u> only served to reconfirm this for me. I was horrified when I learned about the practice of <u>castrating</u> Black men during lynchings and placing their genitals in their mouths or in jars to be displayed in community stores as trophies or warnings.

The other family stories I vividly recall were about the Cummings family from my father's side and the Pearson family from my mother's.

The Cummings Family

According to my father, my great-grandfather "Gramps" was a slave in his youth and always carried the scars of the beatings he received as a child. One of the stories I recall was about Gramps' mother. She was the child of a slave woman and a White Virginia plantation owner. Apparently she resembled her father so much that the owner's wife became upset and had the child sold off. Because of her father's betrayal, the child hated Whites so intensely that she married the darkest man she could find.

There were several interesting stories about Gramps himself. At the age of 16 he was freed from slavery. As an adult he became a land owner in Laurens County, Georgia. He learned to read and passed his love of reading on to his children and grandchildren. He gave his daughters an education so they would not have to work in "Miss Anne's"[2] kitchen, and he gave his sons land. Gramps was one of the first people in his county to own a car. As the story goes, the Whites did not like the idea of a Black man owning a car when the vast majority of Whites could not afford them. So Gramps had to carry a shotgun with him to protect himself from jealous Whites.

The stories about Gramps and his family reinforced what I had been told about the evil of White men. I was shocked that a father would sell his own flesh and blood. As I grew up, I came to believe that being White was nothing to be proud of and that the light skin color of some Blacks (including myself) was a badge of shame. It seemed to me that Whites would resort to any means—even murder—to keep Blacks beneath them.

I later learned other families in the Black community educated their women so that daughters would not have to work in the homes of Whites. This strategy helps to explain, in part, why Black women often had more education than Black men and why this difference did not create tension in the Black community.

My father's stories about his own life also influenced me. Among the most vivid were those of his experiences during World War II. My father was a Tuskeegee Airman. He was very proud to have been part of a U.S. Army experiment to test whether Black men were intelligent enough to fly airplanes. The Tuskeegee Airmen units that ultimately served in Europe and North Africa had one of the most distinguished records of the war. After the war, however, Black pilots were not hired by the airlines unless, perhaps, they were interested in being janitors.

Some of the most painful memories of my childhood revolve around my father's business. Since he couldn't get a job as a civilian pilot, he fell back on skills he learned as a boy in Georgia—masonry and carpentry—and started his own contracting business. But racial discrimination followed him here as well. My father often complained that when Whites contracted with him, they would pay him less than what they paid the White contractors for the same work. Even after he finished the work, some would not pay him for weeks or months. However, I began to notice that not all Whites were alike. Jews seemed to be different. They would pay for quality regardless of whether a Black or White man did the work. At least they were more likely to hire and less likely to delay payment.

Perhaps the most important lesson I learned from my father's stories, that would later be reflected in my own life and the lives of my children, was the idea that many Whites fail to see the talents and accomplishments of Black people—even when the evidence is right before their eyes.

The Pearson Family

The stories about Whites from my mother's family were less violent and shocking. Nat Pearson, my grandfather, was also a land owner. He lived in Wheeler County, Georgia. According to my mother, Whites respected "Mr. Nat" and his children. He was a hard-working and fair man. His wife was also respected in the community. She took food to the sick and the poor, Black or White, in addition to taking care of her nine children.

The Pearson family emphasized the importance of getting a college education. My mother and her eight siblings all attended college and earned degrees. (In my generation it was just expected that all 26 of us would earn at least *one* college degree.) In my mother's generation, the older children helped the younger ones through college by providing financial support. The family stuck together, helping one another. That was very important.

My mother emphasized different things than my father did when she talked about race. For example, she stressed how my grandmother helped poor Whites. My mother did not believe in any way that Blacks were inferior to Whites. She was very proud of her family, and there was no false humility here. However, as the mother of daughters, she did give us one race-related warning: "There is only one thing a White man wants from a Black woman." She warned that Black women should be wary of White men, because, in the event of rape, the White man would probably go unpunished. We should never think of marrying a White man, because, according to her, a Black woman's virtue meant nothing to Whites.

My Pearson cousins were another source of information about race. While I was going to racially integrated schools

> *The most vivid race-related stories of my youth were about the treachery and violence of White men, how Whites could get away with any crime committed against Black people.*

in the North, most of them attended segregated schools in the South. I was amazed that they had all Black teachers, just as they were amazed that mine were all White.

My cousins and their friends loved to tease and tell jokes. They sometimes used <u>profanity</u> just out of hearing distance of the adults. During one of our visits to Georgia, I learned an interpretation of the origin of the word "motherfucker." They said it was used by the African slaves in the Old South to describe White men who raped their African slave mothers.

Beliefs and Stereotypes of My Youth

From these significant stories of my youth emerged a set of beliefs and <u>stereotypes</u> which provided a backdrop for my own lived experience. These beliefs and stereotypes about Blacks and Whites can be summarized as follows:

Black People

■ Black people are "just as good" as White people—and in some ways (e.g., morally) better.

■ Black people are just as smart and capable as White people, if not more so.

■ Black people should always be prepared to fight for fair treatment from Whites.

■ Black people have to be twice as good as Whites to be considered half as good.

White People

■ White people are often violent and <u>treacherous</u>.

■ White people probably have some kind of inferiority complex which drives them to continually "put down" Blacks and anyone else who is not White.

■ White men often rape Black women. If they say they love a Black woman, they are doing so to gain sexual favors. A White man would never marry a Black woman.

■ Most White people do not want to see Blacks rewarded for their abilities and accomplishments.

■ Most Whites, especially Northerners, cannot be trusted. They can hardly ever be a real friend to a Black person.

■ White men are usually arrogant. White women are usually lazy.

■ There are some good White people, but they are the exceptions.

These childhood beliefs and stereotypes, however, did *not* become an intellectual prison of my self-identity or beliefs about Whites. Below, I address how these beliefs and stereotypes blended with my own experiences. From this dialectical interaction, my racial identity emerged.

The Dialectic of Family Stories, Culture, and Identity

Earlier, I suggested that the construction of personal identity is a dialectic between self and culture. In some circumstances, families may reinforce the messages of the dominant culture, but as we have seen in my case, my family's messages ran counter to it. The social-cultural milieu of the integrated North in the 1950s was rife with overt and covert messages about Blacks. Whites often pretended that there was no prejudice in the North. Yet the dominant culture portrayed Black people as stupid, lazy, dirty, dishonest, ugly—and invisible. We were unwelcome in many public places, even if it was legal for us to be there. If my self-image had relied solely on the messages of the dominant culture, I might have grown up with low self-esteem and seen no value in being Black.

Instead, my family's stories gave me pride in my people and in myself. They encouraged me to reject the dominant culture's scripts and embrace those from my family and the Black community that said I was a person of value and worth. The stories became a sort of metaphorical shield that protected me from the larger, hostile culture. In high school, I learned that there were many times I did not need the shield, e.g., with some of my White schoolmates. But I also learned that, because racism is a constant feature of our culture, I would be a fool to ever throw that shield away.

Moreover, I had to revise my stereotyped ideas about Whites and Blacks— hence about myself. For example, I learned that race was not a good predictor of violence—gender was; and that race was not a good predictor of intelligence— income and opportunities were. I further came to believe that all people, regardless of color, deserve to be treated with dignity and respect. We are all equal in God's eyes and in principle in American cultural mythology. Finally, I learned that prejudice existed on both sides of the color line, but sometimes for different reasons.

Through this dialectical process, my beliefs and stereotypes changed and evolved. I made definitive choices about how I would relate to others. Unlike some Blacks who preferred to socialize only with Blacks, I chose to have friends of diverse backgrounds, including Whites.

I am now the mother of two girls. What is the role of family stories related to race in *my* family? I have already had to reassure my four-year-old that "brown" people are good and beautiful. I have stressed the importance of reading and education in our family—values which span generations. And I have passed along my parents' stories, along with my own experiences. For example, I have told my twelve-year-old how as children my sister and I used to run excitedly into the living room whenever there was someone Black on TV. In the 1950s, it was a rare occurrence to see someone Black on TV. And I told her how beauty pageants such as the Miss America Pageant celebrated only European standards of beauty, so Miss America was always White.

In the course of my daughters' childhoods, Black women have finally been crowned Miss America. But when I was a child, I secretly yearned for a Black Miss America. To me that would have been a sign that our culture was learning to value Black women—that we could be viewed as beautiful, smart, and virtuous.

As I grew up, I fantasized about what my life might have been like were race not such a socially significant construct in the United States: after World War II my father would have been hired as a commercial airline pilot and our family would have flown the world for free. I would have been able to afford the Ivy League school I could not attend for lack of funds. I would have studied in Paris, become an anthropologist/pilot, and gone to Africa. . . .

As for Miss America? I would have been too busy traveling to have cared about her.

NOTES

[1]The use of the upper case "B" in the word "Black," when Black refers to African Americans, is a convention dating back to the 1960s and is still currently utilized by some writers. In the late 1960s and early 1970s, the common usage of the word "Negro" changed to "black." However, since black referred to a people and not just a color, some writers thought the upper case "B" in Black seemed more appropriate and dignifying. (Some of these writers also adopted the equivalent use of the upper case "W" when referring to Whites.) Also, since terms used to describe other ethnic and racial groups utilized upper case first letters, for the major descriptor for Black to appear with a lower case "b" seemed an unfortunate, yet grammatically correct, way to reinforce the stereotypical view of Blacks as less important. Black writers using this convention recognized the subtle power of language and that rules of language and grammar are arbitrary and evolve over time. These writers chose to take an active role in promoting what they viewed as a useful change.

[2]"Miss Anne" is an unflattering term referring to White women.

Word Count: 3309

COPYRIGHT NOTICE

WHEN MISSISSIPPI CHINESE TALK

by Gwendolyn Gong

Some of the difficult words in the article are listed below in the order in which they appear. In the text, these words are underlined. As you preview, look at the context in which the words are used.

enigma	snippet	fray
assimilated	linguistically	estrangement
ilk	phenomenon	coyly
complementary	inauspiciousness	juncture
valorize	reverence	saunters
defunct	queried	culinary
milieu	engendered	self-effacing
populace	invoke	sumptuous
epitomized	auspicious	auspicious
Southern Genteelism	prejudicial	reminisces
rhetorical	broaching	alluding
deference	demeaned	divulgence
deftly	espousing	ruminate
felicitously	bravado	construed
reciprocate	KKK and NAACP	embodiment
acquiescence	mete out	

A group of Chinese people born in the Mississippi Delta area refer to themselves as Mississippi Chinese (MC). The author, a Mississippi Chinese, writes about the sound of her speech and the way that she and other MC express ideas.

As an undergraduate at the University of Mississippi during the early 1970s, I can recall thinking about how I spoke and how I sounded to others. When I went to graduate school in Indiana, my Hoosier peers and professors saw me as some sort of enigma—an oddity. They would joke, "The picture's fine but adjust the sound." This same type of remark followed me to Texas, where indeed another version of English is spoken. "Adjust the sound." What did that mean? Hadn't these folks ever encountered a Mississippian before? The truth was that they had. But I was different. I was a Mississippi Chinese.

Though my family heritage traces back to an ancestral village in Canton, China, I am a Chinese American, born and reared in the Mississippi Delta. Since the late 1800s, this lush farming area has served as a homeland for approximately 1200 Cantonese Chinese from Southern China who have gradually assimilated into being Southerners of another ilk: Mississippi Chinese (MC). As a consequence, the MC represent a melding of primarily Confucian and Southern Genteel cultures, distinct yet powerfully complementary in terms of thought and action. For example, despite the apparent geographic and physical European-versus-Asian or Western-versus-Eastern contrasts, both cultures valorize the past, family, elders, traditions, secular rituals, land, business, hospitality, and propriety. And it is this mutuality of values, along with an unyielding emphasis on education, that has allowed the MC to adapt successfully in the Mississippi Delta, not only surviving but flourishing in a place lost in time, a place time has lost.

My family operated a general store in Boyle, a small, dusty town located on Main Street. This location—like most everything in the Delta— represented for us a strange and wonderful cross-cultural intersection. Our store sat in close proximity to the Post Office, City Hall, and the defunct Fire Station and Depot—landmarks that suggested the Caucasian milieu of the plantation South. Our business was also tightly sandwiched between two dirt and gravel alleys where most of the

African Americans in town lived. Thus, my family and I were situated in the middle of a populace whose convictions, behaviors, and social and linguistic conventions epitomized Southern Genteelism. It is from this perspective that I now write about the communicative interactions of the MC with others and among themselves.

In my experience, one of the most interesting ways by which I have observed how Southern Genteelism and Confucianism reveal themselves is in the talk of the MC. A major rhetorical feature that typifies MC speech is deference, the courteous yielding to others, which may manifest itself in two forms: accommodation (i.e., making the non-MC speaker feel comfortable and welcome) and topic shifting (i.e., changing the subject of the conversation). Ironically, accommodation that may provide comfort for the non-MC listener may, on occasion, result in discomfort for the MC speaker; conversely, topic shifting oftentimes provides relief and control for the MC speaker but frustration for the non-MC listener. As an MC, I know that the discomfort and frustration which non-MC listeners may experience is very recognizable by MC listeners. As an in-group participant in this communicative act, I find myself keenly aware of the MC speaker's conversational shifts, which are designed to manage the conversation and my level of involvement in it, no matter how deftly and graciously these rhetorical strategies are executed. My recognition of the linguistic turns enables me to interact felicitously and reciprocate with my own conversational deference: accommodation. For non-MC speakers and listeners, understanding how deference operates among the MC helps to provide a more effective, informed exchange between these two groups.

Deference and Accommodation

Deference refers to the submission or <u>acquiescence</u> to the opinion, wishes, or judgment of another speaker. The courteous yielding of the floor results in an MC accommodating the topic designated by a speaker, whether or not it may be interesting, logical, tasteful, or pertinent. Part of the motivation of this act may be to seek approval, to demonstrate respect, to allow others to perceive that they are respected or even "superior" to the speaker, or simply to cooperate and not "make waves."

Most of the time, accommodating others' topics in conversations can be quite easy, mutually satisfying, and pleasant. I recall customers like Mr. Schaefer (the town sheriff, who insisted we call him "Uncle Charlie") and Preacher (an African American Southern Baptist lay minister), who would stop in the store at supper time to pick up groceries and chat with my father about the weather and fishing.

"How hot was it today, anyhow?" Uncle Charlie would ask Daddy, chomping on his King Edward cigar. "Summers are gittin' hotter every year, don't ya think?"

Daddy would reply, "It was a scorcher, all right. But I didn't see no monkeys dancin'. Now that's when I know it's really hot."

"Monkeys dancin'. Yep, that'd be mighty hot, hell yeah," the sheriff would agree.

Then Preacher would break in, "Good thing we wasn't on the lake in this heat, though. The water's probably so hot the fish ain't bitin'—they just put out a sign sayin' 'Out to lunch' or some such."

They would all laugh and lean on the counter top, while my mother or I totaled their bill, took their money, and sacked their groceries. The chit-chat would end at this point, everyone feeling as if an enjoyable conversation had taken place and that something significant had been said.

As I reconsider this <u>snippet</u> of talk, I realize now it was more than mindless chatter and mere politeness. These three men, all of different races, professions, ages, and socio-economic backgrounds, were interacting socially and <u>linguistically</u>. The Caucasian sheriff initiated the talk and the subject, and my MC father accommodated him, as did the African American minister. This exchange illustrates deference and accommodation in its purest form as both a Confucian and Southern Genteel <u>phenomenon</u>. The MC speaker, as well as the Southern non-MC preacher, courteously participated and played the linguistic game, partly out of respect for the sheriff, partly out of a code of social etiquette—convention or propriety—and partly out of their own genuine interest in the topic and their ability to communicate as equals in this informal rhetorical situation.

While this example of deference is one in which all participants—MC and non-

MC alike—accommodated one another and felt "at home" with the conversation, this is not always the case. For MC, certain topics or types of discussion are simply inappropriate, in both an MC to MC as well as non-MC to MC context. Topics such as death (especially a violent one), terminal illness, and sex are seen as particularly personal and private. MC subscribe to the notion that living things,

> *While food-talk is not the focus of this essay, it is such an unquestionably important subject to all Chinese that it deserves further mention here.*

good fortune, and happiness should never be intermixed with the dead, bad luck, or inauspiciousness in either their conversations or their activities. Consequently, in my parents' home, my mother would never place a photograph of my deceased older brother, Dwight Arnold, among other family pictures of the living. In fact, until I was six years old, I never knew I even had another brother, for Arnold was never talked about.

My first memory of Arnold was when I noticed his name on a headstone at the cemetery the day our family went to "bow

three times in silence" to pay honor and respect to our ancestors. Though his bronzed baby shoes and faded snapshots were treated with reverence, I later learned, these reminders of him were segregated from all other items that families typically display—reunion and wedding pictures, annual school photos, trophies, awards, baby books, and so on. Even in my siblings' and my own home, no picture of Arnold is displayed. I keep my photographs of him in a filing cabinet drawer, along with the portraits of my father's deceased parents. Moreover, I have never queried my parents about the brother I never knew. To accommodate myself about this topic would have caused them great pain and discomfort. Even writing about this now is troubling for me and would be unsettling for my family, were they to read these words. As this clearly illustrates, the MC valorize the family, the past, and secular rituals in very specific, often nonverbal ways.

That example shows how I, an MC speaker, could have engendered discomfort for other MC listeners, such as my parents, in order to satisfy my own need to know. Instead, I understood the delicate nature of death and the need to respect my elders, as well as family, ritual, and MC's tendency to accommodate others; thus, I refused to invoke the tragic subject of Arnold. There are other people and events I long to know more about: my father's involvement in World War II and the Korean War; the KKK's burning of our original family store in Merigold, Mississippi; and Principal Akins, who had a fist-fight with a prominent school board member in his attempts to ensure Chinese Americans would be allowed to attend the Boyle public school. Out of my sense of deference and accommodation, however, I have never asked my parents to explain these parts of our family past that surely must have shaped their lives over the years. For propriety's sake, I have refrained from mentioning anything from the past, especially if it was traumatic. Most MC hold that the "unlucky" past lies behind us, yet the past also represents auspicious events and times such as weddings, births, and family traditions. Consequently, most MC can learn from the auspicious past how to proceed with the present and the future.

Unfortunately, however, this sensitivity in regards to accommodating others may not always be contemplated or realized in conversations between MC and non-MC speakers. A number of years ago at the institution where I was teaching, I developed a friendship with a colleague. This woman was a master teacher who spoke with authority and often openly revealed to me her earnest but prejudicial concerns about me as a person. Occasionally, we would see each other in passing and chat:

"Hi, Gong. I went to a Thai restaurant on Sunday. I asked for some soy sauce, and the waiter looked at me like I was crazy. What was wrong with askin' for some soy sauce? The food was so bad— like bad Chinese food—that I covered it with everything. Why was the guy so mad at me?"

"Asking for soy sauce isn't a crime. I don't know why your waiter was upset," I replied sheepishly. I was not certain why she was broaching me on the topic of Thai food; I'm no expert on it, though I do enjoy that particular cuisine.

"We ought to have lunch. What's your schedule?" my colleague inquired.

"I've already eaten. Plus, I've got so much work to finish in my office today. Sorry that I can't join you while you eat." I was uncomfortable, yet truthful.

"What'd ya eat? Betcha had egg rolls, eh? Gong, you're always eatin' egg rolls—at least you used to. Remember when you first came here years ago? I couldn't believe it—a Chinese, teaching English—with a Southern accent, too. I used to share an office with a fellow named Joe, who'd eat tacos and avocados all the time, and then I'd see you across the hall, eatin' egg rolls. Right, Gong? Don't ya remember?"

"Well, no, I really don't remember, but I suppose it's true," I replied, trying to go along with my colleague. "I do recall Joe and I ate take-out food sometimes. It was a quick way to have lunch," I added, my voice trailing off, diminishing with every syllable. I wished I was anywhere else but here, "talking" with this person. It was embarrassing enough that she made these kinds of remarks to me at all, much less within earshot of other faculty and students. Where could I hide? I thought to myself: "Hang in there; it'll be over soon."

This is only one conversation among many that this professor and I have shared. Out of my deep belief that she did care about me and out of my respect for her professional accomplishments, I always accommodated this individual's topic selection and conversational moves. I self-consciously defended her, rationalizing that she was just "tone-deaf" and didn't understand her audience very well. She admitted that she never knew an American-born Asian like me before. As a result, I reasoned to myself that I should give her a break, help her avoid "losing face," and prevent her from feeling awkward. Despite my desperate efforts to excuse her inappropriate comments, I always experienced regret that I voluntarily subjected myself to being bullied, <u>demeaned</u>, and belittled by someone <u>espousing</u> true friendship. Yet I can still hear her explanation regarding her response to me as a colleague: "I've never known a 'foreigner' who wasn't a foreigner, like you are." She offered this remark with great <u>bravado</u>.

In these types of conversations, the non-MC speaker initiates talk and the MC allows it to continue. In other words, I reluctantly contributed to the communication pattern created in this relationship. Why? Were my attempts to ignore this colleague's insensitivity somehow linked to gender? I don't think so. Was it linked to age? After all, this woman was older than myself. Again, I don't think so. Instead, so that the non-MC speaker didn't lose face, I deliberately chose to let her go on at my own expense—despite the extreme distress and humiliation she was causing me. I wondered to myself: "If I were an African American, would she announce that surely I must eat fried chicken and watermelon in the office?" In this way at least, she would be treating all the people in our office "equitably." This passive strategy in speech is mirrored in most MC behaviors, giving rise to perpetuating the stereotype of Asian submissiveness.

This kind of tolerance can be likened to a Southern Genteel social convention, wherein Southern speakers will casually invite folks to "stop by and visit us whenever you're in the neighborhood; we've got lots of room." True Southerners realize that, while the warm intent of such a speech act is very genuine, it is rarely meant literally. As a result, when those folks—virtual strangers—do appear on the speaker's doorstep, no one is more surprised than their host. All make the best of the situation: The host extended the invitation and must now honor it. It would be impolite to do otherwise; these guests have no idea that they have just missed the implicature (the underlying meaning in, or "real" function of, the literal utterance). Here, accommodating actions reinforce verbal accommodation. MC act too, but they often do so through inaction. For example, I now carefully avoid this colleague, aware that, if I don't cross paths with her, then I won't have to endure her abusive talking—thus, action through inaction. In this non-confrontational and Confucian way, I can prevent this non-MC speaker any opportunity to control our conversations and my role in them, while still "accommodating" her if I have to.

I do not always tolerate her racist talk with passive and indirect accommodation. Sometimes I pursue her subject, refuting her views with vociferous debate. When this occurs, it usually pertains to subjects beyond "self"; that is, when her attacks are personal, I try to ignore or avoid interacting with her. But when they are directed toward others or issues, I am compelled to respond. This is certainly true when she once asserted, for example, that there is no difference between the <u>KKK</u> and the <u>NAACP</u>. If we in society can see the NAACP as respectable, she adamantly asserted, then we should do likewise for the KKK. After all, "they're both merely special interest groups." I wondered, how can she broach such matters with me? Should I be honored that she looks at me, hears my Southern drawl, and then "accepts" me as just a salt-of-the-earth country woman? Or should I be absolutely offended that she fails to realize that I am a person of color whose family has experienced firsthand the ways that groups like the KKK <u>mete out</u> their own particular brand of "special interest?" At times like this, I cannot be silent and passive. Deference and accommodation serve no purpose in these instances. As I illustrated earlier, I believe that I can hear this person's verbal jabs directed at me, and I can weather and survive them by staying above the <u>fray</u>. This is an opportune time to present another conversational strategy that enables MC speakers to participate conversationally with greater ease and comfort: deference and topic shifting.

Deference and Topic Shifting

Ironically, accommodations that may at times provide a sense of deferential comfort for the non-MC speaker may instead result in <u>estrangement</u> and embarrassment for the MC speaker. Accordingly, MC often use a second strategy: topic shifting. This is a linguistic strategy which turns the tables, oftentimes providing relief and empowerment for the MC speaker and confusion and frustra-

tion for the non-MC listener. To understand this type of conversational move requires that we explore when and why topic shifting may occur, as well as consider which topics MC speakers may commonly switch to.

Topic shifting happens most frequently when an MC speaker is the subject of discussion, whether being complimented or spoken of in any positive way, but does not want to respond to the issue. For example, this scenario:

"Good morning, Annie," says Mrs. Alexander warmly, dressed in a floral-patterned knit dress.

"Hello," replies my mother, Annie Gong, busy hauling two massive platters of food into Fellowship Hall. Annie and Mrs. Alexander are both in their early 60s, attending a Sunday potluck lunch at the Boyle Baptist Church.

"I made deviled eggs, my specialty. They go like hot cakes ever' time I make 'em. You make sure you sample one." Scooting over a crystal bowl containing a mustard potato salad, Mrs. Alexander positions her egg plate smack dab in the center of the long table dedicated to salads. "Whatcha got there? I surely do hope it's Chinese food. You make the best Chinese food, Annie."

"I love deviled eggs," my mother says to shift the topic, as she concentrates on removing tin foil from her cashew chicken and sweet and sour pork. She continues to talk, never looking up. "How do you make your filling so tasty?" Garnishing her dish, she persists in her egg-talk: "Some folks just put Miracle Whip or mayonnaise in their filling; some like Underwood deviled ham mixed in with their mashed yolks. What do you think, Mrs. Alexander? I trust what you do."

Mrs. Alexander, however, prefers to talk about Annie's food. "How do you do it? How did you learn to cook like this, Annie? Now, that's sweet and sour, isn't it? And what's that other dish with the nuts? Can it be chicken almond ding? No, well. Last year, you brought fried rice, too. There wasn't a grain left inside of ten minutes when the line started moving. Wish you'd give lessons on Chinese cookin'. Everybody at the church would be your student in nothin' flat. Mark my words."

But Annie just <u>coyly</u> smiles and begins her egg talk once more. "Your eggs, do you boil them all at once? Put sweet or dill pickles or relish in them? And what about white or black pepper, because that's something I've never understood about makin' that." Annie stuffs her tin foil back into her bag and looks Mrs. Alexander in the eye. "I'm fixin' to go back to the car to get the chow mein. Before I do, though, you tell me about your recipe, okay?"

At this <u>juncture</u>, Mrs. Alexander commences telling Annie her deviled egg recipe. "Well, you know, I always go out and buy the freshest dozen of eggs I can find. I put all my eggs in one pot at room temperature. Never try to boil an egg straight out of the ice box."

Relieved by this egg talk, Annie listens intently, nodding her head as each ingredient and instruction is described. "I never had anybody teach me about cookin' in the formal way," she then says. "I just learn from good cooks like yourself and by doin'—makin' mistakes." With that, the small MC woman <u>saunters</u> out of Fellowship Hall to fetch her noodles, breathing a sigh of relief that she avoided having to talk about herself or her cooking without being perceived as rude by not accommodating Mrs. Alexander.

As is evident, Annie diverts attention and conversation away from "self," a subject that she is uncomfortable with, despite the fact that Mrs. Alexander's topic selection would allow this MC speaker a chance to showcase her personal accomplishments as a cook. Annie can't take a compliment, a common phenomenon among most MC. Rather than demonstrate her deference to Mrs. Alexander by accommodating her topic selection, Annie is deferential—polite and respectful— through her topic shifting to highlight the <u>culinary</u> skill of the other speaker. To cap it off, she is even a bit <u>self-effacing</u> at the end of the exchange, thus countering the compliment. This topic shifting, consequently, is a move to accomplish modesty. That is, by persistently re-introducing her egg-talk, she eventually leads Mrs. Alexander to talk about *her*self and *her* dishes, two topics in which most any Southern Genteel woman excels. Hardly any other region of the U.S. compares to authentic Southern cooking and the talk that goes with it.

While Annie didn't choose to talk about the entree that she prepared, she does engage in talking about food. This is a topic to which most MC shift routinely, especially with in-group speakers or non-MC they regard as close friends. To share food talk with an MC is, by and large, a sign of trust and acceptance. In my own MC family, food-talk epitomizes being Chinese. Be it good or bad fortune, the event can be ritualized with <u>sumptuous</u>, bountiful amounts of food. The more impressive or <u>auspicious</u> the occasion, the longer the menu. Rituals require ceremony, and ceremony always entails food. For example, weddings call for nine-course dinners; births—"red egg and ginger" banquets and a vat of *gai djil gahng*, a chicken-whiskey soup often referred to as "mother's brew"; birthdays— chicken, noodles, and a cake with some shade of Chinese red in or on it. (Chocolate cakes and frostings are perceived by many superstitious MC as inappropriate for happy celebrations.) Red is a good-luck color and a standard for every celebration; in fact, brides often don bright red, silk *cheung sahms* (a type of Chinese dress) to their wedding receptions and banquets.

While food-talk is not the focus of this essay, it is such an unquestionably important subject to all Chinese that it deserves further mention here. After all, one conventional way to greet someone in Chinese is "Nay heck fan?" (Have you eaten your rice?) The MC maintain this traditional valorization of food and the Confucian notion of dining rather than eating. As I was once admonished by my sister, "When planning any MC event, always remember that, if everything else is a disaster but there are lots of good, exotic dishes, then you're okay. Everyone will leave bragging about what a great time they had because all they'll remember and tell others about is the food."

Here is another example of topic shifting: Every week I phone my parents in Mississippi. Inevitably, I always spend the majority of the call reviewing the MC current affairs with my mom. She and I cover the general topics—health, work, and family—rather swiftly. Then, without any linguistic cue at all, Mama commences with the food talk:

"Grilled chicken, that's what we ordered. Daddy and I went to our exercise class at the Mall this morning and ate at the Food Court. I like that. It was grilled, yes, not pan-fried with no liquid smoke," Mama speculates. She carried on this dramatic monologue of sorts: "Daddy didn't like it 'cause of the mayonnaise; he likes his sandwiches dry." Reminded of my sister-in-law's poultry, Mama then <u>reminisces</u>: "On Monday, Josie barbecued chicken. It was real good—she left the skin on."

I hear my daddy's voice in the background. "The girls didn't have tennis or basketball—they're all playing sports now, you know—so we all went over there and watched football," he says, <u>alluding</u> to my brother Stephen's big-screen TV and the Monday night NFL game.

Without skipping a beat, my mother returns to revealing the supper guests and their contributions to the buffet. "And Annette made homemade rolls and a broccoli-rice casserole—too rich, but Daddy likes it. Ginger and Eddie ate there, too; think Ginger had a tin of brownies, still warm from the oven. And that Lynette. She made a batch of cookies, and I sampled one—everybody fussed at me, said 'Mama, better watch your diabetes.' Juanita just phoned and told Josie she and her family had already eaten, but she'd come on over later, if she had time. She had laundry and house cleaning to do. Just like a family reunion."

Throughout this part of the phone call, I never get a word in edgewise—nothing but an intermittent "a-huh," barely audible amidst Mama's recollection of the communal meal (i.e., an important interpersonal function that unites everyone, strengthens family ties, and provides a sense of "village" life from Canton) at sister-in-law Josie's. From her food-talk, I intuit that everyone there is fine. My siblings and their spouses are well; the grandchildren are doing well in school; Daddy's blood pressure and cholesterol are reasonably low, but Mama's sugar is high. Among MC speakers who know each other well, food-talk can be as natural, effortless, and meaningful for MC speakers as alternating between English and Cantonese in a single conversation. One MC's <u>divulgence</u> of the context, people, and events, along with a cataloguing of the edibles, can provide information for another MC—data that could only be otherwise fathomed by folks who were present at the family gather. This food-talk demonstrates our common bond as individuals in family and culture; it serves as a vehicle to express our love and respect for one another as members of a single, cohesive community whose "separateness" is merely geographic. A

seasoned food-talker myself, I usually sense there is more to the story than the abbreviated menu suggests. I <u>ruminate</u> on my suspicion, wondering what Mama *isn't* telling me in what she *is* saying.

There is a pregnant pause on the other end of the line, and I chime in, "What was the reason you all decided to eat at Stephen and Josie's, Mama? Didn't you all do turkey and dressing for Stephen's birthday the day before? Goodness, what'd y'all do with all the leftovers, anyway?"

"Oh, C.W. had a stroke, and Audrey drove him to town to see a specialist." C.W. is Mama's nephew, Audrey his wife. "They were supposed to stop by Stephen's to see all of us and have a bite before the drive back, but all they did was call. They have a daughter in town here now, see." There's another lull in the conversation. "We warmed 'em up. Flavor's the best the next day when the turkey and dressin' have set awhile," Mama then says. "We don't waste leftovers here."

I understand now, having discovered the missing link: Mama had arranged the family's Monday night communal potluck at my brother's house because relatives were in town; they had expected C.W. and Audrey to drop by and visit. But the couple never showed up. Never mind that their expectations were never fulfilled. They still enjoyed their own informal reunion, an interpretation that my mother <u>construed</u>. And even more important was this ultimate reality: They had lots of delectable home cooking. Given a satisfying meal, a body can strive to overlook the out-of-town guests who never came to dinner—and C.W. was, after all, sick. The graciousness with which Mama handles this situation is both very Confucian and Southern. But one should never be deceived by the surface politeness: C.W. and Audrey's minor transgression will not be soon forgotten. And you can bet your last shiny penny that I'll hear about this matter next week, when Mama shifts into food-talk. Her message will be loud and clear.

Food-talk is but one topic that MC speakers are predisposed to shift toward. It is a rather clever, witty, and powerful topic, though, for it enables speakers to shift to or intermingle with additional topics. These topics tend to be in narrative form, stories of self-disclosure about the MC's family, cultural, or historical past and traditions. Some of the narratives are "stock" or "ritualized" tales, repeated in public again and again; others are akin to "sacred texts," seldom uttered under any circumstances. The more "ritualized" the narrative, the less trustworthy or familiar the MC speaker may feel toward the other speech participants. Conversely, the more "sacred" the text, the more the MC speaker may identify with and have regard for the other speakers in the communicative act. To break out of the safe, ritualized narratives in topic shifting means risking greater self-disclosure and thus greater vulnerability. Perhaps my best example of the trust and deference involved in topic shifting is apparent when examining the narratives that I have chosen for use in this essay. I really don't know you, my readers. Yet, I am con-vinced that you will be as interested in MC talk as I am, as I have topic shifted to some very "sacred" subjects: my family, its cultural and historical past, and its rituals. The conversations reconstructed here are the <u>embodiment</u> of one of the most precious revelations of all: the way we MC talk to ourselves and to others.

Lotuses in the Land of the Magnolias

When I was in high school, I remember Mama, brother Stephen, and myself driving an old aunt from Canton to visit my cousins in Duncan, a neighboring town some 35 miles north of Boyle. It was fall, the weather was cold and wet, and the expanse of rice and cotton fields were flooded, reflecting an eerie mirror image of the full moon on the black water. The ribbon of road we drove along was surrounded on either side by encroaching rain water. We were all concentrating on the road, silent; my brother drove fast, nonetheless. Then the silence was broken by our elder's deep voice, difficult to decipher because she really spoke no English. She muttered softly. Mama translated: "This looks like Canton." The old aunt scanned the landscape, waving her hand toward the window as if to bless the land itself. We heard her utter more sounds. "No wonder you live here; it's just like home," relayed Mama, fixing her own eyes on the blackness. My mother broke the silence once more: "Home." With this, she peered out her fogged window and reached over to grasp the old woman's hand. Three generations of our family drove the narrow

Delta road that night—Chinese with cultural and linguistic roots in two Southern regions: Canton and the Mississippi Delta.

❖ ❖ ❖

To explain and exemplify deference as it manifests itself in accommodation and topic shifting during MC talk, I have offered here a very small sample of the linguistic interaction of Chinese Americans from the Mississippi Delta as I know it; the milieu that I depict is from my own perspective, as seen through my own eyes. Furthermore, the conversational strategies that I have selected represent linguistic phenomena drawn from my own experiences as an MC speaker.

As mentioned in the introduction, I have always been sensitive to voices—mine and others'. I have always been conscious of how I and other MC were distinct yet complementary in the way we sounded and expressed ideas. My hope is that understanding deference and the ways by which it can be expressed through specific rhetorical strategies will provide keys to greater appreciation for the culturally distinct communicative acts of the Mississippi Chinese lotuses living in the land of the magnolias.

Word count: 5724

APPENDICES

- **NARRATIVE AND EXPOSITORY PROSE**
- **LEARNING NEW VOCABULARY**

Appendix A

NARRATIVE AND EXPOSITORY PROSE

Authors write for four main purposes: 1) to tell a story, 2) to describe, 3) to argue or persuade, 4) to explain. In many articles, two or more purposes are combined. Articles that tell a story (narratives) usually contain description, and articles that explain something (exposition) often contain persuasive techniques. As a reader, you will want to determine whether you are reading a story or an explanation because you approach each type of article differently.

Expository Writing

An expository article is organized logically rather than chronologically (by time). This makes such articles difficult to visualize and impossible to divide into time segments. All of the articles in Part One and most of those in Part Two of this book are expository articles. For this type of writing, the approach taught in Chapters One through Six is recommended. This appendix is designed to offer approaches to narrative writing.

Narrative Writing

There are several ways to approach narrative writing. Three of the most common ways are listed below.

1. **Look for time markers.** A narrative, or story, is organized by *time*. The classic beginning of a fairy tale is "Once upon a time...." One approach, then, is to look for time markers. Time markers, as the name suggests, indicate time and therefore can help you divide a narrative into sections, making it easier to summarize. Here are examples of just a few common time markers:

At 10:30 a.m...	In the morning...
Later that day...	Before he left the house...
Ten minutes later...	After dinner...

You get the picture. If a word or phrase tells you the specific time or gives you some information about time passing, it is usually a time marker and can help you divide a story into parts. These parts are often major details of the story and can be written in an outline similar to what you practiced in Chapter Three.

2. **Play a movie in your head**. In order to remember details of a story, play a "movie" in your head. Visualize the characters (at least the main ones). The author usually gives you information about the characters such as their height, weight, hair color, and age. Use these and other descriptive details to form a picture of the people in the story. Also, picture them acting. Imagine them running, working, driving a car, riding in an airplane, or whatever the author says they are doing at the time. If you can imagine the characters and action, you will probably remember the story.

3. **Understand story parts.** Stories have structural parts and can be broken into the following parts:

Setting: the time and place of the story. Can you tell if it is modern times or the nineteenth century? Does the story take place in a city, on a farm, in and around a castle?

Characters: Identify the main character(s), especially the most important one (often called the *protagonist*).

Beginning event (or problem): Usually a story contains an event or problem which gets the action started.

Plot (or Action): What action takes place? What does the main character do to solve the problem? These are often the major details of a narrative, divided by time markers.

Outcome: Is the main character successful in overcoming the problem? Does the character learn anything from the events in the story? How do you know?

Personal thoughts: What did you learn from this story? How might you have acted differently than the protagonist? Are there any possibilities for a different ending to the story? (This part is individual and personal, and, like the response to an article as described in Chapter Five, there are no right or wrong answers to these questions.)

MODEL: The parts of a narrative

Read the following short story. It is an adaptation of a fable attributed to Aesop, a Greek who lived in the fifth century B.C. Then read the comments on how this story might be divided into parts.

DOUBLE TROUBLE

In his downtown office, Harry Gordon finished his work for the morning and decided to take an early lunch. He took the elevator down to the parking garage and got into his new, shiny, 1992 Corvette. He seemed a happy man when he arrived at his favorite restaurant.

Meanwhile, things were not going so well at home, for Harry had two wives. It was legal to have two wives in Harry's time and place, and his wives got along well. However, there was one problem. One wife was older than Harry, and one was quite a bit younger. His young wife, Diana, wanted Harry to look young and handsome; Gloria desired her husband to look dignified and mature, a perfect match for the woman she thought she was.

It was hard to tell Harry's age. He had a full head of hair and kept fit by exercising at a fitness club. However, gray hairs were creeping into his otherwise dark brown hairdo. Gloria thought to herself, "Maybe I can streak some silver into his hair when he is asleep, or maybe even pull out some dark ones without him knowing it. He's a sound sleeper, and I'll pull just a little at a time." Diana had secret thoughts, too, but quite different ones. "Maybe I can pull out all the gray hairs while he naps on Saturday or Sunday in front of the TV," she thought.

Each wife put her plan into effect whenever she had a chance. As the months passed, it became evident that each was succeeding. The success was soon thought of as a failure, however, because poor Harry woke up one morning to feel a cold draft on the top of his head. His foolish wives had pulled every hair out of his head, and now neither of them found him attractive. Harry was obviously not pleased with either of his wives.

SETTING: It is clearly modern times because of the TV, elevator, 1992 Corvette, office building, fitness club, etc. Often the approximate time is clear; in other stories it is not given, and you can just say "sometime in the past." The place seems to be in a city (or at least a town), for we wouldn't find office buildings and parking garages in a rural setting.

CHARACTERS: There are only three in this short story: Harry, Gloria, and Diana. In a longer story it is not usually necessary to list all of the characters, but it is important to mention the main ones. In this story, all three obviously need mentioning.

PROBLEM: The problem or beginning event is the wives' unhappiness with Harry's appearance. This sets the story in motion.

PLOT: The plot, or sequence of events, is simple in this narrative. Diana begins pulling out Harry's gray hairs, and Gloria begins pulling out his dark ones. Soon Harry is bald.

OUTCOME: The outcome can be considered a success in one way: each wife accomplishes her immediate goal; however, the overall outcome is not good. All characters are unhappy with the ultimate results.

PERSONAL THOUGHTS: This story, originally a fable, has an obvious moral about being happy with what one has. However, most stories will get you to thinking more about the characters and events and will allow you to write a short or long response to the story. For instance, you often put yourself in the place of one of the characters. This way, you can decide how you would have acted in the circumstances presented in the story. Sometimes you can draw on personal experiences which seem similar to those in the story. You may even want to try your own hand at writing a narrative, true or fictional.

To sum up, try to determine if you are reading a narrative. If you are, use one or more of the methods described above to summarize an article rather than the methods you use for expository articles and textbooks.

Appendix B

LEARNING NEW VOCABULARY

Using the Context

One of the easiest, most common ways to learn new words is through the **context.** Context means the words, sentences and paragraphs surrounding the word that is new to you. Your success at determining the meanings of words from the context depends on the presence of context clues and your ability to recognize those clues.

Sometimes the context actually provides you with a definition of the word as is the case in the following sentences from *Biology: A Journey Into Life* reprinted in Chapter Six of this book. The definitions are highlighted with italics.

> "We will travel to spaces as small as the nuclear landscape within a single nerve cell and as large as the **biosphere**: *the entire fabric of life that covers the planet we call home.*"

> "You will learn about **natural selection**, *the major evolutionary mechanism that has produced the variety of living organisms*, and **ecology**, *the study of interactions of living things with one another and with their environment.*"

> "You will study the lives of plants, fungi, bacteria, and *single-celled organisms* called **protists.**"

COMMENTS: Authors indicate that they are providing a definition in a number of ways. In the first sentence, the word "biosphere" is followed by a colon (:) and the definition. In the next sentence, the definitions of the two words in bold immediately follow the word and are set off with commas. Sometimes the definition comes first, as is the case in the third sentence.

Other times, clues or hints to the meanings of the words are provided through techniques such as examples and inferences and by the way the word is used. Notice the various clues in italics in the following sentences from articles in Part Two of this book.

"While I interviewed the other players, he **preened**, *rearranging his hair and pumping out his chest like a turkey.*"

COMMENTS: Even if you are unfamiliar with the word "preened," you can tell by the way it is used that it is a verb--an action that someone is doing. Then the context clue (the description of what he was doing) helps you create a mental image of that action.

"You should also avoid overdosing on **carbohydrates**, *such as pasta and bread.*"

COMMENTS: The phrase "such as" often signals an example. Other words that may indicate that examples follow a word are "for example," "like," "especially," and "for instance."

"Teasing is a problem that dates back at least to the *first inkwell and pigtail*, and **pubescent** girls have long suffered truly degrading abuse from *adolescent boys.*"

COMMENTS: The hints in this sentence are more subtle and depend on a reader's experience or background knowledge. If you know of the long past practice of grade school boys dipping girls' pigtails in inkwells and/or that adolescents are teenagers, these clues may help you understand that "pubescent girls" are girls who are in their early teens and just beginning to mature physically.

By paying attention to the way a new word is used, you will gain some sense of its meaning. You are likely to start noticing the word in other material you read, and gradually, it will become a part of your own vocabulary.

Looking Up Words in a Dictionary

When context clues are missing or insufficient, you will need to look up the words in a dictionary. Sometimes you may want to look up the new word even if there is a context clue in order to get a more complete understanding of the word. Remember, the context can reveal only one meaning or partial meaning of a word.

The information about a word is listed in what is referred to as an *entry*. Each entry gives a wealth of information about the word, and it is especially important to pay attention to the pronunciation and spelling, the part of speech, and the definition.

1. *Pronunciation.* When you use a dictionary, pay attention to the word's pronunciation. Because of the peculiarities of English spelling, it is important to understand how to use the pronunciation key in your dictionary. Every dictionary uses slightly different symbols, so you need to become familiar with the key in the dictionary you

are using. A pronunciation key is usually provided at the bottom of every other page or in the front of the dictionary.

2. *Part of speech.* The part of speech usually follows the pronunciation. Frequently, a word can be used as more than one part of speech, so you need to look at the context in which the word appears to choose the correct part of speech and definition. The most common abbreviations you will see for parts of speech are

n.	=	noun
v.	=	verb
vt.	=	transitive verb
vi.	=	intransitive verb
adj.	=	adjective
adv.	=	adverb

3. *Definition.* Most words have several meanings recorded in the dictionary. Therefore, it is important that you check the sentence or paragraph where you found the word in order to select the correct definition. The part of speech can also help you choose the correct definition.

Reviewing New Vocabulary

In order to learn the words that you find while reading, it is a good idea to make a flash card for each word. A flash card is a blank file card. Put the word and its pronunciation on one side. On the other side, write the definition, the part of speech, and a sentence that uses the word correctly and makes the meaning of the word clear.

Front	**Back**

PREEN (prēn) *"Block that Mental Block," p.121*	*to dress oneself carefully or smartly; primp* *verb* *I knew my son had reached puberty when he began to spend a lot of time in the bathroom, showering, fixing his hair, and preening in other ways.*

Studying vocabulary flash cards

Flash cards are easy to carry with you, and reviewing them frequently will help you learn them. Look at the front side of the card, say the word, then test yourself by trying to recall the meaning. Then turn the card over and check yourself. Later, do just the reverse; read the definition to see if you can remember the word.

Once you think you know the word, test yourself or have someone else test you on the words by using the flash cards. If you correctly recall the definition, put a check in a corner on the front of the card. Once you have earned two checks, you probably know the word and just need to review it periodically.

Improving your general vocabulary

As mentioned above, by paying attention to new words in their context, the number of words you know will gradually grow. However, for a more drastic improvement in your vocabulary, you need to make a more concerted effort. Try selecting five words every week from each article that you read in Part Two or one word a day from the articles. Study the words by carefully examining the context, looking up the words in a dictionary, making flash cards, and reviewing them.

For more ideas about learning new vocabulary, refer to Tony Randall's article on "How to Improve Your Vocabulary" in the section entitled "Learning Strategies" in Part Two.